Y0-BTA-852

Chinatown and Little Tokyo:

Power, Conflict, and Community Among Chinese and Japanese Immigrants in America

Stanford Morris Lyman

ASSOCIATED FACULTY PRESS, INC.
Millwood, N.Y. • New York City • London

ASSOCIATED FACULTY PRESS, INC.

MINORITY STRUCTURES AND RACE AND ETHNIC RELATIONS SERIES

Stanford M. Lyman and John Cooper
Series Editors

Lyman, Chinatown and Little Tokyo: Power, Conflict, and Community Among Chinese and Japanese Immigrants in America

McMorrow, Ideology and Immigrant Culture: The Nineteenth Century German Political Immigrant and the Construction of American Culture and Thought

Millette, New Grenada in Brooklyn

Chang, The Rise of the Martial Arts in China and America

Manufactured in the United States of America

Published by
Associated Faculty Press, Inc.
Millwood, N.Y.

Library of Congress Cataloging in Publication Data

Lyman, Stanford M.
Chinatown and Little Tokyo.

(Minority structures and race and ethnic relations series) (National university publications)
Bibliography: p.
1. Chinese Americans—Social conditions. 2. Chinese Americans—Ethnic identity. 3. Japanese Americans—Cultural assimilation. 4. United States—Foreign population. I. Title. II. Series.
E184.C5L95 1986 305.8'951'073 83-26569
ISBN 0-8046-9352-8

In Remembrance Of

Robert Stewart Culin
(1858-1929)
pioneer ethnographer of Asian America

[F]ortunately social life gives us favorable conditions for comparative studies, . . . in the coexistence of. . . civilized societies sufficiently alike in their fundamental cultural problems to make comparison possible, and differing sufficiently in their traditions, customs, and general national spirit to make comparison fruitful. And from the list of these civilized societies we should by no means exclude those nonwhite societies, like the Chinese, whose organization and attitude differ profoundly from our own, but which interest us both as social experiments and as situations with which we have to reconcile our future.

W.I. Thomas and Florian Znaniecki
The Polish Peasant in Europe and America

Contents

About the Author

Stanford M. Lyman was born in 1933 in San Francisco. In his youth he became closely associated with that city's Chinese and Japanese communities.

Lyman studied sociology and political science at the University of California, Berkeley, where he obtained an A.B. (1955), M.A. (1957), and Ph.D. (1961). In 1957, via the university extension program, Lyman introduced "The Oriental in America," the first course in Asian American studies offered at an institution of higher learning in the U.S.A. Subsequently, he helped to launch Asian American studies programs in colleges and universities along the Pacific coast.

Author of 12 books and numerous articles and reviews, Lyman presented a radio series subsequently published as "The Oriental in North America," in Canada in 1962. He has written *The Asian in the West* (1970); *Chinese Americans* (1974); and *The Asian in North America* (1977).

His other books are: *The Black American in Sociological Thought: A Failure of Perspective* (1972); *The Seven Deadly Sins: Society and Evil* (1978), and the forthcoming *Southerner, Slavocrat, Sociologist: Essays and Papers of Henry Hughes (1829-1862), of Port Gibson, Mississippi.* With Marvin B. Scott, Lyman has written *A Sociology of the Absurd* (1970); *The Revolt of the Students* (1970); and *The Drama of Social Reality* (1975), the latter translated into Japanese in 1981. With Richard H. Brown, he edited *Structure, Consciousness, and History* (1978). Yale University Press will soon release his and Arthur J. Vidich's *American Sociology: Worldly Rejections of Religion and Their Directions.*

Lyman's essays and reviews have appeared in *Pacific Affairs, The Pacific Historical Review, Phylon Quarterly, The Bulletin of the Chinese Historical Society of the United States, The Bulletin of Oriental and African Studies, The American Sociological Review, Canadian Review of Sociology and Anthropology,* and *Hyoron Shakaika-gaku* (Social Science Review of Doshisha University, Japan).

Professor Lyman has received recognition and awards from the Japanese Citizens League, the Chinese Historical Society of America, the Southern California Chinese Historical Society, and the San Gabriel Valley Chinese Cultural Association.

In 1975 Professor Lyman served as Senior Member, Linacre College, Oxford University and in 1981-82 he presented courses and lectures on Asian Americans as Fulbright Lecturer in Japan. Through the auspices of the United States Information Service, Dr. Lyman has lectured in Taiwan, Hong Kong, and Singapore. After having taught sociology and Asian studies at the Universities of California, British Columbia, and Nevada, at Sonoma State College, and at the New School for Social Research, in 1985 Dr. Lyman was appointed Visiting Distinguished Professor at the University of Tulsa and then Robert J. Morrow Eminent Scholar at Florida Atlantic University, whose endowed Social Science chair he holds currently.

Preface

This study attempts to describe and account for the isolation and autonomy of Chinese communities in the United States and to compare their situation with that of the immigrant Japanese.

The overseas Chinese have maintained in the past, and to a considerable extent, maintain to this day, a social, economic, and political life within a quarter of the city commonly known as Chinatown. The existence of this ethnic island amid the teeming life of a modern city is usually attributed to ethnocentrism.[1] Although Sinophobic pressure has contributed much to the enforced segregation of a racially visible and culturally distinct people, it does not account for the establishment and maintenance of autonomous, commercial, criminal, and legal institutions within that isolated community. Moreover, Chinatowns are found in almost every place to which Chinese have migrated,[2] and they appear to thrive even in the absence of racial discrimination.

Another Asian people, the Japanese, although also subjected to a bitter barrage of discrimination and frequently forced into separate residential enclaves, have not established autonomous communities similar to those of the Chinese. There has been little conscious effort on the part of the Japanese in the United States to maintain an existence apart from the larger society. "Little Tokyo" has not thrived as a Japanese residential community or as an immigrant-constructed tourist attraction,[3] nor has it developed a community-wide political structure comparable to that found in Chinatown.

These differences between Japanese and Chinese community

organization suggest that the former have become more integrated into the larger society than the latter. A people may be said to be integrated into the larger society insofar as they share with the members of the larger society the belief that the political and legal institutions of that society have legitimate jurisdiction over them. Nonintegration can be said to exist when a people do not recognize the larger society's political and legal jurisdiction except at the diplomatic and international levels, when self-governing, autonomous communities circumscribe their lives, and when the laws, customs, and institutions of these autonomous communities are different from, and in conflict with, or only complementary to those of the larger society. Integration and nonintegration are viewed here as the extremes on a continuum.[4] The immigrant Japanese are much closer to the integration pole, while the Chinatown Chinese are nearer to the other extreme.

The integration of an alien people into a larger society is one aspect of their acculturation. The speed with which the Japanese have adapted to American life and the resistance of the Chinese to American ways have been cause for comment in the studies of Asian life in America. Leonard Broom and John I. Kitsuse, on the basis of their detailed study of the Japanese, write:

> The rapid acculturation of the Japanese population in America and Hawaii and its adjustment to the dominant society has frequently been remarked upon. Considering the apparent gap between the American and Japanese cultures and the differences between the English and Japanese languages, the speed of this acculturation is doubly notable. . . an achievement perhaps rarely equaled in the history of human migration.[5]

The proassimilationist Chinese sociologist, Rose Hum Lee, laments the fact that "The Nisei (second-generation Japanese) exhibit, within sixty years, greater degrees of integration into the American society, than has been the case with [the] Chinese, whose settlement is twice as long,"[6] and castigates her Chinese American peers for maintaining an isolated community life inside a ghetto.

How can this difference in the integration of two peoples be explained? A major assumption of this paper is that the patterns of community life and hence of the thrust toward or away from integration were set by the interplay of cultural adaptations, social experiences, and demographic features among the early immigrants. This interplay was in great part affected by the cultural and environmental "givens" of the respective immigrant settings.

As with many other dilemmas, the problem of Asian integration into American society becomes more manageable when reformulated into separate questions. Accordingly, I have tried to answer the following questions in this paper:

Why did the Chinese and Japanese initially come to the United States?

What aspects of their culture and social organization were transplanted by these peoples to the New World?

What intramural and external factors affected the survival and structure of their respective immigrant institutions?

On what bases have the less integrated people; the Chinese, organized their communities?

What features of the Chinese community organization function to maintain the isolation of that people from the larger society?

In attempting to answer these questions I have also tried to throw additional light on the general processes facilitating or hindering the integration of immigrants into the larger society.

NOTES

1. See, for example, James A. Quinn, *Urban Sociology* (New York: American Book, 1955), pp. 191-200.
2. Separate Chinese quarters of the city are found throughout Southeast Asia, Oceania, Latin America, and the Caribbean.
3. For a study of Japanese housing conditions completed at the time my own researches were in progress, see
   Harry H.L. Kitano, "Housing of Japanese-Americans in the San Francisco Bay Area," in *Studies in Housing and Minority Groups* eds. Nathan Glazer and Davis McEntire, (Berkeley: University of California Press, 1960), pp. 178-197.
   For information on Chinese residential patterns in the same period, see Davis McEntire, *Residence and Race* (Berkeley: University of California Press, 1960), pp. 46-47, 69-71.
4. My definition here is complementary but not equivalent to that of
   Arnold Rose, *Sociology: The Study of Human Relations* (New York: Knopf, 1956), pp. 125, 267, 303, 563.
   See also the discussion of integration in
   Harry M. Johnson, *Sociology: A Systematic Introduction* (New York: Harcourt, 1960), pp. 54-56.
5. Leonard Broom and John I. Kitsuse, "The Validation of Acculturation: A Condition of Ethnic Assimilation," abridged in *Principles of Sociology: A Reader in Theory and Research,* eds. Kimball Young and Raymond

Mack (New York: American Book, 1960), p. 118, originally published in *American Anthropologist* 57 (1955) 44-48.
6. *The Chinese in the United States of America* (Hong Kong: Hong Kong University Press, 1960), p. 425.

Acknowledgments

My research on the Chinese and the Japanese in North America has been aided by both scholars and friends. Acknowledgment here can only indicate my incalculable debt to them.

My dissertation, "The Structure of Chinese Society in Nineteenth-Century America," from which the present work is adapted, was supervised by Kingsley Davis, H. Franz Schurmann, and Edward A.N. Barnhart of the University of California at Berkeley. Each gave me the benefit of his theorectical, ethnological, and methodological expertise, while allowing me free rein to pursue the subject in my own way.

My knowledge of Asian studies has been enriched by courses and conversations with the following Berkeley faculty members (1951-60): sociologists: Reinhard Bendix, Herbert Blumer, Kenneth Bock, Wolfram Eberhard, Nathan Glazer, Cesar Grana, William Kornhauser, Seymour Martin Lipset, William Petersen, Philip Selznick, and Tamotsu Shibutani; political scientists: Ernst B. Haas, Paul Seabury, and Sheldon Wolin; historians: Raymond Sontag and Kenneth Stampp; speech professors: Ethel Albert, Jacobus ten Broek, Christian Bay, Woodrow Borah, Floyd Matson, David Rynin, William Shephard, Fred Stripp, and Manfred Wolfson.

I worked on part of the original dissertation at the University of British Columbia. There I learned much from the scholarship of colleagues in the departments of Anthropology and Sociology and Asian Studies, including Cyril Belshaw, Bernard Blishen, George Cheney, Tung-tsu Chu, Ping-ti Ho, Harry Hawthorn, William Holland, Shuichi Kato, Catherine Liu, Kaspar D. Naegele, Anthony Richmond, Reginald A.H. Robson, Wayne Suttles, R.P. Srivastava, and William Willmott. Among the Asian-Canadians who taught me much about Chinese and Japanese life were Yunshik Chang, Kunio Ogata, Kaien Shimizu, William S. Tong, Joe Yamauchi, and George Yano.

The late Rose Hum Lee, then of Chicago's Roosevelt University, corresponded with me for two years, graciously sharing her knowledge of Chinese America. For several years before his untimely death, Maurice Freedman of the London School of Economics carried on a lively, scholarly, and always friendly correspondence with me, debating and discussing our respective interpretations of overseas Chinese social organization.

Manuscripts and other materials were provided by Edward Holsinger, Nikita Kuschelevsky, Wesley Chen, Jack Tschen, Kathy Keller, Linnea Osth, and Tony Carnes.

Many habitués of San Francisco's Chinatown—some of them classmates of mine in high school and college—showed me the folkways of Chinese community life. Among those I am most grateful to are Clifford Chang, Robert Chang, Christopher Chow, Galen Chow, Anita Jung Chow, Richard Bung Dick Chun, James Fong, Wilson Fong, Simon Gin, Randolph Hong, Albert J. Hum, Gilbert J. Hum, Thomas Y. Hum, Raymond Joe, Sam Law, Benson Lai, Roberta Chiu Lai, Elliott Lee, Henry Lee, Robert Lim, Donald Loo, Charles Liu, Lindbergh Moy, Alva Owyang, Hanson Quock, William Shem, Myron Tong, Donald Wong, Rodney Wong, Yee Fung Wong, and Osla Young.

In 1951, I was invited to join "the Barons," a young men's association that had been formed a few years earlier by some Nisei youths from San Francisco's Little Tokyo under the guidance of Yori Wada (later to become the first Japanese American regent of the University of California). In the three decades that have followed I have benefitted from the unswerving friendship, insightful knowledge, patient advice, and astute criticism of this group and their families. I am especially grateful to Mr. and Mrs. James Akashi, Ted Amino, Mr. and Mrs. Peter Asano, Mr. and Mrs. Tadashi Asano, Mr. and Mrs. Michisuke Fukuda, Mr. and Mrs. Nobusuke Fukuda, Mr. and Mrs. Saburo Fukuda, Hideo Bernard Hata, Mr. and Mrs. John Kobayashi, Mr. and Mrs. Harold Masamori, Mr. and Mrs. Yosuke Mizuhara, Mr. and Mrs. Ed Nagase, William Nakahara, Jr., the late Donald Katsumi Sakuma, Mr. and Mrs. Tom Shimizu, Mr. and Mrs. Harry Suzuki, Mr. and Mrs. Tio Yamamoto, Masaji "Sam" Yamoto, Shogo Yamoto, Mr. and Mrs. Akira Wtanabe, and Takashi Watanabe. I have also learned about Nisei and Sansei life from Mr. and Mrs.

Hiroshi Fukuda, Mr. and Mrs. Koichi Fukuda, Mr. Hisashi Kitano, Mr. and Mrs. Jerry Nomura, Mrs. Fumi Quong, Mr. and Mrs. Hiroshi Shimizu, Mr. and Mrs. Eugene Yokoyama, and Mr. Douglas Yoshimura.

Many professionals from California's several Japanese-American communities have assisted me in my research and offered their friendship. Among the most helpful have been the late Reverend Taro Goto and Mrs. Goto, Mr. and Mrs. Leo T. Goto, Mr. and the late Mrs. Howard Imazeki, Dr. Tetsuden Kashima, Dr. Paul Takagi, and Dr. Ronald Takaki. Gordon Hirabayashi and the late T. Scott Miyakawa have shared their experiences and knowledge of Japanese-Canadian and -American situations with me.

Over the years Herbert Hill has enlightened me about the racial bases of labor discrimination in the United States. The late Horace R. Cayton deepened my understanding of race relations theory. Benjamin T'sou furthered my knowledge of Chinese sociolinguistics.

In the years since I completed the research for my dissertation, I have learned much from the works of Ying-jen Chang, Philip Choy, Him Mark Lai, Ivan Light, Dean Lan, Dennis Lum, Robert Seto Quan, Henry Tom, and Charles Choy Wong. Richard H. Brown, Charles R. Freeman, and Marvin B. Scott have given me much helpful advice and criticism.

The introduction has benefitted from the advice and criticism of Tetsuden Kashima and Arthur J. Vidich.

The British Psychological Association kindly invited me to present my findings on Japanese character and culture before their annual convention during my term as senior member, Linacre College, Oxford University in 1975.

In 1975-76, under the auspices of the United States Information Service, I was able to lecture on and discuss my Asian-American research with sociology faculty members and students at National Taiwan University and Tung Hai University in Taijung, the Chinese University of Hong Kong and the University of Hong Kong, the University of Singapore, and selected audiences in Nagoya and Tokyo, Japan.

In 1981-82, the Japan-United States Educational Commission invited me to become a Fulbright lecturer at two universities in Kyoto, Japan. While teaching at Ryukoku University, I served as consultant to the interdisciplinary Japanese-American Research Project directed by Sohken M. Togami. Conducted by Professor Togami, our Friday afternoon seminars provided us with the opportunity to exchange ideas and learn from the research of Toru Fukuda, Kozo Ikemoto, Kenji Hayashi, Yoshio Kawamura, and Tetsunen Yamada. Dean

Kesaji Kobayashi provided a warm and friendly attitude highlighted by our many discussions of the military history of the Pacific War and its effects on the Japanese in Japan and America, and by the research project's field trip to Mio Village, Wakayama Prefecture, the "Amerika-Mura" that prospered from the remittances of overseas Japanese. I also gained much personal and professional knowledge while serving as a voluntary faculty adviser to the English-Speaking Society of Ryukoku University and discussing matters of rhetoric and culture with ESS President, Hiroyoshi Yamamoto, President-elect Tamotsu Tsubakihara, Chief of Debate Ken Kondo, and Public Relations Officer Minoru Yoshida.

At Doshisha University I had many opportunities to test my theories and perceptions of Asian-American society, minority problems, and the changing foundations of American sociological thought with Professor and Mrs. Hideo Higuchi and with Yasuhiro Aoki, Kikuji Ito, Leo Loveday, Nobunao Matsuyama, Makio Morikawa, Kazunori Oshima, K. Oshimo, and Akira Shigeno. A conference on race relations sponsored by the United States Information Service at Sapporo permitted me to discuss the socio-legal aspects of many United States Supreme Court cases involving Chinese- and Japanese-Americans with Ms. Kinuko Kubota, Japan's leading jurisprudent.

The original dissertation manuscript was typed by Vorna Johnson. Subsequent copies and additions have been prepared in appropriate form by the ever-enduring Daria Cverna-Martin, who also provides inestimable service as critic as well as constant intellectual encouragement. I am grateful for the sharp editorial eye of Marilyn Silverman. Mr. and Mrs. Kenneth Brown and Dr. Richard Koffler of Associated Faculty Press have been the kind of publishers that every author hopes for.

None of the above is to be held responsible for errors of fact, omission, or interpretation. These are mine.

New York City, January 31, 1984 — Stanford M. Lyman

Introduction

Chinatown and Little Tokyo is adapted from my doctoral dissertation, *The Structure of Chinese Society in Nineteenth-Century America*, completed at the University of California at Berkeley, in 1961. Publication by Associated Faculty Press is its first presentation to a wider public. Because it is one of the first monographs in Asian-American Studies and represents a revisionist approach to the sociology of minority communities, I have let the original stand except for excisions of statistical tables, material on European immigrant communities, and a discussion of European and African secret societies.

The dissertation was researched formally from 1957 through 1961, but had as its background my intimate association with Chinatowners and Japanese-Americans since my high school days, and my experiences from 1939 to 1955 at my parents' grocery store on Octavia Street, where San Francisco's black and Japanese communities conjoined. The argument of my dissertation reflected my intellectual dissatisfaction with the state of sociological thinking on race relations in general and on the Asian-Americans in particular. A debilitating ahistoricism had so overtaken those fields of study that social processes were virtually severed from historical occurrences. Race relations, it was argued, especially by the disciples of Robert E. Park, proceeded through patterned stages—contact, competition, and acommodation—until they ended in assimilation.[1] Although prejudice, discrimination, and economic conditions slowed the pace, hindered the progress, and laid obstacles in the path of a racial or ethnic group, the cycle of race relations was held to be progressive, determinate, and irreversible.

Racial groups that had achieved a rewarding position in the occupational order and had overcome predjudice and discrimination were praised for their efforts if they assimilated, but were stigmatized as sociological malingerers if they remained within the confines of their ethnic community. The group basis of ethnic identity was under attack by a benevolent liberal ethos holding up the superiority of an American Commonwealth of individualism: "America does not consist of groups," Woodrow Wilson had said some thirty years earlier: "A man who thinks of himself as belonging to a particular national group in America has not yet become an American."[2] By this criterion neither the Chinese nor Japanese in the United States were yet Americans.

Sociological perspectives on the Chinese and the Japanese had contributed much to the establishment of the assimilationist solution to America's race and ethnic problems. The arrival of Chinese immigrants had challenged the admissions criteria of the new covenant that Social Gospel sociologists hoped would resolve all issues of the Social Question.[3] Assimilation[4] became both a panacea and a prerequisite for admission to the sociologists' version of a coming American utopia, but few believed that either the Chinese or the Japanese could adapt. W.I. Thomas doubted whether the Chinese immigrants' intelligence could reach beyond rote learning and wondered how they could contribute to American progress.[5] Edward Alsworth Ross opposed the admission of either the Chinese or the Japanese, proposing instead that America redeem itself by limiting immigration to German and Scandinavian smallholders.[6] Charles Horton Cooley concluded that the popular animus against the Japanese was a compelling justification for excluding them from the United States.[7] Albion Small believed that the racial and cultural differences between Asiatics and white Americans were too great to be bridged by the social processes.[8] Franklin Henry Giddings held to his thesis that Japanese immigration threatened "the sociological fact that a democratic republic can be maintained only if the population is on the whole homogeneous."[9] Park, analyst and champion of the race relations cycle, became pessimistic about the possibility that the Chinese or Japanese could overcome the prejudice against them,[10] and, later, repudiated his earlier assurance that assimilation would be the final stage of every cycle of race relations.[11]

The "Oriental Question" became a topic for sociology at the University of Chicago and in the satellite departments that were in its perspectival orbit from the 1920s to the end of World War II. Inspired by the promise and worried over the obstacles that Park's race relations cycle held out, such sociologists as Ting. C. Fan, Chin-Chao Wu, Paul C.P. Siu, Helen MacGill Hughes, Roderick McKenzie, Jesse Steiner, Emory Bogardus, Bradford Smith, Edward K. Strong, S.

Frank Miyamoto, Jitsuichi Masuoka, Andrew W. Lind, and Clarence E. Glick invesigated aspects of the assimilative process, reaching sometimes more, sometimes less sanguine conclusions about the future of Asians in the United States. The last of the uncritical adherents of Park's race relations cycle was Rose Hum Lee, who, in 1960, concluded her lifetime study of the Chinese in America with the exhortation, "There should be but one set of norms which apply to human beings anywhere, encompassing sincerity, honesty, integrity, humanity, dignity, humbleness, and concern for the general welfare." Lee believed that these norms were embodied in the social institutions of postwar America. Accordingly, she instructed her fellow Chinese-Americans, "Regardless of where the peoples of the United States originated, they must strive to fit in to the new social climate which emerged in American society and the world after World War II."[12] The new social climate, however, no longer pressed the older demand for deracinated individualism. The wholesale incarceration of America's Japanese had given the lie to the civic benefits of assimilation, and, except for analysts of race and ethnic relations, few postwar sociologists relied on the old formula.

My own disappointment with the failure of sociologists to develop a fresh perspective on race and ethnic relations led me to undertake a critical assessment of the assimilationist thesis as it applied to Asian-Americans and to investigate the social, cultural, and economic backgrounds to Chinese and Japanese community formation, development, and change. My research proceeded to show that American Chinatowns were not solely an institutional consequence of white racism; similar kinds of community organization were to be found wherever Cantonese had migrated. Chinese immigrants to the United States had brought with them ideas, customs, ways of life, and social institutions that they creatively adapted to their situation in America. Once established, this institutional and cultural complex developed an inertia of its own, persevering in the changing climate of American race relations, maintaining its basic mode of operation in the face of both internal dissent and external assault. Chinese Old World organization made its way side by side that of white America.

Japanese culture, social organization, kinship, and engrained ways of life were also carried abroad in the hearts and minds of its immigrants, but were different from those of the Chinese. Japan had begun to "modernize" two centuries before emigration began. Its cities were closer to the "Occidental" type than those of China; its family system permitted branch nucleation at places of settlement distant from the originating stem. When overseas, the Japanese adapted their organization of communities to an environment of small-holding peasantry and urban ghetto shopkeeping. Their American-born children entered into the maintstream as claimants for civil rights and occupational opportunities. What counted among the first two generations of the Japanese was personal character and living up to the ideal of struggle symbolized by "the Japanese spirit," (Yamato Damashii).[13] Far less significant were the immigrant's associations (*kenjinkai*) that, in contrast to the family-less Chinatowners' clans, *kongsis*, and secret societies, declined during the 1930s, and, after the wartime imprisonment, became associations of nostalgia. Because Japanese community organization complemented that of white America, some analysts mistakenly supposed that their Old World culture had utterly eroded and that nothing but the physical characteristics of race and the attitudes toward them kept Japanese-Americans from disappearing into the mainstream.[14]

Both the Chinese and the Japanese were segregated from white America, but their communities were not alike. The Chinese resided in Chinatowns where in less than splendid isolation they reconstituted the folkways and lived under the guidance of institutions common to city life in traditional China: clans, *landsmannschaften*, and secret societies. Barred by many states' miscegenation laws from marrying outside their own race and prevented by Chinese custom and, later, America's Exclusion Act from bringing their wives and sweethearts to join them in the overseas venture, most Chinatowners sojourned in America as homeless men, served by and serving their Old World associations and working for the day when they might return to China. Their communities contained few women and children; the teenagers to be found there often had been sired in China on one of the infrequent home visits an immigrant paid to his wife and relatives, and had joined their fathers overseas as soon as they had become mature. Chinatown had a solidarity, but it was not supported by internal harmony or a sense of mutual affection. The clans, speech-and-territorial associations, and secret societies competed with each other for control over the communal polity and economy. Their antagonisms strengthened the commitment of Chinatowners to their respective associations, divided these into warring groups, and consolidated their differences as communalized enemies. For much of its history Chinatown was an arena of intramural conflict, isolated from the society that enclosed it.

The Japanese immigrants had established a number of prefecturally based kenjinkai in America, and also formed the Japanese Associations of America, but such groupings could not sustain community-wide authority. Able to marry and settle down on small plots of ground in the Pacific coast hinterlands or to dwell in the Little Tokyos of cities in California, Oregon, and Washington as laborers, domestics, or keepers of *kai-sha* ("Japanese businesses"), the Japanese differentiated themselves according to occupations, urban or rural residence, and, most significantly, by generation. The only people in America to measure group identity in accordance with geo-generational distance from the country of origin,[15] the Japanese distinguish between the *Issei* (the immigrant generation); the *Nisei* (the American-born children of the Issei); the *Sansei* (the American-born grandchildren of the Issei); the *Yonsei* (the American-born great grandchildren of the Issei); the *Gosei* (the American-born great-great grandchildren of the Issei); and the *Kibei* (Nisei educated in their formative years in Japan and returned to America). Each group is said to have its own social character, formed on the basis of its unique experience as *Nikkei* (Japanese in America). The Nikkei are united around their system of geo-generational lineage but divided by social status and by age and respective group personalities. Community conflicts sometimes break out between generational groups, but these never become violent. In fact the deportment of the Japanese-Americans during and after their wartime imprisonment (1942-45) and their integration into the larger economy in the years thereafter led some white observers to regard them as peaceful and highly acculturated. During the racial and ethnic conflicts of the 1960s, one sociologist and a number of journalists nominated them as a "model miniority."[16] There are no "tong wars" in Little Tokyo.

At the same time that I was carrying on my research on Chinatown and Little Tokyo, other sociologists were attempting to formulate a new definition of the American social compact and of the social processes that functioned to keep it viable.[17] Instead of calling for the assimilation of all racial and ethnic groups within the United States, they reconceptualized Park's "coordination of sentiments"—the simulacrum of assimilation—and rejected the necessity of a culturally homogeneous national community.[18] Theirs was the new creed of pluralism. Encouraging consensus around the vital interests of American domestic and international security, the pluralist perspective called for toleration of a healthy diversity among the peoples and cultures of the United States. Racial and ethnic problems were subordinated, becoming but another factor that required management in the new corporate liberal state. Hoping to supersede the doctrines of both left and right, social scientists proclaimed the end of ideology and the opening of a new era in which administrative reform and rational social management would replace anachronistic ideologies and resolve intergroup conflicts. The thesis of American pluralism arose as part of the cold war, and, as I have noted elsewhere, sociology enlisted in this struggle as it had in World War II.[19]

The pluralist end-of-ideology thesis was disconcerting for many Asian-Americans. Enunciated only a few years after the incarceration of the Japanese-Americans, it posed questions about the beliefs and conduct appropriate for Chinese- and Japanese-Americans caught up in America's global struggle against communism. Nationalist China could claim effective sovereignty only over the island of Formosa after 1949, but the United States would recognize and support the Kuomintang regime for almost three decades after its retreat from the Communist-dominated mainland. Chinatowners, apprehensive about what could happen to Asiatics accused of disloyalty to the United States, joined in the anti-Communist crusade. The authority of the Kuomintang, which had infiltrated the oligarchic elite structure of Chinatown years before,[20] was reinforced by cold war policies. Paradoxically, an unacculturated Chinatown could now appear as a small but important bastion of American security, more reliable than the patriotic Nisei of 1942, United States citizens who had volunteered to fight against Japan. Lee's 1960 proposal that the Chinatown Chinese give up their allegiance to traditional associations, depart from the ghetto, and acculturate as rapidly and completely as the Nisei, failed to grasp the status conferred on Chinatown by the cold war.[21] Chinatowners could see that American pluralism might not trust deracinated people to be loyal, but that it did tolerate a diversity of races and cultures even while restricting their ethnic expressions to contributions to aesthetic, athletic, gastronomic, or occupational advances, and to America's national security. With the onset of the cold war, Chinatown's workers' brief flirtation with left-wing labor came to an end. The Chinese Consolidated Benevolent Association granted a permanent seat on its executive board to a representative of the Kuomintang and reasserted its claim to be the sole representative of the Chinese community.[22] Whatever the fate of other ideologies in the era of the "end-of-ideology," the cold war rendered unreserved assimilatin obsolete and redefined the socio-psychological frame for Chinese- and Japanese-Americans.

The advocates of the new pluralism did not envision the reaction their tolerance would arouse among America's racial minorities. Central to the former's perspective was preservation of the institutions of social control and America's basic values. The liberal corporate leadership, who hoped to hold together what Arthur Schlesinger, Jr., called "the vital center,"[23] shared a common faith in the legitimacy of America's institutions, the righteousness of its foreign policies, and the assurance of its moral triumph throughout the world. Asia became the first major international test of the new consensus. In 1950, the United States, under a United Nations mandate, conducted a "police action" in

Korea, putting its troops into combat with not only the North Koreans but also the Communist Chinese; in 1960, American military advisers were sent to Indochina to begin an undeclared fifteen-year war that would eventually engulf Cambodia, Laos, and Vietnam; compel thousands of Asian refugees (a number of them Chinese from Cholon, that is, the Chinatown district of Saigon) to seek safety overseas; and, ultimately, undermine the moral authority of America's vital center.

Because sociologists had contributed to the legitimation of the vital center thesis, angered students and alienated minority group spokesmen began a critique of sociology. The paradigm of structural functionalism identified the United States as a dynamically equilibrating social system inspired by the values of universality, achievement, and individualism, each kept in progressive motion by the voluntary association of its citizens.[24] So pervasive had this perspective become by the end of the 1950s, that Kingsley Davis pointed to the myth of functional analysis as a special variant of sociology; functionalism and sociology were coextensive.[25] And the United States, what Seymour Martin Lipset called the first new nation, would, or at least should, inspire the postcolonial states in Asia, Africa, and Latin America to model their own social development after that of its Founding Fathers. But, as Lipset noted, in the United States equality could not be achieved by a policy of gradual increments; the race question was the Achilles's heel of America's unblemished history of stability in the midst of change.[26]

By the 1960s, Clark Kerr and Edward Shils discovered that the American social system had both a center and a periphery.[27] The center was emptying out as students, minorities, and supposedly assimilated ethnics revolted against America's mass culture, middle-class morality, and warlike foreign policy. Social observers began to speak of the rise of the unmeltable ethnics and the decline of the WASP.[28] Functionalist sociologists began to retreat in the face of the critiques offered by their opponents.[29] However, no paradigm seemed able to embrace the totality of American society or to account for America's aroused racial and ethnic minorities.

One casualty of the conflicts of the 1960s was the concept of assimilation and its attendant ideal, Americanization. In 1980, Philip Gleason found it necessary to repudiate Wilson's assimilationist dictum: "American nationality...does not preclude the existence of ethnicity in the subgroup peoplehood-sense." However, he felt compelled to add that "respect for American principles cannot help but be weakened when the very words *Americanism* and *Americanization* are treated as terms of abuse and when earlier efforts to articulate the nation's values and to give them symbolic expression are dismissed as hypocrisy or worse."[30] In the same year Harold J. Abramson reassessed assimilation and pluralism in American society, reminding his readers that Harriet Martineau had described the United States as a society of "many countries" and that Alexis de Tocqueville had pointed to both voluntary and involuntary association as keys to democracy in America. By 1982, Hubert M. Blalock found it unnecessary to include assimilation in his discussion of the basic processes of race and ethnic relations.[31] In contrast to those pre-World War II sociologists, who had emphasized a unilinear march of all races and cultural groups into the nonethnic oblivion of assimilation, Abramson asserted that "the fluidity of American life...has resulted not in the disappearance of ethnic diversity, but in the persistence of group cultures and structures;... not in the tyranny of pluralistic group life, but in change and diversity within distinctiveness."[32] The consensus demanded by the politics of the cold war failed to hold, partly because of the ineffectiveness of those politics, and partly because the internal divisions in the American people could not fail to assert themselves in the changing culture and political economy of postwar America. When the vital center virtually collapsed, the inner racial and ethnic conflicts were discovered not only to be unresolved but also to have taken on newer and more complex dimensions. Such sociologists as Gleason, Abramson, Blalock, and others are seeking a new vocabulary and a new formula for understanding American race relations, but thus far both have eluded them. The fires of the assimilating melting pot have never blazed hot enough, and the benign domesticity of the pluralistic "salad bowl" does not contain the ethnics or solve their problems. The numerical, distributional, occupational, and educational disproportions among the several racial and ethnic groups in the United States seem to call for a new measure of justice: affirmative action, quota systems, preferential treatment, and, perhaps, monetary reprarations. However, these calculations of a new equality are opposed by the older moral calculus of meritocratic individualism, and by those racial and ethnic group members who have attained middle-class status and power through it. At present there is no sociological or policy consensus on the definition, solution, or resolution of the racial and ethnic problem in America.

The year I completed "The Structure of Chinese Society in Nineteenth-Century America," 1961, coincided with the first expressions of an awakened ethnic consciousness among Asian-Americans and other minorities. On college and university campuses Chinese and Japanese students began a campaign against the administrative benevolence that guided the social and curricular policies of the liberal pluralists. Together with the spokesmen for blacks, Hispanics, Native

Americans, and other minorities, Chinese and Japanese students denounced the sociologists and corporate liberals and asserted their own right to define the meaning of racial identity, establish the grounds for its legitimacy, and chart its development and future in the United States. In so doing they rejected both assimilationist and pluralist models, but found it difficult to formulate an acceptable perspective to replace them.

My work on Chinese- and Japanese-Americans has roused controversy and dissent. *Chinatown and Little Tokyo* will no doubt do the same. For some critics—despite my critical, Weberian reanalysis of America's racial policies as having evolved from total institutionalized subordination on slave plantations and Indian reservations to what I call partially institutionalized sequestration in ghettos such as Chinatown[33]—my perspective is insufficiently detached from the assimilationist and managerial pluralist outlooks. They complain that it "implicitly," "unconsciously," or "indirectly" lends support to the neoconservative model minority thesis.[34] Such "structuralist" reproaches by persons who practice pseudo-psychoanalysis misapprehend both the nature of the problem and the character of my work. Of greater concern is the debate over immigrant Chinese sojourners, and the allegation that sojourner status derogates, misapprehends, or obscures the position and prospects of the immigrants and their descendants. The issues here are substantive, epistemological, and methodological. Often they reflect the rivalry of disciplinary perspectives, especially age-old disputes between historians and sociologists. Sometimes they mask chauvinistic or ideological leanings, claiming that only certain methods or a particular hermeneutic will produce the "correct" understanding. In Asian-American studies the rush to critical judgment has preceded the careful establishment of sound criteria for it.[35]

That most of the original Chinese and Japanese immigrants perceived themselves as sojourners is not contestable. Nevertheless, controversies arise over explanations of the social and cultural conditions that fostered or discouraged sojourner status among the overseas Chinese and Japanese and the effects of designating these immigrants as sojourners. A leading exemplar of this type of critique is Roger Daniels.[36] Preferring to classify both the Chinese and the Japanese as "Westerners from the East," Daniels virtualy acculturates them before their arrival in the United States and obliterates the constraints their respective systems of kinship imposed on them, placing sole responsibility for their suffering as well as their community organization on American legislation and white racism. From this position it is but one step to criticizing my sociocultural analysis of the Chinatown clan situation as a species of "familistic determinism." Aside from its attribution of passivity, deracination, and mere reaction formation to the Asians—the kind of error that Ralph Ellison found in Gunnar Myrdal's analysis of America's black communities[37]—Daniels is at a loss to explain and, in fact, does not bother to explain, why Chinese women did not accompany men to America during the period (1847-82) when their migration was not severely restricted, or why a womanless condition was to be found among overseas Cantonese and Fukienese throughout Southeast Asia, the islands of the Pacific, Latin America, and the Caribbean; that is, in areas where American racist laws were inoperant. Insisting that a subtle racism is behind any attempt to see the Orientals as "different," Daniels acknowledges cultural differences among the Asian peoples only to dismiss their significance by invoking the *tu quoque* argument: European immigrants are also divisible along cultural lines; hence all cultures are cancelable as factors in immigrant social organization because each people possesses one! For Daniels, "[U]ntil uncontrovertible evidence to the contrary is offered, the generalizations which apply to most immigrants also apply to Asians."[38] Having solved the cultural issue by declaring the cultures of the Chinese and Japanese off limits for analysis, Daniels then asserts, "The Chinese and Japanese were Westerners, and largely Californians at that...[T]he chief difference between [these two examples of] immigrants was that one group became industrial proletarians while the other became agricultural proletarians."[39] Unfortunately for this vaguely Marxist thesis, the historical facts will not bear its ideological weight. Within a period of three decades (1880-1910) the Chinese were driven out of their precarious places in the industrial labor force by the racist agitation of American unions. They retreated into Chinatown where they became the much exploited labor and service workers of a nonindustrial commercial colony organized along the lines that Max Weber had described for the Oriental city.[40] Nor did the Japanese remain an agricultural labor force for much more than three decades (1890-1910). Adapting their homeland's *hokonin* system[41] to California's farm situation, most settled down as smallholders, sent for wives from Japan, and became much beleaguered farmers. They were assisted in accomplishing all of this by their creative exploitation of three elements of Japanese life that they grafted onto the American scene: the *hokonin*, "labor organization," the *shashin-kekkon*, "arranged marriage,"[42] and the *ie*, "lineage" and *honke-bunke* systems of stem-branch familism.[43] Converting Chinese and Japanese immigrants into proletarians might satisfy the kind of millennial wish fulfillment that led Marx to see the solution to the Jewish question in the emancipation of society from Judaism,[44] but neither Judaism nor Asian identity is likely to commit ethnocide to satisfy such an apocalyptic nightmare.

Still another critique of the sojourner thesis holds that it is a myth foisted on the Chinese and on Sino-American scholarship by politicians and leaders of the anti-Chinese movement.[45] There can be no doubt that their situation as absentee husbands was used against the Chinese by demagogues and labor leaders,[46] but for the Issei bringing wives became grist for the anti-Japanese movement.[47] The fact that racists exploited the womanless conditions of the Chinese laborer and that American laws (the Page Law of 1875 and the Chinese Exclusion Act of 1882) made it virtually immpossible for the wife of an overseas Chinese laborer to join him should not be taken as indications that the Chinese did not desire to return to China, or that they quite matter-of-factly left their wives in China in the protective hands of their parents. Both the Kuomintang and the Chinese Communist regimes have regarded the overseas Chinese as groups exploitable for remittances and remigration. The "homeland" tactics employed by the representatives of both Nationalist and Peoples China in Chinatown are well documented.[48] In the Chinese case the sojourner orientation was sometimes passed on to children born in or brought to America. Two decades after the first Republican revolution, some San Francisco Chinatowners urged their children to acquire a technical education in the American public schools and then move to China where they might contribute to its modernization. After the establishment of the Peoples Republic in 1949, a few Chinese-Americans went to China to participate in the continuing revolution. In 1984, the Peoples Republic reopened its campaign to reconnect with the twenty million overseas Chinese, inviting them to visit China, adding an article to its constitution that "protects [their] legitimate rights and interests," and urging them to promote contacts between their country of settlement and their homeland. Since 1949, according to Wang Chunliu, director of the Office of Overseas Affairs at Xiamen (formerly Amoy), one million immigrant Chinese have remigrated: "Most are very old people who want to spend their final years in their homeland."[49] It seems clear that the realities and complexities of the sojourner situation cannot be dismissed as a myth merely because some vested interest groups have exploited the sojourner's situation.

By the same token, Japanese sojourners could afford to give up or postpone until old age[50] their reunification with the ie, returning in retirement to the village honke after they had established a bunke[51] in America. In the United States some Issei and Nisei adapted this system to the rural-urban communal economy. One cohort of the Nisei came of age just as the Great Depression set in. Seeking employment in West Coast cities, they found little that was remunerative. A number of farm-bred Nisei opened fruit and vegetable stands, their produce supplied by trucks from their parents' fields and orchards. Such adaptations suggest that the complex culture of Old World Japanese familism played a vital part in their economic adjustment in America.

Another orientation toward the Asian as a sojourner seeks to retain sojourner status but strip off its specific cultural content. This approach is taken by economic determinists and by neo-Marxist sociologists who replace the liberal pluralists' image of the Asian-American as a "model minority" with that of a "middleman." Both Marxist and liberal sociologists agree on the primacy of economic functions, and each wishes to downplay an independent noneconomic function for Chinese and Japanese Old World norms, immigrant institutions, or character and personality. They disagree in their attitudes toward capitalism and achievement. Liberals, (or neoconservatives) eager to reduce the state's obligation to affirm economic opportunities for minorities, attempt to show that the Asian immigrants' culture and personality have contributed to their advance in a laissez faire economy. Thus, for William Petersen, Japan's "Tokugawa religion" becomes the functional equivalent of the Protestant ethic, instilling the drive to succeed across three generations of Nikkei;[52] while for Thomas Sowell, America's Chinese and Japanese are among the more profitable investors of the "whole constellation of values, attitudes, skills, and contacts that many call a culture and that economists call 'human capital,'"[53] and their abilities therein provide "the most dramatic evidence" that "subjective prejudice" is not always translated into effective economic discrimination.[54] Neo-Marxists and other economic determinists treat the sojourner status as an artifact of early capitalist imperialism, a stage in its development when select opportunities were offered to Japanese "middlemen," brokering labor and commercial relations between white entrepreneurs and proletarians of all races.[55] Ethnic identity among these "middlemen minorities" is regarded, virtually, as a false cultural consciousness,[56] blocking self-understanding of the actual function that strategically placed ethnics serve in capitalist development. Presumably these illusions of ethnicity will be exposed in one of three outcomes: the capitalist apocalypse; by the Japanese rising further, perhaps to executive positions; or, regardless of the fate of capitalism or the mobility of the Nikkei, through Asian-Americans' validation of the middleman minority thesis by abandoning their claim to ethnic identity.[57]

For both the liberals and the neo-Marxists the cultural complexes of Asian-Americans are dichotomized in acordance with the interests or dissolution of capitalism: liberals regard those elements that encourage hard work, honesty, chastity, and obedience as eufunctional; that favor indolence, promiscuity, crime, and rebelliousness, dysfunctional.[58] For the neo-Marxists, Japanese and, to a lesser extent, Chinese middlemen are either dupes of the capitalist exploitation of a racially split labor market, opting for a veneer of cultural autonomy instead of forging a proletarian class identification across racial lines, or transients in the final stages of eth-class development, living out the last vestiges of a self-deluding subnational life.[59] In both cases the ethnics are virtually invited to sanitize their cultural heritages according to the respective demands of the liberal or neo-Marxist approaches to American capitalism. The extent to which either the liberal or neo-Marxist positions is adopted by Asian-Americans will indicate the degree and direction of their acculturation, providing a new index of minority acceptability.

Still another position seeks to overcome the assimilationist and liberal pluralist orientations by choosing the ghetto colonialist thesis, first put forward by Robert Blauner.[60] The United States is conceptualized as an imperialist state that established much of its "empire" in the form of internal colonies. Hence, "The Chinatowns of America may be viewed as neocolonial enclaves in which a business class has been able to gain wealth and political power within the ethnic community. In the larger society, however, the Chinese are utlimately powerless, controlled by outside political or economic arrangements."[61] The Japanese are pictured as the only Asian people whose homeland had resisted Western domination. Their "colonization" is depicted in the many discriminatory laws that affected them and in their victimization as an incarcerated enemy people during World War II.[62] The specific contents of the Asian-American cultures are given no special notice, and apparently they are irrelevant to this type of analysis. In the 1960s, Blauner justified revolts against the ghetto because he believed that the "colonized must have the choice between participating in the larger society [or] in independent structures of their own."[63] The choice between restive Chinatown "homelands" or anti-imperialist struggles for integration fails to grasp the complex dynamic that relates one to the other and both to the changing cultural, political, and socioeconomic conditions of the United States in the world.

A more recent modification of Blauner's thesis opts for benevolent Constitutionalism and provides no role for Asian cultures in the maintenance or dissolution of overseas Chinese and Japanese communities. Benjamin Ringer[64] treats the Chinese and Japanese experience in the United States solely in terms of California's statutes, congressional legislation, executive orders, and the decisions of the Supreme

Court.[65] Whatever "colonial" status the two peoples occupy is perceived in terms of what Ringer designates as the white "peoples domain," the WASP sociocultural arena that is his critical view of what the liberal pluralists considered the vital center. Because many of the inequities imposed by America's peculiar variant of internal colonialism continue "to fester and to contaminate the American society and its People's Domain," Ringer exhorts the "dominant whites" to remove them.[66] For Ringer, as for Myrdal, America's minorities are for the most part passive, capable only of responding to the machinations of the ever dominant whites, and not able to shape their own lives according to their own lights.

As this study of the interplay of Chinese, Japanese, and American sociocultural institutions goes to press, the basic issues that inspired it are still outstanding. Students of race relations in general and its Asian-American variant in particular have for the most part rejected the older assimilationist and liberal pluralist models in favor of paradigms of study or programs of action that emphasize cultural radicalism, internal colonialist reactions, middleman minority theses, or participatory integration within mainstream political, economic, cultural, and social institutions.[67]

In virtual agreement that they have passed some distance beyond the melting pot, Chinese- and Japanese-Americans live quite varied lives. Chinatown has been invigorated by the Immigration Act of 1965, permitting a balancing of the sex ratio, reunification of families, and the immigration of thousands of Chinese from Hong Kong, Taiwan, Singapore and, since the thaw in American relations with the Peoples Republic, a handful from mainland China. Revolutions in Cuba and Indochina have resulted in an exodus of Chinese from these two areas; these peoples are settled in various parts of the United States, some outside of, others in Chinatown. In 1980, the census reported 805,000 persons of Chinese ancestry living in the United States, making them the largest Asian group in America, 23 percent of all Asian-Americans. Chinatown is no longer the single place of work or residence for the Chinese in America. Suburban Chinese communities are to be found near major cities that have Chinatowns.[68] The Mississippi Chinese, who never developed a Chinatown, are beginning to move out from the grocery store community they had established in black neighborhoods on the Delta.[69] Foreign and American-born Chinese engineers, chemists, physicists, physicians, pharmacists, and other health and science personnel are to be found in the major industrial, hospital, and professional institutions of the United States.[70] The technological revolution in microchips has captured the imagination of some Chinese, Japanese, and Korean technicians and entrepreneurs in northern California's silicon valley and Los Angeles's "hi-tech" centers.[71]

At the same time Chinatown's old institutions persevere. The balancing of the sex ratio, the aging of the sojourner bachelor population, and the decline of prostitution have caused them to readjust priorities and to reorganize the kinds of goods and services they offer. Tourism continues to be a major attraction. The commercial exploitation of waiters, busboys, clerks, and garment workers is thriving as new immigrants, unable to speak English or lacking marketable skills, fill the places once occupied by sojourners. Large amounts of capital are being transferred from Taiwan and Hong Kong to Chinatown, as is evidenced by the new banks, theaters, and newspapers to be found there. Chinese-American organizations, established by the American-born, have attempted to reform or to revolutionize the Chinatown scene, but they have had little visible success thus far. The International Ladies Garment Workers Union, long indifferent to the fate of Chinatown's garment workers, has recently made a modest effort at organizing the immigrant seamstress.[72] The aged of Chinatown "have chosen separate residences more to avoid potential conflicts over family roles than because of a genuine preference for independent living."[73] A number of sojourners who cannot go home again commit suicide every year. Youth gangs, organized among alienated adolescents from Hong Kong and Taiwan, or by American-born Chinese dropouts who have not opted for college, a profession, and the suburbs, violently vie for "turf" and the profits to be made from extorting money from Chinatown shopkeepers, or they allow themselves to be co-opted by the secret societies[74] as mercenaries and as guards of the illegal gambling establishments that still operate out of Chinatown basements. In both San Francisco and New York, Chinatown has quietly expanded into the adjacent "Little Italy" neighborhoods and spawned "second" or satellite Chinatowns in the Richmond District and Brooklyn, respectively. The Chung Hua Kongsi continues to exert community-wide authority in Chinatown, its legitimacy untoppled by acculturative developments in the United States, or by the changing international situation affecting Taiwan, Hong Kong, and the Peoples Republic of China.[75]

The situation of Japanese-Americans is even more varied. In 1980, the census reported 701,000 persons of Japanese ancestry to be living in the United States, making them 20 percent, or the third largest, of the Asian-American and Pacific Island peoples in America, outnumbered only by Pilipino- and Chinese-Americans. Despite relaxation of the immigration laws, few Japanese migrate to America. Those who do come are the new sojourner business and banking trainees, doing a term of service in the large Japanese industrial, commercial, or financial concerns established in the United States. Specialized service operations—language schools, Japanese food and bookstores, and restaurants and bars where the businessmen might find *karaoke* (Japanese music that they can sing to the accompaniment of a piano or a recorded tape)—have opened up in New York City, San Francisco, and Los Angeles. Despite acculturation, Japanese religions—Konko-kyo, Tenri-kyo, and Buddhism—continue to flourish side by side with Japanese-American Protestantism.[76] Although Nihonmachi (literally "Japan town") is now a commercial and tourist attraction built over the federally bulldozed ruins of San Francisco's Little Tokyo, and Los Angeles boasts a rebuilt Little Tokyo to celebrate the Sansei and the Japanese businessmen's revitalization of Japanese culture, no territorially enclosed Japanese-American community comparable to Chinatown is to be found in America's cities.

Since 1923, much of the growth of the Japanese population of America has occurred through natural increase; the Nikkei can now count as many as six generations in America, although the bulk are Nisei and Sansei. Intermarriages by the Sansei and subsequent generations have amalgamated the Japanese with the white population but not eliminated their sense of ethnicity. The Supreme Court's decision in the *Lau* case[77] has compelled the public schools to ensure that knowledge of the language and cultures of Asia is part of the curriculum for both Chinese- and Japanese-American children. The occupational spectrum among the Nisei and the Sansei has broadened to embrace a number of professional, managerial, and technical fields as well as noticeable representation in local, state, and in a few instances, national politics.[78] The discrimination experienced by the third and fourth generations is subtle and more likely to be hidden in superficially neutral bureaucratic rules or behind the barriers to private clubs where executive decisions are made. However, the murder of Vincent Chin, a Chinese-American mistaken for a Japanese by two disgruntled laborers, and the light punishment—probation and a fine—meted out by the judge, aroused widespread protests by Asian-American groups throughout the United States.

Among Japanese-Americans the wartime imprisonment looms as a decisive experience and as an unresolved issue. The matter is relived and reconsidered annually in the New Year's edition of the Japanese-American Citizens' League newspaper, *The Pacific Citizen.* Among Nisei and Sansei spokesmen there is considerable debate over whether it was due to intracommunal activities that the Japanese were declared an enemy people and whether the consequences of their forced removal were beneficial.[79] In 1976, President Ford revoked Executive Order 9066 by which Japanese-Americans had been imprisoned in 1942; he also pardoned Iva Toguri D'aquino, a Nisei charged with being "Tokyo Rose" during World War II.[80] In 1980, Congress established a Commission on Wartime Relocation and Internment of Civilians to review the facts and circumstances attending the relocation, removal, and detention of Japanese-Americans and other Asians (the Aleuts of the Aleutian and Pribilof islands) and to recommend appropriate remedies to the injured parties.[81] In June 1983, the commission recommended *inter alia* that Congress establish a fund and provide a one-time per capita payment of $20,000 to each of the 60,000 survivors of the wartime exclusion.[82] At the same time, invoking a *coram nobis* procedure,[83] Gordon Hirabayashi, Min Yasui, and Toyosaburo Korematsu applied to the Supreme Court to consider the constitutionality of their wartime convictions for resisting the curfew and detention orders issued against Pacific Coast Japanese.[84] In November 1983, a United States district court judge set aside Korematsu's conviction, pointing out that in his case the Supreme Court's 1944 decision has been "based on unsubstantiated facts, distortions, and misrepresentations."[85] Continued interest and social action in reference to the wartime exclusion testifies not only to Japanese-Americans' interest in securing their civil rights as citizens of the United States, but also to the geo-generational and sociocultural distance from Meiji-Taisho Japan traveled by successive generations of Nikkei.[86]

Chinatown and Little Tokyo is written from a civilization perspective. Aspects of a migrating people's culture and social organization are regarded as chattel, carried abroad to places where they interpenetrate with the culture and social institutions of the host society and adapt, reorganize, complement, or erode in the face of the opportunities and constraints imposed by the latter. The communities established overseas by the Chinese and the Japanese are treated in terms of their fundamental sociocultural components: local origin, speech and dialect, economic condition, institutions of community power, and normative superstructure.[87] Contact between cultures always leads to disturbances in the institutional and normative realms and can lead to a reconsideration of fundamental beliefs and ways of life. However, such potentials for wholesale change must be considered in relation to the tendencies toward conservation, resilience, and adaptability in the respective peoples' outlooks, cultures, and modes of social organization.[88] The Chinese and Japanese experiences in America are contrastive cases—the former toward persistence, the latter toward change and adaptation. In neither case, however, did the norms, beliefs, institutions, or ways of life fade away gradually and orderly under the supposedly inexorable attractions of Americanization. Moreover, what Americanization has occurred should be seen in light of Gustav Ratzenhofer's 1893 prediction about the future of race relations in the United States:

> ...[T]he time will come when the population will have become dense. The struggle for existence will have to be more carefully planned... When the situation comes about, the memory of racial extraction may at last be reawakened. The different languages may become the rallying centers for different interests. Thereupon for the first time will America confront decisively the problem of its national unity.[89]

The time for reevaluation of the basis for American national unity is now at hand. However, the sociological imagination guiding this reexamination seems to be limited by an incapacity to see beyond alternatives of unreserved assimilation, benevolently managed pluralism, or radical eth-class revolution. Common to all of these is the acceptance of the legitimacy of the state as an instrument of group authority. This uncritical commitment to the efficacy of state authority persists in the face of the erosion of a public philosophy and the decline of the religious foundations for the American compact.[90] Asian-American studies are thus relegated to playing a minor role in "bringing the state back in."[91]

The first ethnographer of American Chinatowns, Robert Stewart Culin (1858-1929) proceeded from a nonstatist global perspective on civilizational development. He hypothesized that the cultures of China, Japan, and Korea had originated as adaptations of the autochthonous Paleolithic culture carried by migrating Amerinds into Asia,[92] and that the cultural ideas of these civilizations had, through subsequent contacts, spread to the Middle East, Africa, and Europe, ultimately returning to America as European art motifs, designs, and ways of daily life and, in more pristine form, as the gambling games, divination ceremonies, and communal folkways of the Chinatowners.[93] Opposed to the powerful nationalistic and ethnocentric illusions of its age, Culin's thesis had no takers; utterly neglected, it was never subjected to empirical investigation.[94] It is not my intention to advocate the validity of his thesis, but rather to invoke its spirit of intellectual independence. Its basic assumption, later to be incorporated in Emile Durkheim and Marcel Mauss's theory of civilization,[95] was that culture movements could transcend political organization, territorial boundaries, and formal constraints. That idea deserves attention in any reconsideration of the nature, or the wisdom, of national unit. *Chinatown and Little Tokyo* is dedicated to the revitalization of an independent sociocultural imagination.

NOTES

1. For my critique of sociological theory in race relations see Stanford M. Lyman, *The Black American in Sociological Thought: A Failure of Perspective* (New York: Putnam, 1972).
2. Quoted in Thomas E. Finegan, "The Education of the Illiterate Immigrant," *The Annals of the American Academy of Political and Social Science* XCII (January 1921): 173.
3. See Arthur J. Vidich and Stanford M. Lyman, *American Sociology: Worldly Rejections of Religion and their Directions* (New Haven: Yale U.P., 1984).
4. As both a process and concept, *assimilation* was introduced into the lexicon of sociology in 1901-1902, by Sarah E. Simons: "Social Assimilation," *American Journal of Sociology* VI (May 1901): 79-82; (July 1901): 53-79; (November 1901): 386-404; (January 1902): 539.556. The term received its imprimatur in the discipline when Robert E. Park and Ernest W. Burgess devoted an entire chapter of their path-breaking *Introduction to the Science of Sociology* [Chicago: U. of Chicago, 1921), pp. 734-84] to examining it. The term was always ambiguously defined. Charles Richmond Henderson noted that it indicated "a field of observation and of critical interpretation of intercourse between members of groups, races, or nations" ["'Social Assimilation': America and China," *American Journal of Sociology* XXIX (March 1914): 640.].
5. W.I. Thomas, *Sex and Society: Studies in the Social Psychology of Sex*, Chicago: U. of Chicago, 1907, New York: Arno Press, 1974), pp. 285-87. For Thomas's conflation of Chinese and Japanese cultures and a debate with other scholars over his fears about an Asian conquest of America, see
   Thomas, "The Significance of the Orient for the Occident," *Publications of the American Sociological Society: Papers and Proceedings* II (1907): 111-39.
6. Edward A. Ross, *The Changing Chinese: The Conflict of Oriental and Western Cultures in China* (New York: The Century Co., 1911); *The Old World in the New: The Significance of Past and Present Immigration to the American People* (New York: The Century Co., 1914); *The Social Trend* (1922; reprint ed., Freeport: Books for Libraries Press, 1970).
7. Tasuku Harada, ed., *The Japanese Problem in California* (San Francisco: Privately printed: 1922; reprint ed., San Francisco: R. and E. Research Associates, 1971), pp. 17, 35.
8. Ibid., pp. 34, 38.

9. Ibid., p. 35.
10. Ibid., pp. 15-16, 23, 27-28.
11. Park, Introduction to *Interracial Marriage in Hawaii: A Study of the Mutually Conditioned Processes of Acculturation and Amalgamation*, by Romanzo Adams (1937; reprint ed., New York: Macmillan: Montclair, N.J.: Patterson Smith, 1969), p. xiii.
12. Rose Hum Lee, *The Chinese in the United States of America* (Hong Kong: Hong Kong University Press, 1960), p. 430.
13. See Lyman, "Generation and Character: The Case of the Japanese-Americans," in *The Asian in North America* (Santa Barbara: American Bibliographic Center-Clio Press, 1977), pp. 151-76.
14. Leonard Broom and John I. Kitsuse, "The Validation of Acculturation: A Condition of Ethnic Assimilation," *American Anthropologist* LVII (February 1955): 44-48.
15. I am informed by Tetsuden Kashima that Korean immigrants to America might also be counting geo-generationally. Korea was occupied by Japan from 1910 to 1945.
16. See "Success Story of One Minority Group in U.S.," *U.S. News and World Report*, December 26, 1966, reprinted in *Roots: An Asian American Reader*, ed., Amy Tachiki et al. (Los Angeles: Asian-American Studies Center, 1971), pp. 6-9.
17. See Talcott Parsons "Social Strains in America (1955)," in *The Radical Right*, ed., Daniel Bell, pp. 175-92 (New York: Doubleday, 1963);
Daniel Bell, *The End of Ideology: On the Exhaustion of Political Ideas in the Fifties*, rev. ed. (New York: Collier Books, 1962), pp. 275-404.
18. William M. Newman, *American Pluralism: A Study of Minority Groups and Social Theory* (New York: Harper and Row, 1973).
19. See Lyman and Vidich, "Prodigious Fathers, Prodigal Sons: An Essay in Review of *A History of Sociological Analysis*, eds. T. Bottomore and R. Nisbet," *Qualitative Sociology* II (January 1980): 99-112;
Vidich, Lyman, and Jeffrey C. Goldfarb, "Sociology and Society: Disciplinary Tensions and Professional Compromises," *Social Research* XLVIII (Summer 1981): 322-61;
Vidich and Lyman, "Secular Evangelism at the University of Wisconsin," *Social Research*, vol. 49, no. 4 (Winter 1982): 1047-72;
Vidich and Lyman, *American Sociology: Worldly Rejections of Religion and their Directions*, (New Haven: Yale U.P., 1984).
20. Brett de Bary and Victor Nee, "The Kuomintang in Chinatown," in *Counterpoint: Perspectives on Asian America*, ed. Emma Gee (Los Angeles: UCLA Asian-American Studies Center, 1976), pp. 146-51.
21. Lee, *Chinese in the United States*, pp. 405-430.
22. Peter Kwong, *Chinatown, N.Y.: Labor and Politics, 1930-1950* (New York: Monthly Review Press, 1979), pp. 131-47.
23. Arthur Schlesinger, Jr., *The Vital Center*, rev. ed. (London: Andre Deutsch, 1970).
24. Parsons, *The Social System* (New York: Free Press, 1951), pp. 182-91.
25. Kingsley Davis, "The Myth of Functional Analysis as a Special Method

in Sociology and Anthropology," *American Sociological Review* XXIV (December 1959): 757.

26. Seymour Martin Lipset, *The First New Nation: The United States in Historical and Comparative Perspective* (New York: Basic, 1963), esp. pp. 318-42.

27. Clark Kerr, "Marshall, Marx and Modern Times: The Multi-Dimensional Society," The Marshall Lectures, 1967-68 (New York: Cambridge U.P., 1969), pp. 74-130;
Edward Shils, "The Calling of Sociology," in *Theories of Society*, eds. Parsons et al. (New York: Free Press, 1961), vol. II, pp. 1421-26.

28. Peter Schrag, *The Decline of the Wasp* (New York: Simon & Schuster, 1971);
Michael Novak, *The Rise of the Unmeltable Ethnics: Politics and Culture in the Seventies* (New York: Macmillan, 1972).

29. See Lyman, "The Rise and Decline of the Functionalist-Positivist Paradigm: A Chapter in the History of American Sociology," *Doshisha University Hyoron Shakaikagaku* [Social Science Review], no. 20 (March 1982): 4-19.

30. Philip Gleason, "American Identity and Americanization," in *Harvard Encyclopedia of American Ethnic Groups*, ed. Stephan Thernstrom (Cambridge, Mass.:' The Belknap Press of Harvard, 1980), p. 57.

31. Hubert M. Blalock, ed., *Race and Ethnic Relations* (Englewood Cliffs, N.Y.: Prentice-Hall, 1982).

32. Harold J. Abramson, "Assimilation and Pluralism," in Ibid., p. 160.

33. Lyman, "The Significance of Chinese in American History," in *Asian in North America*, pp. 25-38.

34. See Amy Tachiki, Introduction to *Roots: An Asian-American Reader*, eds. Tachiki et al. (Los Angeles: UCLA Asian-American Studies Center, 1971), p. 4;
Linda P. Shin, "Review of Stanford M. Lyman, *Chinese-Americans*," in *Counterpoint*, ed. Gee, pp. 39-40.

35. Asian-American studies are plagued by a methodological debate over the language of research sources. Critics of my work have stated, incorrectly, that I have not used materials in the Chinese language. For example, Shin observes, "While Lyman...uses no Chinese language sources, he has been able to draw upon a ...range of scholarly work on China and the United States." ["Review," p. 39.] Referring to my essay on power and conflict in Chinatown, Akira Iriye asserts that the analysis is "based entirely on English-language material" [Introduction to *The Asian-American: The Historical Experience*, ed. Norris Hundley, Jr. (Santa Barbara: American Bibliographic Center-Clio Press, Inc., 1976), p. xi] Shin and Iriye make these remarks in passing, but Michael H. Hunt has built this canard about language into a challenge to the veracity of my work. According to Hunt, my conception of the nature of power and conflict in Chinatown is "crude and unsupported by... evidence" because I have "fallen prey to prevailing contemporary stereotypes" and violated "the Zen Buddhist injunction against mistaking the

finger pointing at the moon for the moon." [Hunt, *The Making of a Special Relationship: The United States and China to 1914* (New York: Columbia U.P., 1983), p. 330.]

There are three issues here: first, whether I have in fact used Chinese language sources; second, whether the validity of a source is dependent on the language in which it is expressed; and third, whether my conceptualization of Chinatown power and conflict is valid.

My use of Chinese language sources includes my discovery and supervision of the translation of the rules of a Chinese secret society; my interviews with Chinese-speaking informants; my analysis of the English language versions of various *hui kuan* regulations, translated by missionaries; and my many years of association with Chinese- and English-speaking Chinatowners. (My contributions to Japanese culture include Hiroshi Shimizu's commision and translation of my essay, "Evreinoff, Our Contemporary" as the introduction to his Japanese edition of N. Evreinoff's *The Theatre in Life* [Tokyo: Sanyo-sha, 1983), pp. 1-17].) In regard to the present work, it is worth noting that the most indefatigable researcher in Chinese language materials on America's Chinese, Shih-shan Henry Tsai, reports that in "the last decade before the demise of the Ch'ing dynasty in 1912, there were a few reports on Chinese immigration to America. . . [but, for] the most part. . . the Chinese did little serious historical research on immigration. . ." Tsai employs my estimation of the political authority of the Chinese Six Companies as part of his own analysis, and cites with approval my criticism of other scholars' failure to exploit the available documents on secret societies. [*China and the Overseas Chinese in the United States, 1868-1911* (Fayetteville: University of Arkansas Press, 1983), pp. 157, 37, 124; see also Tsai's essay, "Chinese Immigration Through Communist Chinese Eyes: An Introduction to the Historiography," in *The Asian American*, ed. Hundley, pp. 53-66.]

The higher credibility granted to Chinese language sources by Shin, Iriye, and Hunt glosses linguistic, ethnic, and cultural distinctions and imposes a xenophilic expistemology on Asian-American studies. Information might be written or spoken in Chinese by a native-born Chinese, an overseas Chinese, a China-born non-Chinese, or a linguistically versatile non-Chinese born and educated outside of China. It might be written or spoken in English or in some other language, say Japanese or French, by any or all of the same categories of writers/speakers. Translations of documents or interpretations of interviews might also proceed with the same categories of ethno-linguistic types. Some scholars of Chinese affairs are multilingual and employ several languages in doing and presenting their research, for instance, Wolfram Eberhard, Franz Schurmann, Ping-ti Ho, Shuichi Kato, and Jean Chesneaux. Students of Chinese historiography have long recognized that Chinese language documents are but one of the reliable sources for valid information. [See Donald D. Lesie, Colin Mackerras, and Wang Gungwu, eds., *Essays on the Sources for Chinese History* (Columbia:

University of South Carolina Press, 1973). The criterion for a source's validity should not be made to depend on its language, culture, or ethnicity or those of the scholar who analyzes it. See Robert K. Merton, "Insiders and Outsiders: A Chapter in the Sociology of Knowledge," *American Journal of Sociology* LXXXIII (July 1972): 9-47.]

Because Hunt's invocation of the Zen Buddhist injunction distinguishing the moon from the finger pointing at it cannot be taken as the establishment of a religious qualification for engaging in sinological research, it must be treated within the frame of the modern philosophy of science. The demand that "the moon" itself be apprehended rather than any "finger pointing at" it would seem to be an imperative available only to pre-Kantian epistemologists. So long as we continue to be human, we can only know phenomena, not noumena.

Despite their pleas for Chinese language sources and Sinic interpretations, both Shin and Hunt employ a hermeneutic similar to that of Roger Daniels. Shin, disturbed by what she alleges is my "exaggerated" treatment of Chinese secret society criminality in the 1920s and 1930s, wonders why I make no reference "to the flourishing of large-scale criminal syndicates throughout American society during the same period" and calls on me to "remember Al Capone." ["Reveiw," p. 40.] In other words, she wishes Chinatown crime to be treated as a feature of Americanization and assimilation. However, to accommodate her desires would be to betray the realities of the situation. Chinatown's criminal associations were not then and have not since been incorporated into the Mafia or the Unione Siciliano. They do not proceed from the same motives, operate in the same arena, serve the same clients, or share the same values. Fenton Bresler's [*The Chinese Mafia* (New York: Stein & Day, 1981), pp. 75-76] contention that Chinatown secret societies cooperate with the Mafia is not demonstrated convincingly by his evidence. Moreover, the Chinatown secret societies have confined their activities within the ghetto except when they have taken part in China's internal political conflicts.

Hunt, despite his assertion that I am under the illusion of "white fantasies and misconceptions which pervade the contemporary polemical literature," subscribes to the missionary-merchant perspective that treats Chinatown as partially acculturated (designating Chinatown as "at best a flawed reproduction of life in the Canton delta") and governed by a benevolent, law-abiding merchant oligarchy ("the Six Companies, unlike the secret societies, did not use force against the recalcitrant") who struggle valiantly against white sinophobia, ("a way for white Californians to vent frustrations, assuage disappointments, work for a better future, and secure the comforts of group solidarity."). Prostitution in Chinatown is perceived as a form of Chinese sexism: "What began in the early 1850s, as a business conducted in the main by free agents soon fell under the control and protection of Chinese males who recognized the money to be made in organized prostitution." [Hunt, *The Making of a Special Relationship*, pp. 330, 72, 69, 75, 71.) No Chinese language sources lend support to this thesis. It overlooks the role played by secret societies, the sociocultural sources of sex-ratio imbalance among overseas Chinese, and the communal consequences of that imbalance. [See Lucie Cheng Hirata, "Free, Indentured, Enslaved: Chinese Prostitutes in Nineteenth-Century America," *Signs: Journal of Women in Culture and Society* V (Autumn 1979): pp. 3-29.]

36. Daniels, "Westerners from the East: Oriental Immigrants Reappraised," *Pacific Historical Review* XXXV (November 1966): pp. 373-83.
37. Ralph Ellison, "An American Dilemma: A Review," in *Shadow and Act* (New York: Random, 1964), pp. 303-17.
38. Daniels, "Westerners from the East," p. 376.
39. Ibid.
40. Max Weber, *The Religion of China: Confucianism and Taoism,* trans. and ed. Hans H. Gerth, (New York: Free Press, 1951), pp. 13-19.
41. Thomas C. Smith, *The Agrarian Origins of Modern Japan* (Stanford: Stanford University Press, 1959), pp. 109-23;
Yamato Ichihashi, *Japanese in the United States: A Critical Study of the Problems of the Japanese Immigrants and their Children* (1932; reprint ed., Stanford: Stanford University Press: New York: Arno Press, 1969), pp. 160-206.
42. See Bradford Smith, *Americans from Japan* (Philadelphia: Lippincott, 1948), pp. 73, 139-42, 210-12, 232.
43. See three works by Tadashi Fukutake,
Man and Society in Japan (Tokyo: University of Tokyo Press, 1962), pp. 57-61, 198-205, 217-26;
Japanese Rural Society, trans. R.P. Dore (Tokyo: Oxford University Press, 1967) pp. 31-80, 208-17;
The Japanese Social Structure: Its Evolution in the Modern Century, trans. Dore (Tokyo: University of Tokyo Press, 1982), pp. 25-66.
44. Karl Marx, "On the Jewish Question," in *Writings of the Young Marx on Philosophy and Society,* trans. and ed. Loyd D. Easton and Kurt H. Guddat (New York: Doubleday, 1967), pp. 216-48.
For a comprehensive assessment see
Jules Carlebach, *Karl Marx and the Radical Critique of Judaism* (London: Routledge and Kegan Paul, 1978).
45. Anthony B. Chan, " 'Orientalism' and Image Making: The Sojourner in Canadian History," *Journal of Ethnic Studies* IX (Fall 1981): pp. 37-46;
"The Myth of the Chinese Sojourner in Canada," in *Visible Minorities and Multiculturalism: Asians in Canada* eds. Victor Ujimoto and Gordon Hirabayashi (Toronto: Butterworth, 1980), pp. 33-42.
46. Chan, *Gold Mountain: The Chinese in the New World* (Vancouver, B.C. Canada: New Star Books, 1983), pp. 127-30.
47. See V.S. McClatchy, *Japanese Immigration and Colonization: Brief Prepared for Consideration of the State Department, October 1, 1921* (San Francisco: R. and E. Research Associates, 1970), pp. 46-64.
48. Lyman, *Chinese Americans* (New York: Random, 1974), pp. 181-85; H. Mark Lai, "China Politics and the U.S. Chinese Communities," *Counter-*

point, ed. Gee, pp. 152-59.

49. Christopher S. Wren, "China Opens Her Arms to Emigrants Who Made It," *New York Times*, January 6, 1984, p. A2.
50. In an instance witnessed by the author, an aged Issei couple returned to their village of origin in Japan after a fifty-year sojourn in America. Their children, who had gratefully financed their parents' wish to die in the village of their birth, were surprised to welcome them back to San Francisco a few weeks later. As their mother explained, "We didn't realize that San Francisco was our home until we reached the village. No one knew us. It was so changed."
51. As Fulbright lecturer and consultant (1981-82) to the Japanese-American Research Project at Ryukoku University, Kyoto, Japan, I had numerous opportunities to discuss the complexities attending the Japanese ie, lineal-system, and its connections to the honke-bunke process. There is considerable debate in Japan over the economic and noneconomic aspects of Japanese kinship and their effects on overseas Japanese social organization.
52. William Petersen, "Success Story: Japanese-American Style," *The New York Times Magazine* CXV (January 9, 1966). Reprinted in *Minorities in California History*, eds. George E. Frakes and Curtis B. Solberg (New York: Random, 1971), pp. 189-96.
53. Thomas Sowell, *Ethnic America: A History* (New York: Basic, 1981), p. 282.
54. Sowell, *The Economics of Politics and Race: An International Perspective* (New York: Morrow, 1983), pp. 187-88.
55. Edna Bonacich, "A Theory of Middleman Minorities," *American Sociological Review* XXXVIII (October 1973): 583-94.
56. For the observation that the middleman minority thesis constitutes one more example of blaming the victim for his condition, see
    F. James Davis, *Minority-Dominant Relations: A Sociological Analysis* (Arlington Heights, Ill.: AHM Publishing Corp., 1978), pp. 78-82.
    For an arresting challenge to the middleman minority thesis as applied to Jews in China and India, see
    R.A. Schermerhorn, "Jews Without Middleman Status—Their Historic Position in China and India," *Journal of Intercultural Studies* II (1981): 5-21.
57. Harry H.L. Kitano, "Japanese-Americans: The Development of a Middleman Minority," *Pacific Historical Review* XLIII (November 1974): p. 518.
    For a critique of the applicability of the middleman minority thesis to Japanese farmers, see
    David J. O'Brien and Stephen S. Fugita, "Middleman Minority Concept: Its Explanatory Value in the Case of the Japanese in California Agriculture," *Pacific Sociological Review* XXV (April 1982): 185-204.
58. For a thoughtful critical analysis of the liberal pluralist and neoconservative positions see
    Peter Kivisto's untiled review essay on works by Anthony Smith, Sowell,

and Stephen Steinberg, in the *Humboldt Journal of Social Relations* X (Fall-Winter 1982/83): 370-76.

59. The definitive study of the Japanese-Americans as middlemen is Bonacich and John Modell, *The Economic Basis of Ethnic Solidarity: Small Business in the Japanese-American Community* (Berkeley: University of California Press, 1980).

    Insisting on the steady dissolution of ethnic solidarity among Japanese-Americans as they moved through the generational process and out of agriculture and small business into the professions, Bonacich and Modell are at a loss to explain the persistence of ethnic Japanese elements including their geo-generational identification. Ironically, Bonacich and Modell employ the very geo-generational nomenclature in use by the Japanese-Americans without realizing that such terminology signals cultural retention.

60. Robert Blauner, "Internal Colonialism and Ghetto Revolt," *Social Problems* XVI (Spring 1969): 393-408.
61. Blauner, *Racial Oppression in America* (New York: Harper, 1972), p. 88.
62. Ibid., pp. 60-61, 70-71.
63. Ibid., p. 104.
64. Benjamin B. Ringer, *"We the People" and Others: Duality and America's Treatment of Racial Minorities* (New York: Tavistock Publications, 1983).
65. Ibid., pp. 567-943.
66. Ibid., p. 1102.
67. For a thoughtful assessment see
    Michael Omi and Howard Winant, "By the Rivers of Babylon: Race in the United States," *Socialist Review* XIII (September-October 1983): 31-66; (November-December 1983): 35-70.
68. Charles Choy Wong, "Ethnicity, Work, and Community: The Case of Chinese in Los Angeles" (Ph.D. diss., University of California, 1979), pp. 259-93.
69. Robert Seto Quan in collaboration with Julian B. Roebuck, *Lotus Among the Magnolias: The Mississippi Chinese* (Jackson: University Press of Mississippi, 1982), pp. 146-54.
70. See Betty Lee Sung, *Chinese-American Manpower and Employment* (Springfield, Va.: U.S. Department of Commerce, 1975);
    H. Mark Lai, "Chinese," in *Harvard Encyclopedia of American Ethnic Groups*, pp. 227-28.
71. Joel Klotkin and Paul Grabowicz, *California, Inc.* (New York: Avon Books, 1982), pp. 212-14.
72. Stanley Aronowitz, *Working Class Hero: A New Strategy for Labor* (New York: The Pilgrim Press, 1983), pp. 147-48.
73. Charlotte Ikels, *Aging and Adaptation: Chinese in Hong Kong and the United States* (Hamden, Ct.: Archon Books, 1983), p. 245.
74. Bernard Wong, *Chinatown: Economic Adaptation and Ethnic Identity of the Chinese* (New York: Holt, 1982), pp. 84-85.

Although at least one student of the subject [Jonathan Unger, "The Making and Breaking of Chinese Secret Societies," *Journal of Contemporary Asia* V (1975): 89-98] believes secret societies have died out in China, they continue to flourish in New York's and San Francisco's Chinatowns.

75. In the latest offer to settle the Taiwan problem, Peoples Republic Prime Minister Zhao Ziyang has offered the island community virtual extraterritorial status among the provinces of China with respect to culture, economy, and home rule. Speaking to the National Committee on U.S.-China Relations and the Foreign Policy Association on January 16, 1984, Zhao offered Taiwan special regional administrative status with the right to "keep its social system and life-style unchanged." He went on to point out that the "existing party, government, and military setups... can also remain unchanged," that the island could use "the name of 'Taiwan, China'...continue its external economic and cultural exchanges, and foreign investments in Taiwan will be fully protected... In a word neither party will swallow up the other." Excerpts from "Zhao Speech to a Luncheon in New York," *New York Times*, January 17, 1984, p. A12. Should Taiwan accept such an offer, its relative autonomy might in turn be extended to Chinatown, permitting its incumbent communal elites to continue in office without fear of pressure from Beijing. By the same token, should the Peoples Republic adopt a "hands off" policy with respect to Chinatown, local radicals could not look to it for support in their attempts to overthrow the community's old order.

76. See Tetsuden Kashima, *Buddhism in America: The Social Organization of an Ethnic Religious Institution* (Westport, Ct.: Greenwood Press, 1977).

77. *Kinney Kinmon Lau et al. v. Alan H. Nichols et al.*, 414 U.S. 563 (1974). For a discussion see L. Ling-chi Wang, "Lau v. Nichols: History of a Struggle for Equal and Quality Eduation," *Counterpoint*, ed. Gee, pp. 240-63.

78. Vincent N. Parillo, "Asian-Americans in American Politics," in *America's Ethnic Politics*, eds. Joseph S. Roucek and Bernard Eisenberg (Westport, Ct.: Greenwood Press, 1982), pp. 94-98.

79. For the range of Japanese-American opinion on this matter, see
Frank F. Chuman, *The Bamboo People: The Law and Japanese-Americans* (Del Mar, Calif.: Publisher's Inc., 1976), pp. 126-97;
Harry H.L. Kitano, *Japanese-Americans: The Evolution of a Subculture*, 2nd ed. (Englewood Cliff: Prentice-Hall, 1976), pp. 70-90;
Bill Hosokawa, *Nisei: The Quiet Americans* (New York: Morrow, 1969), pp. 207-434;
Robert A. Wilson and Bill Hosokawa, *East to America: A History of the Japanese in the United States* (New York: Morrow, 1980), pp. 160-285;
Petersen, *Japanese-Americans: Oppression and Success* (New York: Random, 1971), pp. 72-81;
Michi Weglyn, *Years of Infamy: The Untold Story of America's Concentration Camps* (New York: Morrow, 1976), pp. 266-81;

Isao Fujimoto, "The Failure of Democracy in a Time of Crisis: The Wartime Internment of the Japanese-Americans and Its Relevance Today," in *Roots*, ed. Tachiki et al., pp. 207-14;
Yuji Ichioka, "Book Review: *Nisei: The Quiet Americans*," in *Roots*, ed. Tachiki et al., pp. 221-22;
Raymond Okamura, "Farewell to Manzanar: A Case of Subliminal Racism," *Counterpoint*, ed. Gee, pp. 280-83;
Kashima, "Japanese-American Internees Return, 1945 to 1955: Readjustment and Social Amnesia," *Phylon* XLI (Summer 1980): 107-115;
Maurice Isserman, *Which Side Were You On? The American Communist Party During the Second World War* (Middletown: Wesleyan University Press, 1982), pp. 143-45;
Personal Justice Denied: Report of the Commission on Wartime Relocation and Internment of Civilians (Washington, D.C.: U.S. Government Printing Office, 1982), pp. 295-302;
John J. Stephan, *Hawaii Under the Rising Sun: Japan's Plans for Conquest After Pearl Harbor* (Honolulu: University of Hawaii Press, 1984), pp. 23-40, 167-78.
Karl G. Yoneda, *Ganbatte: Sixty-Year Struggle of a Kibei Worker*, (Los Angeles: Asian American Studies Center, 1983), pp. 111-68.

80. *Federal Register* XLI (February 20, 1976); Clifford I. Uyeda, *A Final Report and Review: The Japanese-American Citizens League National Committee for Iva Toguri*, Occasional Monograph 1, Asian-American Study Program (Seattle: AASP, 1980).
81. *Personal Justice Denied: Report*, pp. 1-25.
82. Petition for Writ of Error, Coram Nobis, from the Judgment of Conviction September 8, 1942, filed before the United States District Court, Northern District of California, filed January 19, 1983. Copy in possession of author.
83. "Personal Justice Denied, Part 2: Recommendations," pp. 9-10.
84. Peter Irons, *Justice at War: The Story of the Japanese-American Internment Cases* (New York: Oxford U.P., 1983).
85. "Bad Landmark: Righting a Racial Wrong," *Time Magazine*, November 21, 1983, p. 51.
86. The mistreatment of the Japanese during World War II occurred throughout North and South America. For some representative studies see

    Ken Adachi, *The Enemy that Never Was: A History of Japanese Canadians* (Toronto: McClelland and Stewart, 1976);
    John K. Emerson, "Japanese and Americans in Peru, 1942-1943," *Foreign Service Journal* LIV (May 197?): 40-47, 56;
    C. Harvey Gardiner, *Pawns in a Triangle of Hate: The Peruvian Japanese and the United States* (Seattle: University of Washington Press, 1981);
    Gardiner, "The Japanese and Venezuela," *Revista Interamericana* V (Fall 1975): pp. 359-77.
87. Cf. Nicholas Spykman, "The Social Background of Asiatic Nationalism,"

American Journal of Sociology XXXII (November 1926): 396-411. Spkyman, a student of Frederick J. Teggart (1975-1946), integrated Teggart's macro-historical science of continental development with the sociological approach to history and social change developed by Georg Simmel. Teggart had applied his orientation to studies of China and California.

88. Teggart, *Theory and Processes of History* (Berkeley: University of California Press, 1941), pp. 149-50, 196-97, 223-314.

89. Gustav Ratzenhofer, *Wesen und Zweck der Politik*, 3 vols. (1893) sec. 18, p. 165. Quoted in Albion W. Small, *General Sociology: An Exposition of the Main Development in Sociological Theory from Spencer to Ratzenhofer* (Chicago: U. of Chicago; 1905; reprint ed., New York: Arno Press, 1974), p. 256.

90. See the concluding discussion in Vidich and Lyman, *American Sociology*.

91.
> "States conceived as organizations controlling territories and people may formulate and pursue goals that are not simply reflective of the demands or interests of social groups, classes, or society. This is what is meant by state autonomy. . . The limits and the possibilities of public policy are profoundly influenced by historically developed state organizations and their structured relationships to domestic and international environments."

Theda Skocpol, "Bringing the State Back In," *Items: Bulletin of the Social Science Research Council* XXXVI (June 1982): 4, 8.

92. Other eighteenth- and nineteenth-century scholars also supposed that Asian civilization had originated in North America. Among them were Thomas Jefferson [see Bernard W. Sheehan, *Seeds of Extinction: Jeffersonian Philanthrophy and the American Indian* (Chapel Hill: University of North Carolina Press, 1973) pp. 57-58];
Arthur Comte de Gobineau [see Charles G. Leland, *Fusang, or the Discovery of America by Chinese Buddhist Priests in the Fifth Century* (1875; reprint ed. London: Curzon Press, 1973), pp. 175-76];
Charles Wolcott Brooks, *Origin of the Chinese Race, Philosophy of Their Development, with an Inquiry into the Evidence of Their American Origin, Suggesting the Great Antiquity of Races on the American Continent* (San Francisco: Reprinted from the Proceedings of the California Academy of Sciences, 1876), pp. 3-31.
On the other hand, the beginnings of anthropology in California are to be found in debates over the thesis that California Indian languages originated in Asia. See
Stephen Powers, "Aborigines of California: An Indo-Chinese Study," *Atlantic Monthly* XXXIII (March 1874): 313-23.

93. R. Stewart Culin, "America the Cradle of Asia," address before the section on anthropology, American Association for the Advancement of Science, Washington, D.C. meeting, December 1902-January 1903. *Proceedings of the American Association for the Advancement of Science* (Washington, D.C.: Gibson Bros., 1903), vol.. LII, pp. 493-500.

94. I have examined facets of Culin's thesis in four papers:
"Stewart Culin and the Debate over Trans-Pacific Migration," *Journal for the Theory of Social Behaviour* IX (March 1979): 91-115;
"Stewart Culin: The Earliest American Chinatown Studies and a Hypothesis about Pre-Colombian Migration," *Annual Bulletin of Research Institute for Social Science, Ryukoku University* [Kyoto, Japan], no. 12 (March 1982): 142-160;
"Two Neglected Pioneers of Civilizational Analysis: The Cultural Perspectives of R. Stewart Culin and Frank Hamilton Cushing," *Social Research* XLIX (Autumn 1982): 690-729.
'Asian American Contacts Before Columbus: Alternative Understandings for Civilization, Acculturation, and Ethnic Minority Status in the United States," to be published in *Imin ka ra Jirtsu Eno Rekishi Katei (Japanese Americans: Some Aspects of Their Experiences as an Immigrant Group)* in Tokyo in 1985.
95. Emile Durkheim and Marcel Mauss, "Note on the Notion of Civilization," trans. Benjamin Nelson, *Social Research* XXXVIII (Winter 1971): 808-13.

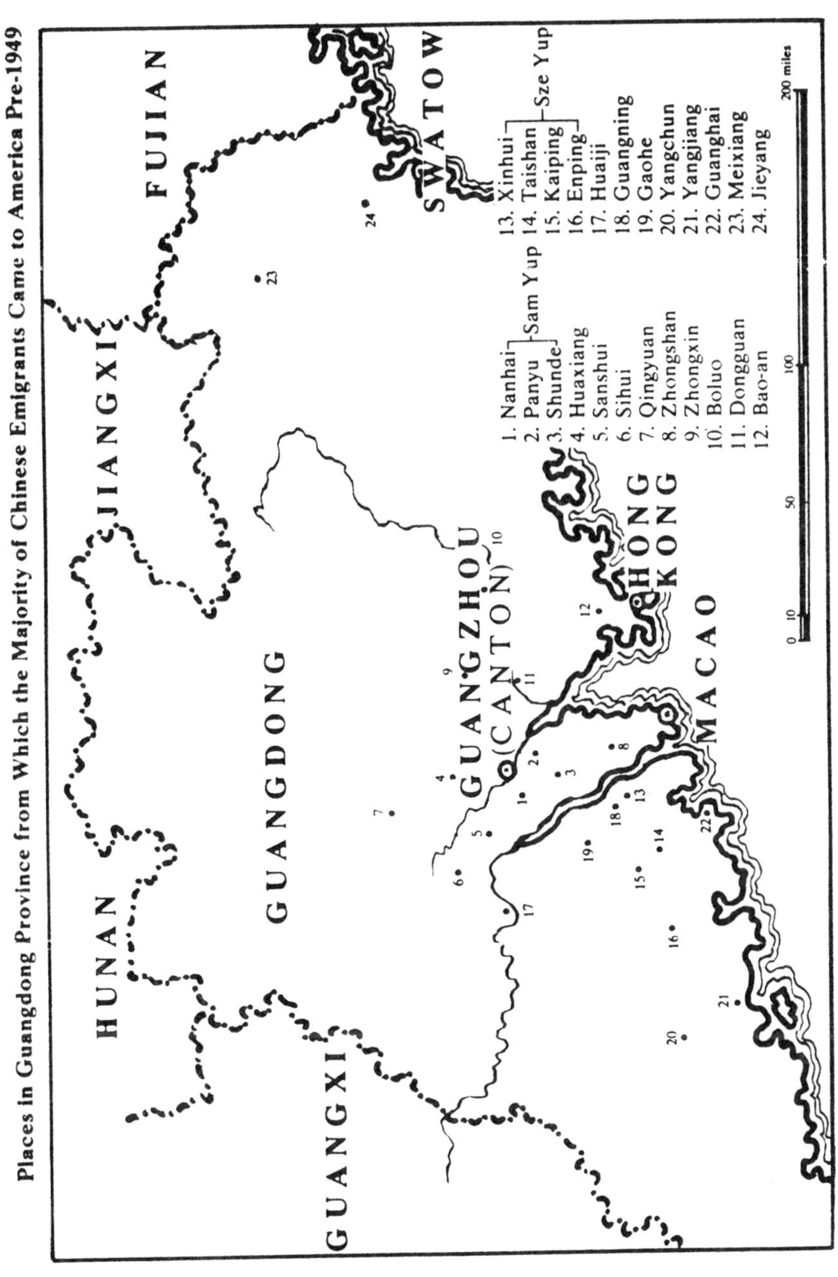

Places in Guangdong Province from Which the Majority of Chinese Emigrants Came to America Pre-1949

Adapted from: Jack Chen, *The Chinese of America*, (San Francisco: Harper & Row, 1980), p. 17.

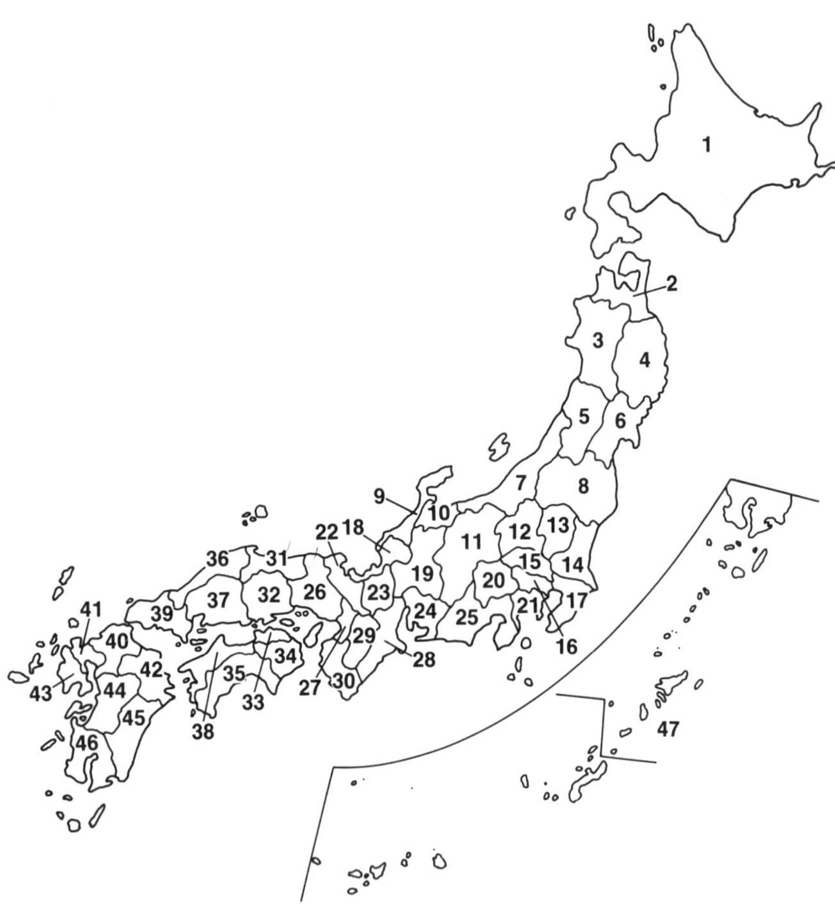
1
2
3
4
5
6
7
8
9
10
11
12
13
14
15
16
17
18
19
20
21
22
23
24
25
26
27
28
29
30
31
32
33
34
35
36
37
38
39
40
41
42
43
44
45
46
47

ESTIMATED NUMBER OF IMMIGRANTS TO THE UNITED STATES BY PREFECTURE OF ORIGIN (1925)

Number/ Prefecture	to USA	to Hawaii	Total	Prefecture %*
1. Hokkaidō	253	38	291	0.11
2. Aomori	293	4	297	0.11
3. Akita	67	6	73	0.03
4. Iwate	213	126	339	0.13
5. Yamagata	146	63	209	0.08
6. Miyagi	1,065	968	2,033	0.79
7. Niigata	1,356	4,050	5,407	2.09
8. Hukisima (Fukushima)	2,808	3,697	6,505	2.51
9. Isikawa (Ishikawa)	506	50	556	0.21
10. Toyama	506	340	846	0.33
11. Nagano	1,264	289	1,553	0.60
12. Gunma (Gumma)	466	163	629	0.24
13. Totigi (Tochigi)	293	63	356	0.14
14. Ibaraki (Ibaragi)	452	50	502	0.19
15. Saitama	213	13	226	0.09
16. Tōkyō	1,490	503	1,993	0.77
17. Tiba (Chiba)	835	327	1,152	0.44
18. Hukui	1,490	340	1,830	0.71
19. Gihu (Gifu)	373	63	436	0.17
20. Yamanasi (Yamanashi)	2,209	528	2,737	1.06
21. Kanagawa	2,462	289	2,751	1.06
22. Kyōtō	492	50	542	0.21
23. Siga (Shiga)	1,624	163	1,787	0.69
24. Aiti (Aichi)	3,021	113	3,134	1.21
25. Sizuoka (Shizuoka)	2,768	453	3,221	1.24
26. Hyōgo	679	101	780	0.30
27. Ōsaka	1,118	126	1,244	0.48
28. Mie	1,783	264	2,047	0.79
29. Nara	240	13	253	0.10
30. Wakayama	13,814	1,182	14,996	5.79
31. Tottori	2,196	163	2,359	0.91
32. Okayama	6,361	780	7,141	2.76
33. Kagawa	586	151	737	0.28
34. Tokusima (Tokushima)	186	38	224	0.09
35. Kōti (Kōchi)	1.477	340	1.817	0.70
36. Simane (Shimane)	1,184	214	1,398	0.54
37. Hirosima (Hiroshima)	39,924	35,063	74,987	28.97
38. Ehime	1,091	553	1,644	0.64
39. Yamaguti (Yamaguchi)	7,133	28,762	35,895	13.87
40. Hukuoka (Fukuoka)	9,489	7,282	16,771	6.48
41. Saga	958	75	1,033	0.40
42. Ōita	479	151	630	0.24
43. Nagasaki	359	63	422	0.16
44. Kumamoto	12,430	19.984	32,414	12.52
45. Miyazaki	240	—	240	0.09
46. Kagosima (Kagoshima)	3,713	289	4,002	1.55
47. Okinawa	998	17,443	18,441	7.12

* Emigration percentage from the prefecture.

Source: "Emigration of Japanese to the United States," Yasuo Wakatsuki, *Pacific Citizen*, January 6-13, 1984, Section B, p. 1.

Emigration from Asia || *I*

1 A Frame of Reference for the Analysis of Emigration

"Social movements can be viewed as collective enterprises to establish a new order of life."[1] Both general social movements and large-scale migrations have their "inception in a condition of unrest and derive their motive power on one hand from dissatisfaction with the current form of life, and on the other hand, from wishes and hopes for a new scheme or system of living."[2] Group emigration gives a spatial expression to such movements,[3] seeking to redress individual statuses and collective identities rather than to reorganize the basic structure of the home society. Emigration movements seek less to change the social order than to alter the position of individuals with respect to that order. Emigration movements are of two types. In one, the migrants permanently sever connections with their own society and seek a new life elsewhere. In the other, migrants temporarily abandon their own society in order to take advantage of opportunities elsewhere; they intend to return home at a later date, having made their fortune, to enjoy the fruits of their efforts in a life-style hitherto unavailable to them. The second type—the sojourner movement—has been characteristics of the Chinese, the East Indians, and the Japanese.[4]

For an emigration movement to develop, conditions must be such that numbers of people feel impelled to pull up stakes and leave. The receiving society must appear to the immigrants as offering advantages that outweigh the emotional and economic costs of relocation.[5] Whether or not the general conditions of unrest in any society, or portion thereof, are channeled into migration abroad rather than into some other kind of conduct is, in part, a function of the presence and potency of certain "catalytic" factors; that is, the linkages which directly connect the conditions of unrest with movement abroad.

ENCOURAGEMENTS TO EMIGRATION

Though it is difficult to state with any degree of certainty the specific conditions attendant upon emigration movements, the general character of these conditions may be suggested. The impulse to move out is likely to arise when some event seriously interrupts the everyday lives of a people. Whether it is a sudden natural calamity such as a flood, volcanic eruption, or climatic change; or a human catastrophe such as war, revolution, economic depression, or religious or political persecution, the essential point is that the "cake of custom" is broken and new ways of life have to be found.[6] It may be fairly assumed that people are, for the most part, fixed in their habitat, and that for a large-scale spatial movement to take place there must occur some major event to shake them out of their inertia.

Obviously, emigration movements do not arise if there is no place to go. Inviting to immigration would be the opening of a frontier where hitherto none had lived, the discovery of precious metals available to the taker, or the sudden need for a labor force in a developing but unsettled area.

However, stress at home and opportunity abroad are in themselves insufficient reasons to induce migration, since domestic conditions of unrest may give rise to reform or rebellion rather than migration.[7] A sedentary people may even accept its lot as inevitable. Linking conditions potential for emigration with the actual departure of people are certain "catalytic" factors. These play the same role in emigration movements that agitation does in reform and revolutionary movements: "to loosen the hold [on people] of their previous attachments, and to break down their previous ways of thinking and acting ...to intensify, release, and direct the tensions which people already have."[8] Four such factors may be listed, although this does not exhaust the possibilities: (1) A history of trade, piracy, or travel from the home country that supplies information about foreign countries and sets the stage for later, larger out-migration; (2) A "pioneer" migration, involving a few persons who provide information about, and incite general interest in, the area of future settlement; (3) The presence of persons, conditions, or institutions through which the original stimuli to emigrate is maintained, re-enforced, or enhanced; (4) The widespread availability of means by which large number of persons can be transported from their homeland to the new area of settlement.

DETERRENTS TO EMIGRATION

The forces discouraging emigration include "counter-push" or "counter-pull" and "counter-catalytic" forces in the home or receiving society respectively. These counteractives tend to weaken or negate the encouraging forces. Technological improvements in agriculture and legal prohibitions on departure are but some instances of the first type. Closing the job market and legal restrictions on immigration indicate some of the forms of the second.

Emigration may fail to catch on because of the insufficiency of any of the catalytic agents or because of "friction"; that is, the tendency in the face of conditions encouraging emigration to resist responding to them. Friction, in turn, appears to depend on the degree to which the society resists change in general and the momentum of the emigration movement itself. Even traditional societies do not resist all innovation; indeed, as one study of political change in Africa indicates, tribally organized societies tend to offer less resistance to new items that are additions to rather than replacements of their cultural inventory.[9] On the other hand, as a study of population movements from Holland suggests, even a modernized people will resist the opportunities to go abroad when emigration threatens cherished values of decisive norms.[10]

The factors contributing to the migration of the Chinese and Japanese to the United States in the nineteenth and early twentieth centuries suggest a complex of encouraging, catalytic, and deterrent factors that helped shape the formations of communities among these peoples in the United States.

NOTES

1. Herbert Blumer, "Collective Behavior," in *New Outline of the Principles of Sociology*, ed. Alfred McClung Lee (New York: Barnes & Noble, 1946, 1951), p. 199.
2. Blumer, "Collective Behavior," in *Sociology*, ed. Lee.
3. Blumer, "Collective Behavior," in *Sociology*, ed. Lee, p. 202.
4. Chinese American sociologists have described the early Chinese immigrants to America as persons "who come for economic gain and return to China when their objectives are accomplished." Homer C. Loh, "Cultural Conflicts of Americans of Chinese Ancestry of Philadelphia" (Ph.D. diss. University of Pennsylvania, 1945), ch. VI, p. 8. Another Chinese Ameri-

can sociologist, having completed a study of the Chinese laundryman, characterized the Asian immigrant as a variant of "the stranger."

> The sojourner is...a deviant type of the sociological term of the stranger, one who clings to his cultural heritage of his own ethnic group and tends to live in isolation, hindering his assimilation in the society in which he resides, often for many years. The sojourn is conceived as a "job" which is to be finished in the shortest possible time. As an alternative to that end he travels back to his homeland every few years. He is comparable to the marginal man.

Paul C.P. Siu, "The Sojourner," *American Journal of Sociology*, July 1952, pp. 34-35.

5. Kingsley Davis, *Human Society* (New York: Macmillan, 1948, 1949), p. 587.
6. See August B. Hollingshead, "Human Ecology," in *Principles of Sociology*, ed. Lee, p. 107.
7. Reform or revolutionary movements and emigration movements are not mutually exclusive. Indeed, they often are concomitants of one another. Revolutions sometimes serve as expulsive factors.
8. Blumer, "Collective Behavior," in *Sociology*, ed. Lee, p. 204.
9. See Ethel M. Albert, "Socio-Political Organization and Receptivity to Change: Some Differences Between Ruana and Urundi," *Southwestern Journal of Anthropology*, Spring 1960, pp. 46-74.
10. William Petersen, *Planned Migration: The Social Determinants of the Dutch-Canadian Movement* (Berkeley: University of California Press, 1955), pp. 64-65. I am indebted to Professor Petersen for the usage of "friction."

The Chinese Emigration ||2

|| GENERAL CONSIDERATIONS

Between 1820 and 1892, approximately 360,000 Chinese emigrated to the United States.[1] In the same period, about 270,000 of the Chinese who had journeyed to the United States returned to China.

The migration of Chinese from the Province of Kwangtung to the United States was but a small fraction of a general out-migration from southeastern China in the second half of the nineteenth century. The United States received only the peoples from a score of prefectures in and around the environs of Canton. British colonies in the south Pacific and certain countries in southeast Asia, Latin America, and the Caribbean received the great bulk of Chinese overseas migrants.[2]

In several respects Chinese migration may be compared with that from India.[3] Peoples from both nations have been drawn to British colonies, tropical regions, and places accessible by water. From both nations a comparatively smaller number of migrants entered the United States.[4] As time went on the migratory movements of both Indians and Chinese became confined to southeast Asia—Malaya, Burma, Ceylon, and so forth—and for much the same reasons: (1) Commerical agriculture, the principal employment of Chinese and Indian laborers is much more lucrative in Asia; (2) There arose a greater demand for seasonal labor with the decline of indentured servitude; (3) The Asian areas, in greater proximity, have been able to employ Chinese and Indian labor on a seasonal basis; (4) Petit bourgeois shopkeeping, the characteristic enterprise of successful overseas

Chinese, tend to reap higher rewards of status and greater economic gains in underdeveloped economies than in industrialized Western nations.[5]

Furthermore, with respect to return movements, Chinese and Indian migration stand in sharp contrast to that from Europe. It is estimated that only 30 percent of the Europeans migrating to the United States between 1821 and 1924, and 47 percent of those going to Argentina between 1857 and 1924, returned to their native lands.[6] But, the conservative estimates for Indians is 80 percent,[7] and for Chinese in the period 1820 to 1892 is 75 percent. The reasons for the ephemeral character of Chinese and Indian immigration are to be found in the conditions under which they went abroad. Both Indians and Chinese went primarily as temporary or seasonal laborers under contract or with the intention of making a fortune and returning home. Racial unrest, economic and cultural conflicts with the indigenous inhabitants of the countries to which they migrated made them unwelcome as settlers.[8] In the case of the Chinese there was a strong inclination to remigrate to the native village where wives and families awaited the return of their menfolk. Given their lack of interest in settlement in the United States, the harsh treatment they received there, and the untold hardships suffered in long separation from wives and families, the fact that even such a small percentage of Chinese immigrants apparently did not return to China, may be attributed less to a positive decision to settle abroad, than to a financial inability to return to China.

|| EXPULSIVE FORCES

Migration out of China was brought about by political and economic changes in China, and by the existence of newly opened and beckoning frontier areas abroad. Emigration to North America was made desirable by the first reports of Chinese "pioneers." What "friction" existed was in large part overcome by a local practice of seasonal migration, which counteracted the tendency to resist emigration in the face of conditions encouraging it. "Counter-pull" forces in America tended to have an effect on the number of Chinese emigrants departing from China in certain years, but were unable to stem the movement entirely. Even after severe exclusionist legislation against the Chinese had been enacted, Kwangtungese smuggled themselves into the United States.

A principal factor encouraging departure from China was the near collapse of its agricultural economy in the mid-nineteenth century, preceded by a rapid rise in population from the latter part of the sixteenth century to the decade prior to the outbreak of the Taiping Rebellion.[9]

Wolfram Eberhard[10] estimates that the cultivated acreage-man ratio was adequate to meet the demands for minimum subsistence for the year 1578. If his estimate is correct, then the general conditions of life in China appear to have grown progressively worse after that year.

Actually, however, the condition of the Chinese peasant was not so dire,[11] since much land went officially unregistered, and that which was recorded only imperfectly represented the acreage under cultivation. Sometimes land registration included cultivated land, sometimes fiscal acreage. The latter was computed according to the alleged yield of the land. In general, all land cultivation statistics of prenineteenth century China must be understood in terms of the various and unsystematic modes employed to collect (and sometimes to obscure) agricultural information.

The increase in population was, for a time, accompanied by tillage increases and crop innovations that met the demand. There was no incentive to emigrate in part because of the change in family size attendant on the modernization of agriculture, and the introduction of fertilizers.[12] In China the development of early ripening varieties of rice permitted two yields per year. Irrigation technology improved. The cultivation of northern and imported dryland crops was introduced among the south Chinese after the sixteenth century. Peanuts were brought into China from abroad. Maize, sweet potatoes, Irish potatoes, and corn found a prominent place in south Chinese agriculture supplementing the production of rice. Even before the sixteenth century, barley, millet, and sorghum had been cultivated. Newly discovered records indicate that the Chinese regarded the doubling of the population in the century after 1662, not as a calamity, but as an unqualified blessing.

Nevertheless, conditions in the seacoast provinces of southeastern China, Kwangtung, and Fukien, were sufficiently unsatisfactory to produce a fairly extensive Cantonese immigration into the Philippines at this time. Piracy, and later, trade, between Canton and Manila promoted a great deal of traffic between the two ocean ports. As early as 1586, there were 10,000 Chinese living in Manila, and in 1596 the king of Spain warned his Colonial governor of their "injuries, expenses, secret sins, scarcities, and witchcrafts." From the earliest days, the Sangleys, as the Manilenos called them, monopolized retail trade and skilled crafts in the Philippine community.[13] From the late sixteenth century to the present day, the Chinese have been a conspicuous commercial minority in those islands.[14] In the Philippines and in other parts of Southeast Asia where Chinese commercial enterprise is especially prevalent, economic resentment is frequently translated into Sinophobia.[15]

Agricultural improvements in China did not keep pace with population growth. To maintain a viable acreage-man ratio it would have been necessary for north China to develop a great series of dykes and canals.[16] Such a system was not possible without advanced technology and might even have been impractical with it. Despite its improvements in rice yields and its dissemination of dryland crops, south China needed a far greater yield of crops to continue to sustain its population after the close of the eighteenth century, and importation of food did not become an important source of sustenance until late in the nineteenth century. China's large-scale but poorly developed internal trade could not stave off an inevitable populaton crisis.[17] Industrialization had been discouraged by China's political structure, by its primitive technology, and by the unwillingness of its gentry to shift from land to industrial investment. A rational system of credit and investment did not develop.[18]

Other factors served to inhibit the maintenance of a balance between the population and its needs. Whereas the Ming leaders had greatly oppressed the peasants by heavy taxes and by the hated corvée that at times depopulated whole villages, the benevolent despotism of the early Manchu rulers restored a modicum of wealth and security to the Chinese farmer and in general, it appears, prolonged the length of life of the peasant.[19] The social misery of the Chinese peasant, so familiar to students of twentieth-century China, arose after a decline in welfare policies instituted by the later Manchus, and in consequence of unequal land and tenure distribution, a matter especially acute in Kwangtung.[20] As the Chinese population continued to increase, overall opportunities for gainful employment were drastically reduced. By 1850, the margin above bare subsistence had become so much smaller than the tradtional living standard that the ranks of the Taiping rebels were swelled by millions of peasants reduced to impoverishment. However, though a more equitable land distribution might have lessened the social misery of the peasant, it alone would not have halted the steady deterioration of the standard of living first noticed at the close of the eighteenth century.

Although other students of Chinese demography have placed the date when the population produced maximum economic welfare later than that of Eberhard, they still agree that by the second decade of the nineteenth century, this point had been passed. An early Chinese demographer, Hung Liang-chi (1746-1809), published two essays in 1793,[21] five years before the publication of Thomas Malthus's *Essay on Population,* which predicted for China those very conditions of overpopulation which the latter was to make so foreboding in his famous work. Hung firmly believed that natural checks like floods, famine, and epidemics would not be able to diminish the surplus population. Thirty years prior to the outbreak of the devastating Taiping Rebellion, Kung Tzu-chen, a noted scholar of his day, viewed the growing disparity between population increase and individual well-being as portentous of imminent violence:

> Those who are now neither scholars and farmers nor artisans and traders constitute nearly one-half of the population.... In general, the rich households have become poor and the poor hungry. The educated rush here and there but are of no avail, for all are impoverished. The provinces are at the threshold of a convulsion which is not a matter of years but a matter of days and months.[22]

However, as Petersen has suggested, an account of emigration "can begin, with some assurance, by rejecting all monistic theories."[23] Emigration movements arise when a series of encouraging factors are strong enough to overcome deterrents to departure. In the case of China, only the Kwangtungese and Fukienese have embarked upon overseas migration. This geographical selectivity would have an important effect on overseas Chinese social organization.

Available information does not permit us to ascertain whether the increase in China's population was more severely felt in Kwangtung and Fukien than elsewhere. What evidence there is would indicate that, although in 1850, population density was greater in Kwangtung and Fukien provinces than in the majority of the provinces of China, there were agricultural provinces with an even greater density than those two which did not produce overseas immigrants. If increase in population pressure were the central cause for emigration we should expect to find provinces other than Kwangtung and Fukien producing migrants. To account for the overseas migration in the latter provinces we must examine other factors encouraging migration.

It appears that only in Fukien and Kwangtung—and especially in the latter—did there develop that concatenation of circumstances that has, in other instances, generated emigration.

Pressure on the population of Kwangtung and Fukien at this time may have arisen from the situation existing in adjacent provinces.[24] Local histories of Kiangsi and Hunan provinces indicate that by the beginning of the nineteenth century, the most urgent economic problem was that of maintaining minimum levels of subsistence. Traditionally the "rice-bowl" of China, Kiangsi's rice-exporting areas had only a small surplus; in some cases it was necessary to import food. Prior to

1850, Szechwan, the areas of the Han River drainage, and the Yangtze highlands had been places of fairly large-scale in-migration for peoples of the overpopulated southeastern and coastal provinces. After that year the situation changed. With Szechwan overpopulated, and the Yangtze highlands and the Han River drainage areas suffering from soil erosion, migrants from the coastal provinces chose other places to resettle. The peoples of Kwangtung could no longer look to inner China for relief.

In 1847, southeastern China was struck by a catastrophe unparalleled in its recent history. During the seventeenth and eighteenth centuries, Manchu officials had maintained the dykes that prevented floods along the Yangtze. The dykes having fallen into disrepair, the sudden rains of that year were calamitous. The annual memorial to the emperor indicated the danger: "The rains have been falling for forty days until the rivers, and the sea, and the lakes, and the streams have joined in one sheet over the land for several hundred *li* [one li = 1/3 mile] and there is no outlet by which the waters may retire." An unsigned article in a California magazine of the day indicated the extent of the disaster:

> [T]en thousand people were destroyed, and domestic animals drowned in untold numbers; crowds even of the first families were begging bread, and (horror of horror to the pious Celestials!) coffins were floating about everywhere on the face of the water. ...Such an inundation is too stupendous for the European mind adequately to comprehend its extent, and is said to have exceeded any similar disaster in China within the memory of the present generation.[25]

Their livelihoods destroyed, landless Chinese flocked to coastal cities in search of work; from there many were induced or coerced to go abroad. "No one will wonder at the emigrating spirit in China," commented a contemporary observer, "when he is informed that the most evils to which the Celestials are subject is that crowning misery, starvation. The population is extremely dense; the means of subsistence, in ordinary times, are seldom above the demand, and, consequently, the least failure of the rice crop produces wretchedness."[26]

The economic disaster spurred social unrest and revolution. Beginning first in Hunan, then in Kwangsi, and spreading throughout southeast China, rebellious peasants united with alienated intellectuals in the Taiping Rebellion (1851-64). It is estimated that over twenty million lives were lost in this bloody revolution and that Kwangtung Province suffered intensely. As a concomitant of this abortive insurrection, thousands of refugees—victims of the changing fortunes of the rebel and imperial forces—fled through Kwangtung to the treaty ports of Canton, Hong Kong, Amoy, and Macao. Villagers who otherwise might never have left their homes sought work and escape ourside their own communities. At the port they purchased or borrowed the passage fare to Singapore or the United States; if unable to pay for their own passage, they would indenture themselves as "credit-ticket" workers bound for the British West Indies, Peru, or Cuba. Those who borrowed money from clan brothers or from representatives of their own prefecture bonded themselves to a period of indentured servitude to their clan or "prefectural association" (*hui kuan*) or to its agents abroad.

The Taiping Rebellion—despite its mammoth destruction—was but one of the wars being waged in southeastern China at this time. The British and French invaded China several times between 1838 and 1860, moving their forces ashore at Canton and Hong Kong and proceeding northward. The Hakka-Punti War (1855-68), fought in Kwangtung Province between the indigenous Punti and the invading Hakka people, added to individual and group dislocation. It had one other consequence: the victory of the Punti over the Hakka led to the sale of Hakka females as indentured servants to overseas Chinese settlements.

ATTRACTIVE FORCES

These "push" factors might not have developed into a migration to the United States had there not arisen simultaneously a forceful "pull" toward that country. The discovery of gold in Calfornia in 1847 spread around the world and induced a world-wide population movement. California was perceived as the place where fortunes could be made overnight. In fact, a vast frontier has been opened, and its need for a labor force, especially in primary industries, was immense. As early as 1852, Chinese were envisioned as the persons to fill the labor vacuum. Some intellectuals prophesied that California's destiny was bound up with the ultimate commingling of the races of mankind:

> The New World commenced the fusion of the varied nations of the Old, but it is on the shores, or in the bosom, of the Pacific that that fusion is to be consummated. There the diverse elements of the population of Eastern America are gathered to a focus, and, blending, with those of China and the intervening isles, will by and by settle in peace in California....Gold is now the great

> lodestone of the nations, and is yet destined to break up the seclusion of the hermit races of India and China. It was gold abroad and distress at home that first covered the Atlantic with ships and its western shores with a new population—and the same agencies of Providence are now doing a like service for the Pacific. But the progress of the human race, though slow and liable to many fluctuations, is, on the whole, ever onward; and, instead of the labor market of the new empires of Oceanica being supplied, like that of Eastern America, by means of violence, and with the captive savages of Negroland, it will be voluntarily by the free and industrious outpourings of China.[27]

|| CATALYSTS

The links between the distress at home and gold abroad were established by both the Chinese and the Americans. Hardly had the announcement of the gold discovery been made when passenger trade between Canton and San Francisco began.[28] By 1852, the route had been secured, and the fare had been fixed at a moderate rate (though still too high for the average emigrant, who was all too often forced to indenture himself).

The discovery of gold brought a few adventurous Chinese merchants to San Francisco.[29] These men established businesses and provided valuable goods and services; in marked contrast to the attitude toward Chinese laborers developed later, the storekeepers and restauranteurs were welcomed by the Caucasian elites of the city.[30] Many years later an old California hand recalled the pursuits of these early Chinese pioneers, contrasting them with the laborers from China:

> It is enough to know that in the fall of 1849, the Chinese in San Francisco numbered several hundred. They were not laborers who came; not of the coolie class at least. Very few of them went into the mining districts, and the writer never saw, never heard of a Chinaman digging for gold in any of the placers that year.
>
> The scarcity of lumber and the enormous prices at which it was sold—from $400 to $500 per 1,000 feet—prompted enterprising parties to ship hither the light frames and prepared stuff for what were known as China houses—structures put up in a few days, with single boarding set on end, battens covering the spaces left between the unjoined boards and roofs similarly laid on. These houses were comparatively cheap, and much better than

> tents. Many of them were brought and put up by the Chinese themselves, some of them working with their queer and clumsy tools in the carpentering, and others occupying the frail structures as shopkeepers, merchants, and dealers in Chinese wares—silks, shawls, and strange commodities never before offered for sale in an American city, or seen by the American people.... Three or four Chinese restaurants were opened, the largest and most patronized on Sacramento Street, between Montgomery and Dupont Streets, and in these the owners accumulated rapid fortunes beyond the expectation of the average Chinaman.[31]

These pioneering Chinese entrepreneurs wrote letters home telling of their successes in the new land; indeed, they went back to China, and acted as agents for their emigrating compatriots. An early letter[32] from two Chinese merchants to the governor of California reports that five of the merchants are importing goods and persons from China. Two of the five boast of sales totaling $10,000 in one day. Inspired by the merchants' reports of profits to be made in America and fabulous stories about gold strikes that sea captains circulated in Canton, Hong Kong, and Macao, numbers of Chinese from Kwangtung embarked for California.[33]

Early emigration from China brought speakers of several dialects of Cantonese to the United States. Why these groups and not others in the "emigration provinces" departed cannot be ascertained without a comprehensive examination of Cantonese social structure and local history, a task beyond the scope of this book. But, several suggestions may be offered:

First, the emigrant prefectures were closest to Canton and most subject to propaganda and pressure by pioneers and employers' agents.[34]

Second, the seafaring spirit reached its fullest development in the coastal prefectures of Kwangtung and Fukien.

Third, seasonal migration to Formosa had originated in this area. This point deserves further comment.

In many countries in which migration movements have been developed, a longtime seasonal migration to more proximate areas has preceded and set the stage for the migration to areas more distant. In Kwangtung the seasonal movements to Formosa laid a basis for migration to America. After the Ming patriot and secret society leader, Cheng Ch'eng-kung had expelled the Dutch from Formosa in 1662 the island attracted seasonal laborers and a few settlers from Kwangtung and Fukien. By 1683, large numbers of coastal Chinese appear to have migrated there. Their way of life was described by Lan

Ting-yuan (1680-1733), a general who suppressed a revolt there in 1721:

> The people of Ch'ao-chou and Hui-chou prefectures of Kwangtung who come to Formosa as agricultural laborers are called *k'e-tzu* (literally, "guest people"). Their places of residence are called *guest* villages. They number several hundred thousands and are all without wives and children. Although they are often described as violent people, their aim is to make a living from farm labor... and they return to Kwangtung after selling their autumn crops. With their income they buy property at home and support their families. By spring they come back to Formosa. They do this year after year.[35]

By 1811, according to Ping-ti Ho, "there can be little doubt that the majority of the Formosan population had...become sedentary."[36] While some seasonal migration to Formosa probably continued throughout the nineteenth century, keeping alive the notion of emigration among the Cantonese, the severe deprivation and distress of the mid-nineteenth century could not be met by Formosa's limited open space. Nevertheless, emigration to Formosa and other parts of Southeast Asia had established a precedent and a pattern for subsequent migration to the United States.

The culture and social organization of overseas Cantonese communities discouraged Chinese from other provinces from joining them. The Cantonese are divided into distinctive, sometimes mutually unintelligible dialect groups. Other cultural traits and practices as well as a well developed sub-ethnic pride divided these groups from one another and distinguished them from Chinese from other provinces. The opening of America by the early Cantonese pioneers tended to attract their *landsmanner.*

An area of migrant settlement becomes fixed as the social distance between it and the homeland is shortened. The emigrant pioneers, in a fashion similar to that of rural Chinese when they moved to a city in China, established hostels for those who came later and helped them adjust to their new life. In the process they established an ethnic community, a "Chinatown," inclusive of persons from their own prefecture speaking their own dialect. Insofar as a particular speech group ould not get a foothold in Chinatown—could not, in other words, establish hostels and its own commerical elite within the ghetto merchant oligarchy—its leaders would not encourage its members to migrate to that Chinatown.

DETERRENTS TO MIGRATION

Deterrents to migration could limit but not halt the flow of persons from China to the United States. Local, city, and state laws, enacted to restrict the opportunities of immigrant Chinese, and violent popular uprisings against them did take their toll on the numbers electing California as a place to seek their fortunes. Customhouse figures on entering Chinese reveal that in the years of severe hardship—the period during which California enacted an oppressive tax on all foreign miners but collected it almost exclusively from the Chinese—the number of immigrants dropped below that of previous or later years. On the other hand, foreknowledge of impending exclusion legislation seems to have been a deciding factor for many Chinese considering emigration. In the ten years immediately preceding the Chinese Exclusion Act of 1882—years in which such an act was a matter of widespread public discussion and in which anti-Chinese violence reached new heights—the number of Chinese arriving in the United States fluctuated: 20,291 in 1873; 5,802 in 1880; 11,890 in 1881; and, in the year before the exclusion law went into effect, 39,579.[37]

The traditonal opposition to overseas migration in the villages of Kwangtung was not strong enough to prevent the outward movement. In Nanching Village, near Canton, for example, a person with wanderlust was reproved: "Pleasant are the thousand days at home, but difficult is even half a day spent on the road."[38] The long history of overseas trade, travel, and piracy emanating from Kwangtung and Fukien suggests that such ideas were more often honored in the breach.

CONCLUDING REMARKS

China's southeastern seacoast was geographically well-suited for overseas traffic. The coastline of Kwangtung and Fukien is enclosed by a belt of islands: "These islands," observed Thomas Taylor Meadows, "with the promontories facing them on the mainland, form along a coast of 1,200 miles in extent a remarkably close series of the safest, landlocked harbors; many of which are at once easy of access and large enough to contain the whole British navy."[39] These coastal advantages were not lost upon the southeastern Chinese. Their seafaring adventures are celebrated as part of the history of Asia.

China remained only intermittently isolated from the West. Trade between imperial Rome, the Middle East, India, and Cathay played an important part in the vicissitudes of ancient economic life.[40] In the days of the Mohammedan ascendance, adventurous Cantonese traders proceeded to the Indian Archipelago and penetrated the coasts of southern Africa.[41] The Ming period (1368-1644) is known for the bold voyagers who always set out from Canton.[42] Migration to the Philippines had already begun in the late sixteenth century. The Ch'ing period (1644-1912) witnessed a diffusion of southeastern Chinese, sending traders, sojourners, and settlers throughout Southeast Asia and into Northern, Central, and South America.[43]

NOTES

1. This figure is probably an underestimate. It has been arrived at by comparing figures obtained from the customhouse of San Francisco, the commissioner-general of immigration of the United States, and the Treasury Department that are presented in
Mary Coolidge, *Chinese Immigration* (New York: Henry Holt, 1909), pp. 498 ff.
2. Ta Chen, *Chinese Migrations, with Special Reference to Labor Conditions*, Bulletin of the United States Bureau of Labor Statistics, No. 340, (Washington: Government Printing Office, 1923), p. 15.
3. Kingsley Davis, *The Population of India and Pakistan* (Princeton: Princeton University Press, 1951), pp. 99-101.
4. Harold S. Jacoby, *A Half-Century Appraisal of East Indians in the United States* (The Sixth Annual College of the Pacific Faculty Research Lecture, May 23, 1956), pp. 1-10.
5. Davis, *Population of India and Pakistan*, pp. 99-100;
G. William Skinner, *Leadership and Power in the Chinese Community of Thailand* (Ithaca: Cornell U.P., 1958);
Donald Earl Willmott, *The Chinese of Semarang: A Changing Minority Community in Indonesia* (Ithaca: Cornell U.P., 1960).
6. Davis, *Population of India and Pakistan*, p. 100, citing A.M. Carr-Saunders, *World Population* (Oxford: Clarendon, 1936), p. 49.
7. Davis, *Population of India and Pakistan.*
8. Ibid.
9. Much of the data on demographic changes in China has yet to be collected. For the best recent discussion see
Ping-ti Ho, *Population of China* (Cambridge, Mass.: Harvard U.P., 1959).
10. Wolfram Eberhard, *A History of China* (London: Routledge and Kegan Paul, 1948), p. 291.
11. The following discussion is based on Ho, *Population of China*, pp. 101-35, 169-95.
12. Ibid., pp. 169-195.
13. William Lytle Schurz, *The Manila Galleon* (New York: Dutton, 1939, 1959), pp. 63-98.

14. J.E. Spencer, *Land and People in the Philippines* (Berkeley: University of California Press, 1954), pp. 20-21, 96-97, 116-17, 198-203, 220.
15. Melvin Conant, "Southeast Asia," in *Race: Individual and Collective Behavior*, eds. Edgar T. Thompson and Everett C. Hughes (New York: Free Press, 1958), pp. 144-49.
16. Eberhard, *History of China*, pp. 291-93.
17. Ho, *Populaton of China*, pp. 196-208.
18. Albert Feuerwerkes, *China's Early Industrialization* (Cambridge, Mass.: Harvard U.P., 1958).
19. Ho, *Population of China*, pp. 208-26.
20. Ibid., p. 219.
21. Hung Liang-chi, *Chuan-shih-ko wen-chi*, Ssu-pu ts'ung-k'an edition, Series A, 1793, pp. 8a-10b. See the discussion of these essays in Ho, *Population of China*, pp. 270-73.
22. Kung Tzu-chen, *Ting-an wen-chi*, Ssu-pu pei-yao edition, 1820, Prose Works, B.6a, quoted in Ho, *Population of China*, p. 273.
23. Petersen, *Planned Migration*, p. 58.
24. For the data from which this analysis is drawn see Ho, *Population of China*, pp. 139-53, 273-94.
25. Both the memorial to the emperor and this quotation are to be found in "The Celestials at Home and Abroad," *Littel's Living Age*, August 14, 1852, p. 294.
26. Ibid.
27. Ibid., p. 298.
28. Commerical Circular, King and Co., Canton, China, January 27, 1852. Quoted by Governor John Bigler in his "Special Message from the Governor of California to the Senate and Assembly of California in Relation to Asiatic Emigration," *California Senate Journal.* 3rd sess., April 23, 1852, p. 375. The passenger trade between Canton and San Francisco became so lucrative that the shipping companies were quite willing to permit the Chinese Benevolent Association to dictate the terms under which Chinese might return to China. Such firms as the Pacific Mail Steamship Company, Koopmanschap and Co., The Oriental Line, and others, were most vociferous in their denunciation of legislative attempts to curb Chinese immigration. Anti-Chinese mobs more than once burned the wharf of the Pacific Mail Steamship Company. This company and others readily admitted violating safety rules in order to include greater numbers of Chinese passengers. U.S. Congress, Senate, Joint Special Committee to Investigate Chinese Immigration, 44th Cong., 2d sess., February 27, 1877, S. Rept. 689.
29. A few Chinese had reached the Hawaiian Islands as early as 1794. In 1835, William French brought a number of Chinese to Hawaii for the purpose of manufacturing sugar. The Chinese played an important role in the establishment of Hawaii's first sugar mills. By 1846, there were eleven such establishments in the islands, at Kohala and Hilo, run by Chinese. On August 12, 1851, the British bark *Thetis*, sailed for China to obtain labor for Hawaii's plantations. It returned on January 3, 1852,

with 200 Chinese from Amoy. These were the first Chinese "coolies" brought to Hawaii.
See Ralph S. Kuykendall, *The Hawaiian Kingdom, 1778-1854* (Honolulu: University of Hawaii Press, 1957), pp. 27, 84, 175, 180-81, 316, 329.

30. *Daily Alta Californian*, May 12, 1851.
31. James J. O'Meara, "The Chinese in Early Days," *Overland Monthly*, May 1884, p. 477.
32. "Letter of the Chinamen to His Excellency, Gov. Bigler," San Francisco, Thursday, April 29, 1852, reprinted in *Littel's Living Age*, July 3, 1852, pp. 32-34.
33. The effects of this propaganda are described in a letter of that era:

> During the past month there has been not a little excitement among people connected with foreigners, and who have means of learning anything of the "gold hills"—more especially among those whose acquaintances in California have described the advantages of the country, or, on returning to China, have spread the report of their good fortune. Letters from Chinese in San Francisco and further in the country have been circulated through all this part of the province; and the accounts of the successful adventurers who have returned would, had the inhabitants possessed the means of paying their way across, have gone far to depopulate considerable towns. The number of men that have gone, and that are now preparing to embark, is so considerable, and the employment which has been thus so unexpectedly, at a moment of great depression of freights, is so remarkable, that we have no doubt the subject will excite the attention of all who are interested in the trade of the East.

Letter of March 27, 1852, quoted in "The Celestials at Home and Abroad," p. 291.

34. The bulk of overseas Chinese in the United States and Canada are from the Sam Yup and Sz Yup, both neighboring the city of Canton and subject to its influence.
35. Lan Ting-yuan, *Lu-chou ch'u-chi*, 1732 edition, 11.33b-34a, quoted in Ho, *Population of China*, p. 164.
36. Ho, *Population of China*, p. 165.
37. Coolidge, *Chinese Immigration*, p. 498.
38. C.K. Yang, *A Chinese Village in Communist Transition* (Cambridge, Mass.: Harvard U.P., 1959), p. 81.
39. Thomas Taylor Meadows, *The Chinese and Their Rebellions* (Stanford: Academic Reprints, 1856), pp. 43-44.
40. Frederick J. Teggart, *Rome and China: A Study of Correlations in Historical Events* (Berkeley: University of California Press, 1939);
G.F. Hudson, *Europe and China: A Survey of Their Relations From the Earliest Times to 1800* (Boston: Beacon, 1931; 1961), pp. 27-102;
C.P. Fitzgerald, *China, A Short Cultural History* (London: Cresset, 1958), pp. 174-201.
41. Pyau Ling, "Causes of Chinese Emigration," *Annals of the American*

Academy of Political and Social Science, January 1912, pp. 74-82; Victor Purcell, *The Chinese in Southeast Asia* (London: Oxford University Press, 1951), p. xxviii.

42. L.C. Goodrich, *A Short History of the Chinese People* (New York: Harper, 1943, 1959), pp. 192-95.

43. "The 'issuing forth into the sea' is wanting to the Chinese of the northern coastland. . . . [B]ut it is long since the South Eastern Chinese—the inhabitants of Kwangtung and Fuh keen, commonly known as Canton men and Fuh keen men—have so issued forth. It is they who, after occupying all inhabitale portion of the belt of islands on their coast, colonized Formosa and Haenan; proceeded then in their junks . . . to Siam, to Manila, to Borneo, Java, Singapore, and the Indian Archipelago generally; . . . They are superseding the aboriginal inhabitants, much as the Anglo-Saxons have superseded the Red men of America. These South Eastern Chinese, these Canton men and Fuh keen men, are in short the Anglo-Saxons of Asia, as sailors, as merchants, as colonists, and indeed as adventurers generally; for I may add, these are the Chinese, whose gainseeking and adventurous spirit is carrying them in thousands to the gold mines of California and Australia, the guano islands of Peru and the sugar plantations of the West Indies." Meadows, *Chinese and Their Rebellions*, pp. 46-47.

The Japanese Emigration ‖3

‖ GENERAL CONSIDERATIONS

The conditions that preceded Japanese migration to North and South America are not basically dissimilar from those in China. Historical circumstances modified the times and places from which Japanese would depart and effected the ways in which Japanese and Chinese immigrants organized their communities in the New World. Emigration from Japan arose under situations of distress at home and opportunities abroad and was catalyzed by propaganda, sponsorship, and other encouragements.

The overseas distribution of Japanese migrants may be divided into three periods during which the destination and social organization of the migrants changed.[1]

In the first period the number and kind of departures were limited by strongly enforced governmental restrictions. Japan's migration to Europe and the United States consisted mostly of students, some under government sponsorship. Itinerant traders and fishermen accounted for the migration to Asiatic Russia, Korea, and China.[2]

Emigration during the next two periods was affected by the interplay of economic and social conditions abroad, and political development in Japan. To satisfy the need for plantation workers in Hawaii, agreements were drawn up between the Japanese and Hawaiian governments permitting the employment of Japanese as contract laborers. With the American annexation of Hawaii in 1898, the lawful importation of contract laborers came to an end.[3]

The shift in migration on the Asian continent was also a product of political and economic forces. Migration to Japanese-dominated Korea continued after the annexation of 1910; for the most part these were officials, professionals, and persons engaged in commerce and transportation.[4] A rapid increase in the indigenous Korean population—consequent upon the reduction in death rates and stability of birth rates that occurred during the period of Japanese rule[5]—tended to discourage Japanese peasants from moving there. Imperial and industrial policies encouraged the migration of officials, manufacturers, and traders to Taiwan, Kwantung, and the Leased Territory in South Manchuria.[6] After the turn of the century Hokkaidō and Karafuto received agricultural migrants almost exclusively from northern Honshū.[7]

After Japan abandoned official isolation in 1868, the slow trickle of emigrants that began to flow to the United States streamed into mass migration. From 1868 to 1884, Japan permitted long-term emigration solely for educational purposes.[8] But starting in 1885, the number of non-student emigrants grew and their social origins and occupational aspirations indicate that, while students did not cease going abroad, the majority of migrants were farmers, laborers, artisans, and merchants. Moreover, the aspirations of the immigrants did not necessarily coincide with the occupations they actually pursued in the United States. Many students found a great hiatus between their intellectual desires and available educational opportunities. An erstwhile student, forced to enter domestic service, complained: "Some say the Japanese are studying while they are working in the kitchen, but it is all nonsense. Many of them started so, but nearly all of them failed."[9] Data on the occupations of the Japanese in the United States indicate that the great majority were, at first, domestics and laborers in primary industries and, later, farm workers and tenant farmers. A small petit bourgeois class did arise after 1904.[10] Nevertheless, the greatest hostility to the Japanese arose where their numbers appeared most threatening—in labor and agriculture.[11]

The small migration of ambitious farmers increased after returning migrants advertised their success. The shift from large-scale enterprises to small intensively cultivated vegetable plots attracted farmers from Hiroshima and adjacent prefectures to California. As an isolated and remote peasantry, the Japanese had less to fear from hostile mobs of urban white laborers who made life so unsafe for Asians seeking employment in the city. This security served as a further inducement, pulling Japanese laborers and newly-arrived immigrants into agriculture, a fact attested to by the increase in farm tenancy among Japanese in California after 1908.[12] The unenforceability of California's Alien Land Law counteracted its intended deterrent effect.[13]

While demographers and sociologists have conducted analyses of the statistical record, overseas distribution, and the age, sex, and occupational statuses of Japanese immigrants,[14] none has explained satisfactorily why the overseas emigration of Japanese commoners—that is, those who were not officials of the government or agents of large business houses—proceeded for the greatest part from certain prefectures in southeastern Honshū and western Kyūshū. Ichihashi, after demonstrating that the *districts* (but not the *prefectures*) from which the migrants departed were not those of the greatest density, ascribes Japanese overseas emigration to general causes of which the most important was the desire to escape from Japan's military conscription.[15] He thus neglects to account for the fact that, though the alleged causes were general, emigration was not. Yoshida emphasizes the density and poverty of the emigrant prefectures and points up the role played by propagands, pioneer migration, and sponsorship, but his analysis is unsystematic and lacks a theoretical framework.[16]

If we examine the conditions present in southern Honshū and western Kyūshū in terms of the framework outlined earlier, some suggestions emerge to help account for the particularity of Japanese emigration.

All of the emigrant areas were scenes of population increase equal to, or greater than, the increase in all other parts of Japan between 1750 and 1852.[17] Overseas emigration was a small part of the general redistribution of the Japanese population that resulted from the Meiji policy of industrialization.[18] The areas of incipient industrialization, construction, and service activities were concentrated in Tokaido and Kinai, areas that absorbed an earlier internal migration. It is probable that overseas migration out of the cities of Hiroshima and Toyoda was, in part, a surplus of that early migration from rural to urban areas that had increased faster then the cities' capacity for absorption.

In the two decades after the Meiji Restoration, pressure in agricultural parts of the emigration districts appears to have become a factor encouraging emigration. Increased population became a perennial threat to industrializing Japan; it still poses a problem today.

The emigrant districts appear to have been the worst off. For Japan in general, the average holding of land cultivated by a single farmer was so small, that according to Yosaburo Yoshida, the "annual yield...[is] even under the most perfect system of utilization,... absolutely insufficient to support a family according to modern standards of comfort."[19] In four of the six emigration prefectures for which information is available, two thirds or more of the farming families cultivated less than the minimally sufficient acreage; in the other two, over half farmed substandard areas. In Hiroshima, the district which has contributed the majority of persons applying for overseas passports, the average amount of cultivated farm land per capita is not only the lowest for the emigrant prefectures, but for all of Japan.

That the material condition of the emigrants from Hiroshima was improved by their sojourn abroad was indicated in a contemporary report:

> ... When they start as emigrants, their land and houses are in the hands of landlords; their position is that of small tenants. But when they come back after four or five years' labor abroad, they usually buy a house and two or three tans of farm land, and become independent farmers or merchants. ... About six tenths of all emigrants succeed in this way.[20]

ATTRACTIVE FORCES

After the passage of the Chinese Exclusion Act in 1882, a labor shortage in primary industries in the western states induced some Japanese to become replacements for the Chinese. A far greater inducement were the new opportunities in small-scale agriculture, particularly in California but also along the entire Pacific Coast and in western Texas. As agriculturalists the Japanese immigrants enjoyed some measure of material prosperity in the New World.

CATALYSTS

Three catalytic forces operated on the emigrant prefectures to overcome the presence of deterrent forces and "friction": (1) an earlier history of piracy, trade, travel, and Western contact in the emigrant prefectures; (2) success stories and other encouraging propaganda spread by Japanese pioneers; and (3) emigration companies which helped the emigrant to overcome the financial obstacles to departure.

Despite Japan's seclusion from the Western and Pacific world for much of its recent history, the emigrant prefectures offered an outlet for the adventurous and the enterprising. In 1263, the Korean monarchy officially complained of the raids of Japanese pirates. In the fourteenth century joint attempts were made by the Chinese and Japanese governments to suppress Japanese corsairs; in the same period the development of overseas trade by Buddhist monks paved the way for the building of port cities on Kyūshū. At the end of the sixteenth century, Shogun Hideyoshi encouraged trade overseas; certain feudatories in Hiroshima and Kyūshū pursued commercial piracy until they were suppressed by Tokugawa power.[21] The importance of piracy is that it stirred Japanese interest in the outside world. As one Japanese historian stated:

> These pirates were really the pioneers of foreign trade. Their ships visited Borneo, Malacca, Annam, Siam, Tonkin, Saigon, Cambodia, and the Philippines, venturing at times as far as Mexico, and carrying the treasures of the southern and eastern ocean backward and forward. So long as they were in a foreign port, the sailors behaved like respectable merchants, and when they returned to Japan and China they brought back so much valuable timber and so many curious jewels that the hearts of all the adventurers in Japan and China were fascinated, and the people were convinced that the islands of the sea were inexhaustible of gold and jewels.[22]

What Canton, Hong Kong, and Macao were to the Chinese villagers of Kwangtung and Fukien, the ports of Hiroshima, Nagasaki, and Wakayama were to Japanese rice-farmers in Kyūshū and southern Honshū. In both areas piracy planted the seed of an overseas movement that took root and flourished as the migrations of the nineteenth century. At all of these Chinese and Japanese ports overseas trade flourished; here also the first and continuous contacts were made with Western missionaries, merchants, government officials, and sea captains—all of whom acted as witting or unwitting catalysts in the emigration process.

Adventurous tales related by shipwrecked sailors and wondrous descriptions of Hawaii and the United States mailed home by pioneer migrants enhanced interest in these areas and kindled the flame of new fortune for distressed Japanese at home. Sailors on junks from Kyūshū and Hiroshima were frequently rescued from shipwrecks by American ships and taken to Hawaii or the coastal states of California or Oregon. Eight such instances are recorded in California and Hawaii between 1806 and 1860. In March 1833, a Japanese junk was driven ashore near Cape Flattery. The survivors of the crew were brought to Fort Vancouver, sent east by the Hudson's Bay Company, and eventually returned to Japan by way of England.[23] Of such rescues the most celebrated was that of Manjiro Nakahama (1841). Nakahama, rescued from a wreck in the north Pacific and taken to Hawaii, eventually traveled to the United States, learned English, and returned to Japan after an absence of twelve years. He became a principal in the negotiations with Admiral Perry in 1854, returned to Hawaii and the United States as a captain in the Imperial Japanese Navy, and related his impressions of America to his countrymen. Another shipwrecked Japanese, Hamada Hikozo, who was taken first to San Francisco and then to Washington, D.C., and educated and naturalized as a citizen of the United States, published a popular account of his adventures in America, and spent much of his time as an interpreter for other Japanese castaways brought to San Francisco.[24] Much of what the later emigrants first knew about the New World came from the lips or pens of these rescued mariners.

Although curiousity about overseas areas was aroused by the stories of shipwrecked Japanese sailore, it was the success of a few of the pioneer migrants that inspired the desire to migrate. Early student migration to the United States seemed promising after a man named Miyama retailed the excellence of its educational system upon returning to Japan, and Yukichi Fukuzawa returned from America to found Keio University. Shoemakers from Hiroshima were attracted by the opportunities in San Francisco advertised by an immigrant named Shiro who established the Japanese Shoemakers' Union in that city.[25] The success of Kinji Ushijima (George Shima) "the potato king," who cleared a supposedly uncultivable area in California and became a millionaire, was broadcast throughout the emigration districts and especially attracted *landsmänner* from his native Fukuoka.[26] An enterprising farmer from Wakayama became known as the greatest flower raiser west of the Rockies and his success attracted immigrants from his former prefecture. Kanae Nagasawa, a rich wine manufacturer, and Jokichi Takamine, a millionaire pharmacological chemist similarly attracted aspiring young men from their own and neighboring districts.[27]

Nor was spectacular success the only factor that encouraged group and later mass migration; a modestly enticing opportunity was often sufficient if the needs at home were great. The events leading up to the establishment of a Japanese fishing village in British Columbia in 1887, undoubtedly had parallels in other villages in the emigrant prefectures.[28] Mio Village, now a prosperous fishing community because of remittances sent by its sons who settled in Canada, was a near-destitute fishing community in nineteenth century Wakayama. In 1887, Gihei Kuno, a Mio carpenter, went to Canda upon the advice of a cousin living in a neighboring village. In Vancouver, this "pioneer" noticed the opportunities for salmon fishing and invited fellow-villagers to come over. Young men began to emigrate from the village, then under greater hardship than before. Despite anti-Japanese sentiment in Canada, the village prospered. Soon the emigrants included not only the poverty-stricken and the fortune-hunting, but also Mio's comparatively better off farmers. By 1926, the peak year for emigration to British Columbia from Mio, the number of its villagers in Canada was nearly equal to that of the population of Mio itself. In its fortieth-anniversary commemorative issue, the bulletin of the Association of Mio-villagers in Canada stated: "Our poor native village now has turned into an 'El Dorado' and people now call it 'Amerika-mura.' "[29]

Transportation and financial aids for Japanese unable to pay their own way abroad were made possible by several large emigrant companies established in Japan shortly after the Meiji government permitted emigration. These companies were commercial capitalist ventures, owned by groups of private investors—some were wealthy Japanese pioneers in the United States—and operated under imperial regulation. The bulk of the emigrants sponsored by this form of assistance went to Peru and Brazil; although American law prohibited the importation of contract labor, it is possible these companies found subtle means to evade or circumvent the customs and labor regulations.[30]

DETERRENTS TO EMIGRATION

Until the exclusion of Japanese immigrants in 1924, deterrents were able to slow but not halt the movement of Japanese into the United States. The "Gentleman's Agreement" of 1907 sought to prevent all male Japanese laborers from entering the United States. Anti-Japanese sentiments and occasional uprisings against Japanese no doubt had some deterrent effect, but on balance, it does not appear that fears of racial oppression kept Japanese from coming to America.

Success stories might have encouraged emigration but reports of failure discouraged it. In 1869, a colony of about a hundred Japanese attempted silk agriculture at Gold Hill, California.[31] The failure of their project discouraged others with the same vocation from joining them.[32] Especially discouraging was failure abroad when conditions in the home prefecture were reasonably satisfactory. After an immigrant named Ito had returned to relatively prosperous Aichi Prefecture with stories of his success in California, a hundred young farmers from Aichi departed for the Golden State. Others soon followed and for a short time farm laborers from Aichi dominated the labor force in the San Joaquin Valley. Their remarkable failure to prosper carried back to Aichi, and emigration to the United States from that prefecture ceased after 1905.[33]

In summary, overseas emigration from both China and Japan

occurred in areas where social unrest stirred up by crop failure, flood, famine, war, revolution, or sudden social and economic changes made the homeland a less desirable place to live. Advertised opportunities abroad directed a portion of this social unrest into emigration. Pioneer migrants incited the migratory interest; propaganda maintained and enhanced it. Departures occurred principally from those depressed areas where once pirates, sea-traders, and adventurers had operated. Various kinds of assistance—the forms of which would profoundly affect the social organization of the immigrants—overcame the financial obstacle to movement overseas. Opposition to emigration while having some effect, was unable to prevent a significant number of Chinese and Japanese from coming to the United States.

NOTES

1. See Yamato Ichihashi, *Japanese in the United States* (Stanford: Stanford U.P., 1932), pp. 401-9;
   Dorothy Swine Thomas, Charles Kikuchi, and J. Sakoda, *The Salvage* (Berkeley: University of California Press, 1952), pp. 3-18, 571-626;
   E.K. Strong, *The Second Generation Japanese Problem in the United States* (Stanford: Stanford U.P., 1934;
   H.A. Millis, *The Japanese Problem in the United States* (New York: Macmillan, 1915);
   K.K. Kawakami, *The Real Japanese Question* (New York: Macmillan, 1921);
   T. Iyenaga and Kenoske Sato, *Japan and the California Problem* (New York: Putnam, 1921);
   Charles H. Young, Helen R.Y. Reid, and W.A. Carrothers, *The Japanese Canadians* ed. H.A. Innis (Toronto: University of Toronto Press, 1938);
   Torajie Irie, "Japanese Migration to Peru," *Hispanic American Historical Review*, May 1951, pp. 437-52; November 1951, pp. 648-64, trans. William Himel;
   Ernest K. Wakukawa, *A History of the Japanese People in Hawaii* (Honolulu: The Toyo Shoin, 1938);
   Romanzo C. Adams, "Japanese Migration Statistics," *Sociology and Social Research*, May/June 1929, pp. 436-45.
2. Maurice R. Davie, *World Immigration* (New York: Macmillan, 1949), p. 318.
3. Wakukawa, *Japanese People in Hawaii*, pp. 15-29, 42-51, 89-111;
   R.S. Kuykendall, *Hawaiian Kingdom, 1854-1874* (Honolulu: University of Hawaii Press, 1953), pp. 66-69, 75-78, 178-233.
4. Ryoichi Ishii, *Population Pressure and Economic Life in Japan* (London: P.S. King and Son, 1937), pp. 192-93.
5. Irene Taeuber, *The Population of Japan* (Princeton: Princeton University Press, 1958), p. 187.

6. Ishii, *Economic Life in Japan*, pp. 192-93;
Taeuber, *Population of Japan*, p. 185.
7. Taeuber, *Population of Japan*, pp. 173-80;
Ishii, *Economic Life in Japan*.
8. Ichihashi, *Japanese in the United States*, p. 54;
Davie, *World Immigration*, p. 318.
9. "The Confessions of a Japanese Servant," *Independent* vol. 59 p. 667, quoted in Yosaburo Yoshida, "Sources and Causes of Japanese Emigration," *Annals of the American Academy of Political and Social Science*, September 1909, pp. 166-67.
10. Ichihashi, *Japanese in the United States*, pp. 116-36.
11. See Jacobus ten Broek, Edward Barnhart, and Floyd Matson, *Prejudice, War, and the Constitution* (Berkeley: University of California Press, 1954), pp. 11-67.
12. Dorothy S. Thomas and Richard Nishimoto, *The Spoilage* (Berkeley: University of California Press, 1946), pp. 20-23;
Yoshida, "Japanese Emigration," p. 161.
Ichihashi, *Japanese in the United States*, pp. 160-78;
Iyenaga and Sato, *California Problem*, pp. 120-48;
Kawakami, *Japanese Question*, pp. 41-62.
13. Thomas and Nishimoto, *Spoilage*, pp. 24-25.
14. See the sources cited in footnote 1.
15. Ichihashi, *Japanese in the United States*, pp. 78-92.
16. Yoshida, "Japanese Emigration," pp. 157-67.
17. Taeuber, *Population of Japan*, pp. 24-25, 46.
18. Ibid., pp. 45-47.
19. Yoshida, "Japanese Emigration," p. 160.
20. *The Osaka Mainichi Shimbun*, November 9, 1904, quoted in Yoshida, "Japanese Emigration," p. 162n.
21. George B. Sansom, *Japan, A Short Cultural History* (New York: Appleton, 1946), pp. 96, 169, 195, 309, 354, 411, 454.
A valuable discussion of the Kyūshū-based *Wako* (so-called dwarf-pirates) will be found in C.R. Boxer, The Christian Century in Japan (Berkeley: University of California Press, 1951), pp. 7-14, 248-307.
22. Y. Takekoshi, *The Japanese Rule in Formosa* (London: n.p., 1907), p. 50, quoted in Ichihashi, *Japanese in the United States*, pp. 83-84.
23. George W. Fuller, *A History of the Pacific Northwest* (New York: Knopf, 1931), p. 44.
24. Wakukawa, *Japanese People in Hawaii*, pp. 3-14;
Ichihashi, *Japanese in the United States*, pp. 19-23, 48-53.
25. Ichihashi, *Japanese in the United States*, pp. 88-89.
26. Yoshida, "Japanese Emigration," p. 164;
Ichihashi, *Japanese in the United States*, p. 89;
John P. Irish, "Reasons for Encouraging Japanese Emigration," *Annals of the American Academy of Political and Social Science*, September 1909, p. 77
27. Ichihashi, *Japanese in the United States*, p. 89.

28. The following is from *Influences of Emigrants on Their Home Village: Report of a Survey of Amerika-Mura,* Population Problems Series No. 8, mimeographed (Tokyo: The Populations Problems Research Council—The Mainichi Newspapers, 1953). This is a summary of a larger work in Japanese edited by Tadashi Fukutake, *Amerika-Mura* (Tokyo: University of Tokyo Press, 1953).
29. [Author's note for 1984 edition: In 1981 I visited Mio Village. A museum honoring the migration to Japan has been established as a joint venture by Canada and Japan. The village seems prosperous and boasts its own historian, writing the narrative of the North American venture. Some homes have an architectural style definitely influenced by that of British Columbia.]
30. See Hart H. North, "Chinese and Japanese Immigration to the Pacific Coast," *California Historical Society Quarterly,* December 1949, pp. 343-50.
31. *Sacramento Daily Union,* November 27, 1869, p. 8.
32. Millis, *Japanese Problem,* p. 2;
    Ichihashi, *Japanese in the United States,* p. 51.
33. Ichihashi, *Japanese in the United States,* p. 88.

Immigrant Adjustment in America II

Chinese and Japanese Communities 4

INTRODUCTION

Chinese and Japanese have reacted differently to their respective positions as immigrants in the United States. This can be seen in the organizational structure and political processes within their overseas communities. The customs, practices, beliefs, and perspectives of the Chinese and Japanese were not the same when the two peoples emigrated nor were the opportunities awaiting them in the New World. Their respective patterns of adjustment were creative responses to the complex interplay of socio-cultural forces and environmental conditions that produced the unique social worlds in which each struggled for existence.

CHINATOWN

Chinatowns may be classified as *communalist* societies. Communalism refers to that political system in which a racially or culturally defined group governs itself, makes its own laws, lives according to its own traditions, and is ruled by its own elites. In its immigrant form it is a special instance of extraterritoriality.[1] Communalism may arise under state sponsorship or informally when a minority's self-regulation of its internal affairs goes unnoticed or unmolested within the state. In some instances a long-standing traditional communalism is recognized as legitimate by the state and left to operate without interference.

Chinese communalism has arisen under state sponsorship in colonial areas; in other kinds of societies the Chinese have been left to manage their own affairs without state interference but with no formal acknowledgment of their communal self-governance.

In Southeast Asia, the Dutch and British practice of indirect rule over the several minorities inhabiting their colonies formally recognized the rights of the Chinese to regulate their own affairs. The "Kapitan China" system, under which British and Dutch colonial authorities appointed a prominent Chinese to be the ruler-representative of his compatriots, legitimized the domination of the Chinese by their own communal elite.[2]

Thai dynasties acknowledged Chinese self-government under appointed "headmen" and permitted Chinese monopolies over tax, opium, and gambling. The Chinese were also permitted entry into Thai officialdom; some even rose to high rank.[3] In nineteenth-century western Malaya, the large mining centers such as Larut, Kuala Lumpur, and Lukut, were beyond the administrative resources of the Malay chiefs to control. To administer the internal affairs of these communities, inhabited largely by Chinese, Malay chiefs recognized the rights of a headman who was "of course always a Chinese and was usually the leading mine manager of the centre. The Malay ruling class thus dealt with the Chinese as groups rather than as individuals."[4]

Voluntary communalism is found in those overseas Chinese communities not under Colonial indirect rule. In the United States, Jamaica, and Great Britain,[5] no formal recognition of Chinese jurisdictional and extraterritorial rights has been made, but informal practices, for instance, the assumption by city mayors that the Chung Wah Kongsi (federation of territorial and dialect groups) is the legitimate spokesman for all the Chinese, or the tacit recognition by city police of the right of the Chinese to regulate criminal matters within Chinatown,[6] has given rise to a communalist form of self-government hardly dissimilar from that under British or Dutch colonial rule. In Jamaica, where Syrians, Greeks, Jews, Britons, and blacks have all established ethnic enclaves, the Chinese community is conspicuous for its isolation and has more than once aroused the enmity of the peoples of the larger society.[7] The Chinese community in Merseyside, Liverpool, appears to regulate its own affairs under the direction of its kongsis and secret societies:

> In most respects the Chinese keep themselves at a distance from European society.... They have formed numerous locality organizations. ... These associations... function as social centers

> and in some respects as friendly societies. ... There is also the Chi Kung Tong or Chinese Masonic Hall, ... a moribund association frequented mainly by the old men of Chinatown. ... A few organizations were set up jointly by the English and Chinese authorities during the last war, in order to deal with the problems raised by the sudden expansion of the Chinese community in Liverpool, but they were not, it is understood, particularly effective and the local authorities have had little cause or encouragement to extend their activities in that direction.[8]

The Chinese inhabitants of New Zealand appear, on the other hand, to live under less self-government than their compatriots elsewhere. Despite the continued existence of a community-wide "association," Chinese social institutions are said to be in a state of disorganization, and there is "no well-defined institution which all Chinese in the community rigorously maintain and support."[9]

The organizational structure of an overseas Chinese community is not too different whether it exists in Semarang or Sarawak, in Singapore, or San Francisco. An oligarchic elite, composed of the heads of the "speech" associations (kongsi), or, in some instances, the chiefs of various secret societies, or both, exercises communitywide authority. It makes and enforces laws, collects taxes and fees, and settles disputes. It carries on "foreign relations" with the official government outside Chinatown, speaks in behalf of the Chinese people, and in the nineteenth century arranged contracts for Chinese labor, and appeared in behalf of the Chinese in the courts. In those countries where their rights are inferior to those of the native citizenry, or where anti-Chinese sentiments are strong, an immigrant's disrespect, disloyalty, or disobedience to the official Chinese community elite carried with it the possibility of a terrible penalty. An offender might be falsely accused of a crime, turned over to the public courts, and left undefended and unprotected.

Opponents of the ruling Chinese elite organized protective and defensive societies. These societies, from time to time, emerged in insurrections against the ruling elite. These conflicts took form as open warfare or subversion. Intramural struggles locked the Chinese together in deadly embrace and, coincident with the effects of racial prejudice and cultural differences, lengthened the social distance between Chinese and non-Chinese.

|| JAPANESE COMMUNITIES

Communalism did not arise in overseas Japanese communities to an extent similar to that among Chinese. The few isolated and largely self-governing Japanese communities—like those said to exist in prewar Brazil[10]—are exceptions to the usual experience of Japanese immigrant life. For communalism to exist there must be community-wide domination of the people in question by a group of institutional elites, the policy they pursue must be directed toward maintaining the separateness of the community and their own authority over the "subjects." Both of these conditions existed in Chinatown; neither in "Little Tokyo."

Japanese communities have not been dominated for any lengthy period by a single set of associations. Instead, a proliferation of limited special interest organizations have arisen to represent the Japanese. Mutual aid societies among Japanese in America have been limited in purpose and short-lived. The relatively rapid balancing of the sex ratio (a phenomenon just now occurring in Chinese communities)[11] operated to create a cleavage between the immigrant generation and the American-born Japanese. This division is a most pronounced characteristic, recognized in their language and in their social organization.[12] Various religious denominations further divided the community. Moreover, the Japanese did not seek a segregated self-governing community for themselves. The American-born pursued a policy directed at public recognition of their own Americanization. The supreme irony of their efforts occurred when, at the outbreak of the Pacific War, all Japanese on the Pacific coast, regardless of generation or citizenship, were alleged to be "unassimilated," forcibly removed from their homes and occupations, and incarcerated.[13]

Among the Japanese immigrants one major community association was the "prefectural society" (*kenjinkai*). However, unlike Chinese kongsis, kenjinkai limited their activity to providing mutual aid and death benefits and did not exercise executive, legislative, or judicial power over the Japanese.[14] Moreover, even these activities of the kenjinkai were short-lived; as the second-generation (Nisei) became the most numerous Japanese group, the importance of kenjinkai in Japanese social life diminished. Even in their heyday, kenjinkai faced the competition of special interest organizations that undermined any attempt at diffusion of kenjinkai authority over the entire community.[15]

For a brief time, kenjinkai did act as employment agencies for newly arrived immigrants. The latter were introduced "to those members who might be able to offer employment; unually a *kenjin* got the first chance of employment...other things being equal."[16] During the first two decades of Japanese immigration, operators of boarding-houses and kenjinkai officials apparently exercised considerable control over the employment of Japanese; this lent itself to abuses, corruption, and in some instance, flagrant exploitation of laborers by their fellow-countrymen.[17] However, as occupational opportunities for Japanese shifted away from wage labor and into independent agriculture, the exploitative power of "bosses" and associations diminished.

The emergence of a highly vocal and ambitious second generation furthered the breakdown of ethnic solidarity among the Japanese. The political voice of the Issei "immigrant" group had been the Japanese Associations of America (JAA), founded in San Francisco in 1900, and established in New York City in 1914. The accommodative policy of this early association (it never appears to have favored communalism as has the political voice of the Chinese, the Chung Wah Kongsi) was bitterly opposed by the organization of the Nisei which sought full assimilation of the Japanese into the larger society.[18]

The Japanese Associations of America enjoyed only a short productive life and even in their heyday did not claim the majority of Japanese as members. Formed in response to early outbreaks of anti-Japanese agitation, these associations were an autochthonous product of Japanese life in America; they were not imported from Japan.[19]

The Japanese Associations of America can best be classified, sociologically, as institutions of accommodation. The provided the immigrants with instruction in English; attempted to foster Japanese understanding of American society and culture; offered legal advice to their fellow-immigrants; and served as a microcosmic functional equivalent of the United States Department of Agriculture Field Service, helping their compatriots to improve methods of agriculture. They conducted censuses of the Japanese population in the United States and made these reports available to the Japanese consulates; aided Japanese who had left the country to obtain reentry permits; acted as agencies, in the absence of consular officials, for the endorsement of certain legal certificates; and attempted to educate American-born Japanese about Japan, and non-Japanese about the culture of Japan and the Japanese-Americans.

However, the right of the Japanese Associations of America to act as the sole public spokesman for the Japanese was challenged by the Nisei association, the Japanese American Citizens' League (JACL, established in 1930).[20] At the local and rural level, JACL activities were, and are to this day, largely social—picnics, talent revues, dances, and the like. In cities and in their national conferences, JACL activities have been directed toward fuller integration with non-

Japanese society; except in a few instances, it disregarded the Japanese consulates and the chapters of the JAA and petitioned the American government directly to ensure civil liberties, civil rights, and equal protection for persons of Japanese descent. Especially active in this regard, the JACL scored some successes in the decade prior to the outbreak of the second world war and many more in subsequent decades.

In both Canada and the United States, Japanese labor unions, in contrast to any similar type of organization among the immigrant Chinese, have shown a great interest in integration with the larger non-Japanese unions. The Japanese Camp and Mill Workers' Union, organized in 1920 for the purpose of promoting trade unionism among the Japanese in Canada, affiliated with the Canadian Trades and Labor Congress in 1927, and in 1931, endorsed the principle of "equality of treatment and full rights of citizenship" for Canadian Nisei at the union convention.[21] As early as 1907, Japanese mine workers in the United States, by a bold move, broke the color bar and secured the right to join the Wyoming local of the United Mine Workers of America.[22]

Many other Japanese immigrant associations, of a religious, commercial, and social nature,[23] sprang up, and by 1920, the Carnegie-sponsored Studies of Americanization described the Japanese as "the most efficiently and completely organized among the immigrant groups" and as "not at all equaled" by any other foreign language minority in "the work of accommodating themselves to alien conditions."[24] In contrast to the Chinese, the Japanese approached immigrant life with the goal of ending their separate status in American society.[25] A sociologist who carefully studied the social life of the Japanese in the United States has written: "The word *assimilation* has two meanings—interbreeding and comprehension of political and social conditions. In the latter scheme, the young Japanese are more readily assimilated than people of several European races."[26]

NOTES

1. The definition is slightly reformulated from that given by J.A. Laponce, *The Protection of Minorities* (Berkeley: University of California Press, 1960), p. 84.
2. J.S. Furnivall, *Colonial Policy and Practice* (New York: New York U.P., 1956), pp. 1-142, 217-512;
   Victor Purcell, *The Chinese in Southeast Asia* (London: Oxford, 1951);
   Ju K'ang T'ien, *The Chinese in Sarawak* (London: London School of Economics Monographs on Social Anthropology, 1953);

Lea Williams, *Overseas Chinese Nationalism: The Genesis of the Pan-Chinese Movement in Indonesia, 1900-1916* (New York: Free Press, 1960);
Leon Comber, *Chinese Secret Societies in Malaya* (Locust Valley: J.J. Augustin, 1959), pp. 70-74, 139-46;
Donald Earl Willmott, *The Chinese of Semarang: A Changing Minority Community in Indonesia* (Ithaca: Cornell U.P., 1960), pp. 147-52.

3. G. William Skinner, *Leadership and Power in the Chinese Community of Thailand* (Ithaca: Cornell U.P., 1958), p. 1-26.
4. J.M. Gullick, *Indigenous Political Systems of Western Malaya* (London: Athlone Press, 1958), pp. 24-25.
5. Rose Hum Lee, *The Chinese in the United States of America*, pp. 147-52;
Leonard Broom, "Jamaica," in *Race: Individual and Collective Behavior*, eds. Edgar T. Thompson and everett C. Hughes (New York: Free Press, 1958), pp. 131-41;
Maurice Broady, "The Chinese in Great Britain," in *Colloquium on Overseas Chinese*, ed. Morton Fried (New York: Institute of Pacific Relations, 1958), pp. 29-35.

> "In Cantonese-American economic activities, as well as in other affairs, there is a marked tendency not to rely upon or follow American legal procedures,"

Milton L. Barnett, "Kinship as a Factor Affecting Cantonese Economic Adaptation in the United States," *Human Organization*, Spring 1960, p. 43.

6. > "Professor Sutherland points out that in Chicago the Chinese have an official court, without political authority, that exercises control over members similar to that maintained in their own country."

Harry Elmer Barnes and Negley K. Teeters, *New Horizons in Criminology* (New York: Prentice-Hall, 1951), p. 169.
See also, Rose Hum Lee, *Chinese in the United States*, pp. 161-68.

7. Broom, "Jamaica," in *Race*, eds. Thompson and Hughes, pp. 140-41.
8. Broady, "Chinese in Great Britain," in *Overseas Chinese*, ed. Fried, p. 32.
9. I find it difficult to accept the conclusion of this report, that there is little communalism among the Chinese in New Zealand. Mrs. Fong's description of the Chinese association leaves one to speculate about its intracommunity domination:

> The only other institution which is sponsored by all the Chinese community is the Chinese association, which is a truly nonpolitical institution. Its work is voluntary; its upkeep is by annual subscription from the Chinese adults in New Zealand. the head office is in Wellington, with branches in the main cities. Every year there is a general meeting in Wellington, attended by representatives from other cities. Each branch also elects its members; monthly meetings are held, or whenever a topic arises which concerns the welfare of the Chinese and has to be discussed and decided. Although the secretary hold office for a year, a chairman is elected at every meeting, there being no permanent chairman. All voting

> is carried out democratically. . . . For the Royal Visit in 1954, the association collected money from its districts to bring out from Hong Kong the Dragon Dance outfit to be used in the general demonstration of welcome.

Later in the report the kongsis with their clan affiliations are described, but the connection between the clans, kongsis, and the association is not mentioned. In another section, we learn that the Sze-yap Association, which is one of the largest kongsis, is the only association to maintain a successful youth club because "the Sze-yap people are perhaps more parochial in their outlook than the Chinese from other Counties." The status barriers to marriage between a Sze-yap and a Chinese from some other areas are still operative to some extent.

The Chinese of New Zealand may also be living under an insular communalism as yet unnoticed by this analyst of the local scene.

Ng Bickleen Fong, *The Chinese in New Zealand* (Hong Kong: Hong Kong University Press, 1960), p. 50, 52-53, 61-62, 94, 100.

10. Kingsley Davis, *Human Society* (New York: Macmillan, 1948, 1949), p. 591.
11. Lee, *Chinese in the United States*, pp. 42-47.
12. Jacobus ten Broek, Edward Barnhart, and Floyd Matson, *Prejudice, War, and the Constitution* (Berkeley: University of California Press, 1954), pp. 274-79.
13. For discussions of the incarceration, relocation, and resettlement of the Japanese during World War II see
    Morton Grodzins, *Americans Betrayed* (Chicago: U. of Chicago, 1949);
    Dorothy S. Thomas and Richard Nishimoto, *The Spoilage* (Berkeley: University of California Press, 1946);
    Dorothy Swaine Thomas, Charles Kikuchi, and J. Sakoda, *The Salvage* (Berkeley: University of California Press, 1952);
    By far the best analysis is that of ten Broek, Barnhart, and Matson, *Prejudice.*
14. S. Frank Miyamoto, *Social Solidarity Among the Japanese in Seattle* (Seattle: Bulletin of the University of Washington, 1939), pp. 118.
15. ten Broek, Barnhart, and Matson, *Prejudice*, p. 276.
16. F. Fukuoka, "Mutual Life and Aid Among the Japanese in Southern California with Special Reference to Los Angeles," (M.A. thesis, University of Southern California, 1937), quoted in Thomas, Kikuchi, and Sakoda, *The Salvage*, p. 50.
17.
    > Some of the Japanese "bosses" are notorious exploiters of labor. Their system of exploitation begins with the hiring of laborers. The various subagents who secure men for the "boss" are paid $5 per man, which is deducted from the wages paid at the end of the season. The book wages of the Japanese laborers vary from $160 to $225 each for the season, or about $40 per month in addition to board and lodging, but the individual who returns to the home port with $30 or more to his credit is considered fortunate. Orientals are ordinarily transported in sailing vessels and the trip is long. The

food furnished is of poor quality and scanty quantity and probably does not cost more than $3 per month per man. However, the "boss" has on board a large supply of appetizing eatables, which he offers for sale at high prices, and which he readily disposes of because of the poor food regularly furnished for the two meals per day. It is said that these goods are sold at 100 per cent profit.

The long period of idleness during the voyage, coupled with the fact that most of the men who are induced to go to the canneries are of a speculative turn, enables the Japanese contractor to practice further exploitation. He provides for numerous games of chance, and places his henchmen or "subbosses" in charge of these. These "dealers" get 25 per cent of the earnings of the tables, and the remainder goes to the head "boss" as profit. This gambling trade is carried on in going to and from the fishing grounds. During the work season at the canneries the Japanese subsist chiefly upon salmon and rice. Other commodities are furnished them by the "boss" at the usual high rates.

The sums spent on wages for the Japanese laborers, in assembling them for the trip and for board during the period of several months, frequently, if not generally, amount to more than the sums paid the contractors by the canning companies. The Japanese "boss" makes his profit, and at times covers a part of his necessary outlay, by selling provisions and other merchandise and from the tables used for gambling. A few small "bosses" reported that their incomes were as much as $2,000 for the year. Doubtless the incomes of the "bosses" who control more men are larger.

U.S. Congress, Senate, Immigration Commission. Immigrants in Industry. *Japanese and Other Immigrant Races in the Pacific Coast and Rocky Mountain States*, 61st Cong., 2d sess., Sen. Doc. 633, vol. III (Washington, D.C.: Government Printing Office, 1911), pp. 406-7. (Hereafter cited as Sen. Doc. 633.)

18. The purpose of these Japanese organizations, both social and economic, was principally to present a common front against discriminatory practices, and secondarily to provide a meeting place for Japanese possessing mutual interests. Although some groups, such as the prefectural clubs, tended naturally to perpetuate old world customs and recreations, the general effect of Issei organizations was to smooth relations with the dominant American community and to facilitate the social adjustment and integration of Japanese in this country. The later organizations of the Nisei, oriented wholly around American traditions and values, were sometimes formed specifically to counter the "Japanese" aspect of the Issei group, and all were positive forces for assimilation and Americanization.

ten Broek, Barnhart, and Matson, *Prejudice*, p. 276.

For the position of Japanese in Hawaii, see

Andrew Lind , *Hawaii's Japanese* (Princeton: Princeton University

Press, 1946);
Edward Norbeck, *Pineapple Town, Hawaii* (Berkeley: University of California Press, 1959), pp. 86-104.

19. For descriptions of the activities of the JAA see
Michinari Fujita, "Japanese Associations in America," *Sociology and Social Research*, Janaury/February 1929, pp. 211-28;
Ichihashi, *Japanese in the United States*, pp. 224-27;
Miyamoto, *Japanese in Seattle*, p. 116;
Thomas, Kikuchi, and Sakoda, *Salvage*, pp. 47-50.

20. Thomas, Kikuchi, and Sakoda, *Salvage*, pp. 51-53;
ten Broek, Barnhart, and Matson, *Prejudice*, pp. 276-79.

21. Charles H. Young, Helen R.Y. Reid, and W.A. Carrothers, *The Japanese Canadians* ed. H.A. Innis, (Toronto: University of Toronto Press, 1938), pp. 111-12.

22.
> In 1907, the Wyoming [coal] field was unionized for the first time. In that year the operators entered into an agreement with the United Mine Workers of America very similar to that in force in northern Colorado. Since a number of Orientals were employed at that time, the operators planned to employ them for a lower wage than that specified in the agreement. However, a delegation of Japanese called on the officials of the union at its convention in Denver and secured a special rule under which Orientals could become union men. It was the first time that the union had admitted Orientals to membership.

Sen. Doc. 633, p. 282.

23. Young, Reid, and Carrothers, *Japanese Canadians*, p. 109;
Thomas, Kikuchi, and Sakoda, *Salvage*, pp. 50-51;
ten Broek, Barnhart, and Matson, *Prejudice*, pp. 277-79.

24. Robert E. Park and H.A. Miller, *Old World Traits Transplanted* (New York: Harper, 1921), pp. 168, 180.

25. For a recent study of housing and the efforts of the JACL in behalf of equal treatment in rights of purchase see
Harry H.L. Kitano, "Housing of Japanese-Americans in the San Francisco Bay Area," in *Studies in Housing and Minority Groups*, eds. Nathan Glazer and Davis McEntire (Berkeley: University of Calfornia Press, 1960).

26. E.K. Strong, *The Second Generation Japanese Problem* (Stanford: Stanford U.P., 1934), p. 26.

27. "Racial Assimilation in Secondary Groups With Particular Reference to the Negro," *Publications of the American Sociological Society* VIII (1913), pp. 66-83, reprinted in Robert E. Park, *Race and Culture* (New York: Free Press, 1950), pp. 204-20, quotation on p. 209.

28. "Behind Our Masks," Survey Graphic, LVI (1926); pp. 135-39, reprinted in Park, *Race and Culture*, pp. 244-45, quotation on p. 249.

The Social Sources of Communalism—With Special Reference to Its Failure to Develop in Japanese Communities 5

INTRODUCTION

Communalism did not develop in overseas Japanese communities, although it flourished among the overseas Chinese, because the institutional base upon which it might have been built had been severely weakened in Japan three centuries before emigration began; and because the New World environments of the Chinese and Japanese, in terms of sex ratios, occupations, and types of settlement, were different. The structure of Chinese and Japanese communities developed out of the interplay of social heritage that each group carried with it and the economic and civic conditions they encountered in the new land.

SOCIAL CHANGE IN CHINA AND JAPAN IN THE PRE-EMIGRATION PERIOD

Overseas Chinese communalism has its roots in the social organization of rural Kwangtung and Fukien. Overseas clans derive from the lineage communities of southeastern China;[1] "speech" associations from the hostelries and trade guilds established in Chinese cities to protect fellow villagers from the depredations of strangers; *tongs* from the secret societies so prevalent in southeastern China.

Before the Tokugawa era (1603-1868), Japan was also organized into lineage communities. Its few cities were in effect congeries of village or prefectural guilds (kenjinkai), each with its distinct regional pride. Bandit gangs composed of pariah classes, masterless warriors, and outcasts preyed upon the countryside. Had extensive emigration to the Americas occurred before the eighteenth century, as indeed it might had the original foreign policy of Tokugawa Iyeyasu been successful,[2] clans, powerful kenjinkai, and secret societies might also have been established by the overseas Japanese.

The social organization of southeastern China remained for the most part unchanged until the twentieth century. Such was not the case in Japan. Political and social changes begun in the century prior to the establishment of the Tokugawa Shogunate sapped the strength of those institutions which, had they remained viable, might have spawned an overseas communalism among the Japanese. Four coincidental developments in feudal Japan—developments that have no equivalents in China until the twentieth century—were to have significant effects on the organization of overseas Japanese communities: (1) the destabilization of the lineage community; (2) the rise of the city; (3) the weakening of the communal loyalties; and (4) the centralization of government.

First, in the fifteenth and sixteenth centuries, Japanese lineage-communities,[3] whose opposite numbers in China gave birth to overseas clans, were dispersed in the wake of peasant revolts and internecine strife among rival clans. The land-based lineage community was one casualty of social disintegration at this time. In the new order that emerged after the advant of Tokugawa, the smaller lineage-household arose as the primary unit of kinship.[4]

The static order of Japan's familistic communities was transformed into a dynamic society. Opportunities for both vertical and horizontal mobility increased. A *samurai* ("warrior") could now terminate his service to a *daimyo* ("lord") at will. The ranks of daimyo were no longer limited by a warrior's hereditary status but could be purchased with rice rents.[5] The enfeoffment of commoners loyal to the Tokugawa banner and the redistribution of fiefs according to principles of political loyalty and military strategy[6] accelerated the speed by which the lineage and the lineage community was subverted. The tie that was to create such a strong sense of social solidarity among overseas Chinese, the tie connecting family—lineage—territory began to erode after the rise of Tokugawa.

Second, kenjinkai, whose Chinese counterpart produced the powerful overseas kongsi, were severely weakened by Japan's early urbanization. Chinese cities, in contrast to those of Japan and the Occident, did not develop an autonomous character, did not receive a charter of political privileges, and did not possess the military or economic perquisites for civic autonomy.[7] As a result of their heterocephalous character, Chinese cities fostered the growth of powerful clans and other rural-based autonomous hostelries (hui kuan and kongsi), representing their members' lineage communities, prefectures, or secret societies, and protecting them from rival groups and the imperial police. A deeply ingrained adherence to local associations was carried abroad by the Chinese migrants and manifested itself in their loyalty to overseas immigrant associations. In Japan, although pre-twentieth century urbanization did not reach the extent of that in the Occident, the establishment of autonomous and semiautonomous urban trade and administrative centers was sufficient to curtail further development of kenjinkai power.

Japan's urban growth dates from the middle of the Muromachi period. Provincial towns and seaports began to flourish as a result of increased trade with China. The number of persons in cities increased as two centuries of war and social disorganization uprooted the countryside.[8] After 1600, urban growth proceeded at an astonishing speed.[9] "Clearly a very large part of the population of the country was urban by the early nineteenth century."[10]

Japanese cities became relatively autonomous civic units, the character that distinguished "Occidental" cities from those of the "Orient." Many were given civic privileges and enjoyed a modicum of self-government. Those inhabited by *ronin* ("masterless warriors") sometimes developed their own corps for civic defense, much like their counterparts in medieval Europe.[11] The aspect of Japanese urbanization that is significant for the later organization of immigrant communities is that the city's central and independent authority eliminated the need for protection at the communal level and restricted the expansion of prefectural trade guilds and kenjinkai. Independent "civic trade guilds" (*za*), arose under the protection of an urban lord or, in some cases, a priest. Some of these guilds combined to form interurban leagues.[12] Urbanization in Japan nipped the rural traditional bud which might otherwise have ripened into a congeries of all-encompassing communal associations among the overseas Japanese.

Third, familistic communalism, which made Chinese lineage communities nearly impregnable to imperial authority and which made Chinatowns largely impervious to the norms and political authority of the larger society, were weakenned along with the lineage community in Japan. In its place there arose a vertical authority stretching from the villager through his protector, the daimyo, and ultimately reaching the Emperor. After 1603, local pride gave way in the face of a new national consciousness. Villages, once the center of social life and the whole world to their inhabitants, now were but units in a larger whole, the empire.

As a result of this transformation of familism and authority, the overseas Japanese migrant felt an attachment not only to his village or prefectural unit, but also to the nation as a whole. And this attachment to the nation was vague and diffuse; in time the overseas Japanese would sense within himself a national sentiment that was independent of his relationship to the kenjinkai. His children, born in America, would be removed from that national consciousness,[13] their loyalty and identity would be to the land of their birth. The Chinese migrant, in contrast, regarded the lineage community as circumscribing his world. Attachment to the clan and kongsi was part and parcel of this identification.[14] He would gain a national consciousness in the twentieth century, partly as a result of his categorical treatment by white Americans, partly through his interest in events surrounding the establishment of the first Chinese Republic.

Nothing illustrates better the transition from family mindedness to public spiritedness in Japan than the contrast between the success of the *pao-chia* system there and its ineffectiveness in China.

Pao-chia is the unsuccessful system by which both imperial and republican governments in China have attempted to bring central authority to bear on lineage-communities. Introduced first in A.D. 1069 by Wang Anshih in order to effect a military draft, the aim of pao-chia was to take advantage of the local kinship structure by subordinating its authority to an appointed official. Households, lineages, and multi-lineage groups were organized hierarchically into a *pao*, composed, sometimes, of over five thousand persons, and headed by an appointed official, who was to report to the prefectural magistrate all cases of "robbery, religious heresy, gambling, runaways, kidnapping, counterfeiting, sale and transport of counterfeit goods, swindling, organization of secret societies, unknown and suspicious characters."[15] Pao-chia proved ineffective in China because it attempted to co-opt the particularist family structure into the universalist order of imperial law; to impose legal rules over local mores; to integrate separate and even hostile bodies; and to broaden the responsibility of persons whose interests were parochial.[16]

In Japan, where pao-chia was introduced from China, it took root along with the uprooting of the lineage-community, the growth of feudalism, and the flowering of national imperium. The new villagers,[17] organized as nuclear families, felt bound to one another not by ties of blood, but by their common service to, and protection from a daimyo, who, in turn, was obliged through his military service and rice-rents to the emperor (actually the shogun). The grouping of families into units of five, regardless of class differences, the redirection of loyalty upward and responsibility downward, and the movement of persons to and from cities, reorganized local loyalties within a national perspective. The village was persuaded to conceive of itself as one part of the interdependent empire. Citizenship was transformed from its original meaning as membership in a lineage-community, to a wider definition, membership in the imperial nation-state.

This comparatively early development toward nation-statehood in Japan had effects on the community organizations established by overseas Japanese two centuries later. The migrant who left his village near Hiroshima still longed for home and still sought out companions from his own ken, but he did not regard his kenjinkai as an organization to which he owed unqualified allegiance and from which he could not sever his connection if the opportunity or inclination arose. Among the immigrant Chinese, "citizenship" was defined in terms of one's obligation to a lineage-community or its overseas equivalent; among the Japanese, "citizenship" was defined in terms of a generalized allegiance to the nation-state rather than in terms of abject loyalty to a local village or prefecture.[18]

SEX RATIO

Similar to the sex ratio of most groups immigrating to a frontier society, that of the Japanese and Chinese was unbalanced, that is, the number of males was far greater than the number of females. However, the Chinese and Japanese tended to respond to the shortage of women in different ways. Japanese men came less and less to depend on their mutual aid societies as they sent for brides and founded families in America; Chinese men required special services of their clan, prefectural and secret societies in order to satisfy their social and sexual needs.

So few Chinese women came to the United States that a relatively evenly balanced sex ratio was not achieved until the middle of the twentieth century. Until that time it is hardly possible to speak of conjugal family life for most of the Chinese in the United States.[19]

MARITAL STATUS

Although statistical evidence is inconclusive, it appears that at least half of the Chinese males who came to California in the nineteenth century were married.[20] In 1910, roughly half of California's Chinese males were married.[21] The very large number of married

Chinese males, when considered in relation to the few Chinese women reported to be residing in the United States, suggests that wives were residing in China.[22]

Unlike the Chinese, a greater percentage of Japanese males in California were single in 1910. As was the case with Chinese females, most Japanese women in California in 1910 were married, (approximately 86 percent). In 1910, the period before the migration of thousands of Japanese women to America, married Japanese male immigrants appear to have been absentee husbands. A sample survey of the same industries from which the marital status of the Chinese laborers was determined, confirms that a greater percentage of the Japanese laborers were single than were the Chinese, and that married Chinese and Japanese males left their wives in the home country.

However, the shortage of women among the Japanese was relieved by a procedure foreign to the Chinese. Commencing around 1910, a number of unmarried Japanese males, many of whom had rented, share-cropped, or leased farm land in the Pacific Coast states, arranged marriages by means of the "picture-bride" system (*shashin kekkon*). Between 1910 and 1920, several thousands of Japanese women crossed the Pacific to join their newly acquired husbands.

One feature of Japanese kinship appears to have facilitated the marriage and overseas settlement of Japanese families.[23] The Japanese family is of the stem-branch type, with the eldest or youngest son designated as heir and supporter of his parents and the other sons permitted to establish families away from the stem site. A son who is able to establish himself financially is not required by custom to return to his home or to live with his parents after marriage. The rural-urban migration to Tokyo in the early days of industrialization was composed of younger sons of peasants for the most part. Poor peasants could not afford to keep their younger sons on the land; those better off sent the second sons for an education. Those second sons who came to California and obtained a piece of farmland were in a good position to abandon sojourner status, send for a wife, and settle down permanently, without doing violence to family custom.

The egalitarian relations among Chinese male siblings, coupled with the expectation that all brothers would live under the same or nearby roofs, made marriage-by-mail or the neolocal residence of a married couple abroad a serious breach of custom.

The superfluity of males in the overseas Chinese communities had as its natural sequel the resort to an informal mode of polyandry; that is, the common possession of a woman by a number of men.[24] In Chinatown, men had such possession only for the time of the sex act itself; polyandry became institutionalized in the ghetto community of lonely sojourners: secret societies purchased or kidnapped girls from China and put them under contract for "prostitution-labor."

In 1890, a compassionate journalist, himself an immigrant, inspected New York's Chinatown and noticed its paradoxical cleanliness, its pungent odors, its dens of iniquity, its exotic religious practices, its incomprehensible inner government, and its seemingly endless number of brothels. His proffered solution to "the Chinese question" was the following:

> This is a time for plain speaking on this subject. Rather than banish the Chinaman, I would have the door opened wider—for his wife; make it a condition of his coming or staying that he bring his wife with him. Then, at least, he might not be what he now is and remains, a homeless stranger among us. Upon this hinges the real Chinese question, in our city at all events, as I see it.[25]

II OCCUPATIONAL STRUCTURE

Introduction

In the United States opportunities for employment differed for Chinese and Japanese immigrants. In the short span of time between the arrival of the first wave of Chinese (1848), and that of Japanese (1890), an economic, technological, and agricultural revolution had taken place. The California of 1848-82 was a different California from that of 1890-1924. Thus the periods of Chinese and Japanese immigration must be viewed almost as if the two groups were coming to different countries.

The kind of job an immigrant could get and the means by which he could get it affected his relation to immigrant associations. The Chinese at first were wage-laborers, subcontracted by, and under the direction of, a headman who was often an agent of the kongsi. Later, driven out of the industries dominated by white labor, the Chinese retreated to Chinatown, where, regardless of their special skills, they were even more dependent on the kongsis, whose leaders provided leads to whatever jobs were to be had. In contrast, the Japanese, after a brief period of labor exploitation by labor contractors attached to their kenjinkai, entered agriculture, where, as relatively independent farmers with wives and a claim to property, they no longer were obligated to their associations for jobs.

The Chinese

During the "Chinese period," California was the scene of two major types of economic activity: gold mining and railroad building. The former activity required long, difficult hand labor and many miners—machinery was almost unknown. When gold mining ceased to be a profitable enterprise, and when attention was turned to California's other mineral wealth, machinery had been invented that replaced much of the labor needed in the earlier period. Similarly, railroad construction reached its peak in the years just after the completion of the Transcontinental Railway (1869), which alone had employed over 10,000 Chinese. As the railroads were completed many Chinese were thrown out of work and into the cities on the Pacific Coast, along the lines of the railway, and—because of a desire for exploitable labor—into the cities of the East.

The Chinese were early employed in gold mining as laborers, service workers, and as miners. But the Chinese population in the mining counties of California shows a rapid decline after 1880 when gold mining, which had been one of the principle attractions to Chinese migrating to the United States, had ceased to be of occupational importance for them.

The Chinese had turned to other occupations even before the mines petered out.

> ...[T]hey perform all kinds of light labor, and that particularly which requires no capital; and they are expert in that which requires dextrous manipulation of the fingers—as the assorting of wool, working in silks, the rolling of cigars, and such matters as that....Laundry work, cigar-making, slippers, sewing-machine-labor, they have very nearly monopolized. They are largely employed as domestic servants and as office-boys. In assorting and repacking teas, in silk and woolen manufactories, in fruit picking, in gardening, in harvesting, in building levees for the restoration of tule lands, in railroad-building, in placer mining, in basket-peddling of vegetables and fruits, in fishing and peddling fish, are among the most noted of their industries, and from these industries I have named they have nearly driven out the white laborers.[26]

But with the exception of migratory harvesting work and a few fruit and produce farms near the cities of Sacramento and Vancouver, B.C., the Chinese did not engage in agriculture to any significant extent. Those who had expected the Chinese to cultivate rice, tea, and silk in California bitterly complained that "not one acre of land has yet been devoted to the culture of rice; not one shrub to the production of tea; not one single industry has been introduced, so far as I am advised, that is peculiar to the Chinese people."[27]

After 1860, the rise of trade unionism in the United States encouraged entrepreneurs to experiment with the Chinese as strike-breakers and as an alternative labor force in the manufacture of shoes, cigars, cutlery, and woolen products. In the South an abortive attempt was made to utilize the Chinese as field workers in lieu of the recently emancipated blacks.[28]

However, job opportunities for the Chinese in the incipient cigar, garment-making, woolen, and gunpowder industries of San Francisco were short-lived. After the completion of the era of railroad building, San Francisco and other west coast cities responded to the violent Sinophobia of unemployed Caucasian laborers by formal enactments and informal pressures designed to drive the Chinese out of the labor market if not out of the country. As early as 1859, the People's Protective League, a union of cigar-makers, began its agitation against Chinese in the industry with boycotts of Caucasian employers of Chinese.[29] Later Samuel Gompers, himself a cigar-maker, was to make an important part of the policy of his federation of craft unions, the American Federation of Labor (A.F.L.), the exclusion of the Chinese from the A.F.L. and from the United States.[30] The first attempts of the exclusionists were unsuccessful, but as the number of unemployed white men rose, the political advantages to be gained by appealing to the white proletarian vote at the expense of the disfranchised Chinese[31] were not overlooked. The net result of the anti-Chinese agitation was to drive the Chinese out of the "white" cigar industry and into Oriental cigar manufactories or into intraethnic employment, and to contribute to the decline of the cigar industry itself. The Immigration Commission summarized the history of the employment of Chinese in San Francisco's cigar industry:

> The races employed in the cigar and cigarette industry of San Francisco have changed radically during its history. The industry was established in San Francisco about 1860, by Germans. However, Chinese were employed to a considerable extent almost from the first. It is estimated that in 1870,...91 percent were Chinese....A few years later strong opposition to the employment of Orientals developed, and by 1880, ...the Chinese constituted only 33 percent of the "hands" at work. The agitation against the employment of Chinese grew stronger, and effective use was made of the "white label" as a basis for discriminating

> against the product of shops in which they were employed. In 1885, the White Labor League demanded that the Chinese be discharged and their places filled by white cigar-makers, large numbers of whom were reported to be out of employment. This demand was acceded to by some of the employers, by so many, in fact, that the number of white cigar-makers was inadequate to meet the demand for them. Cigar-makers were then brought from the East by the union. They proved to be rather unsatisfactory to the employers, while the men themselves were not satisfied with the employment, and many left the shops for more remunerative work elsewhere. Following this effort there was a strike for higher wages, and a number of the manufactories again employed Chinese.
>
> The disturbances in the industry caused by this agitation and the resulting publicity given to the evils of Chinese coolie manufacture tended to demoralize the industry and to encourage the importation of cigars and cigarettes of Eastern manufacture. . . .
>
> From this review it is evident that, largely because of widespread opposition to their employment, but also more recently because of the decreasing number available for such work, fewer Chinese have been employed in white cigar and cigarette factories. Their withdrawal from the industry as a whole, however, has not been so extensive, for as the Chinese gained experience and were forced to withdraw from white establishments, they started small shops of their own. In 1908, according to the report of the assessor for the city and country of San Francisco, 20 of these Chinese shops were in existence.[32]

The same pattern of employment prevailed in the other Caucasian-owned industries which at first employed Chinese. Agitation and pressure forced the Chinese out of work and into self-employment or wage-labor within the confines of Chinatown. The sewing trade, once an important source of jobs for Chinese had but a few Chinese employed by 1910.[33] Chinese-owned sweatshops employing foreign-born Chinese-speaking women, however, are still to be found in San Francisco's Chinatown and are an important, if covert, source of dress manufacture for the garment industry.[34] The gunpowder industry had lost much of its original Chinese labor supply by 1910, although the hazards of this occupation together with the low indemnity paid to the dependents of those killed or injured in explosions had rendered it difficult to find workers to meet the demand. But, in that year Chinese constituted 24.4 percent of the total foreign-born labor so employed and were 84.8 percent of those employed as "powder workers"—the most dangerous job in the factory.[35]

The Chinese were said to be the preferred labor in the salmon-canning industry on the Columbia River, in Puget Sound, and in Alaska and had pioneered that industry from its inception in 1891. However, despite allegations of employers that Chinese were the most skilled and experienced, by 1910 their number had declined considerably, and cannery laborers were obtained from among Japanese, Korean, Filipino, East Indian, and North American Indian workers, usually hired through the intermediary of Chinese contractors.[36]

The exclusion of Chinese laborers from the United States, enacted as federal law in 1882, and renewed every decade thereafter until permanent exclusion was achieved in 1904, not only served to drive the Chinese out of those industries in which they supposedly competed with Caucasians, but also to reduce the number of Chinese available for those industries in which they were the preferred work force. Moreover, because the Chinese in America were predominantly male, they could reproduce themselves only if "free immigration" continued, or by reducing the shortage of females among them. But immigration was cut off,[37] and with Chinese women laborers also excluded, the sex ratio remained unbalanced. As the Chinese population in America that did not return to China grew older, it was not replaced by an equal number of younger men.[38] The older Chinese who retired or were laid off from urban industrial jobs returned to Chinatown either to engage in small-scale merchandising or to work in Chinese-owned stores and restaurants.

In the small towns of the Midwest to which Chinese had migrated after 1880, technological changes, restrictive legislation, and labor union hostility tended to limit their occupations to those they could provide without coming into competition with Caucasians—noodle parlors, curio shops, tailor shops, laundries, cafés and restaurants, rooming houses, and so on. The low number of Chinese in these towns made reliance on community businesses precarious.[39] A sudden change in the town's economic base might undermine the entire Chinatown economy. With the decline of metalliferous mining in the Rocky Mountain states, many Chinatowns failed, forcing Chinese to migrate to the larger Chinatowns on the Pacific and Atlantic coasts and in the cities of the Midwest.[40]

In addition to their employment as miners, railroad-builders, industrial laborers, and strikebreakers, Chinese worked as domestics and in certain service occupations. The latter included intraethnic services and those special occupations—operating Chinese restaurants and laundries—which have become identified with the Chinese. The occupation most frequently associated with the Chinese male, and the one that has stereotyped him to a great part of the American public, laundryman, is worth special comment. Chinese are not by nature or habit laundrymen. Yet in 1880, "[T]here were about 320 laundries in the city and country of San Francisco, of which about 240 were owned and conducted by subjects of China."[41] The explanation for this occupational position lies in the peculiar conditions of life on the frontier.

A noted authority on social stratification has written: "If the talents required for a position are abundant and the training easy, the method of acquiring the position may have little to do with its duties. There may in fact be a virtually accidental relationship."[42] Such is the origin of the Chinese laundryman in America, and to a lesser extent the Chinese cook and domestic as well. No special training is required to operate a hand laundry. That the Chinese entered this occupation had to do neither with its duties nor any peculiarities of Chinese culture. Except one: the Chinese did not regard washing clothes as an occupation reserved especially for women. Most of the Caucasian males on the trans-Mississippi frontier did. And until the turn of the century few women of any race were available in the West to do any of what was considered women's work.[43] At first a Chinese would do the laundry for his compatriots for a nominal fee. As word got around his clientele increased to include the white miners who were glad to find someone to do such distasteful work. That he was Chinese only confirmed in the white man's eyes the low status of the occupation. Soon the Chinese had a virtual monopoly on the occupation. "From the Chinese point of view, owning, managing, and operating a business was far superior to being employed as domestics by whites. Being owners of laundries, restaurants, etc., accorded them proprietary status."[44] Although later on some Chinese came to resent their lowly status as laundrymen, they clung to the occupation out of necessity, and it gradually became identified with them.[45]

However, with the invention of the steam laundry and the coming of Caucasian females to the West, the Chinese monopoly was challenged. No longer was work in a laundry fit only for Chinese men. Caucasian laborers and entrepreneurs demanded their place in the washman's world. Moreover, the laundryman now had competition from another source: the housewife. Chinese laundrymen in small towns were hardest hit by the change:

> In the early days of [Chinese population] dispersion, a lone Chinese or two would be located in a small city or railroad junction and do the cooking, serving food, washing, and ironing in a predominantly male society. This work grew less lucrative as

> more white men settled their families in the Western States. Hand laundries and small restaurants could not compete with the same services normally performed by women in the household. Moreover, municipal laws frequently taxed Chinese businesses out of existence or the local population boycotted their goods and services. Hence more and more Chinese settled in metropolitan cities where single persons desired their services and visitors or lovers of Chinese food preferred Chinese style cooking.[46]

The governments in larger cities, urged on by labor agitators, white laundry operators, and Sinophobes, also attempted to restrict or abolish the Chinese laundry. San Francisco, beginning in 1880, passed a series of ordinances which amounted to a practical denial of the right of the Chinese to be washmen. Some of these laws were upheld by the United States Supreme Court, but the most stringent were struck down, declared to be in violation of the Fourteenth Amendment of the Constitution.[47] The protection afforded him by the Court has contributed in part to the survival of the Chinese laundryman in American society.

Two salient features emerge from this examination of the occupational structure of the Chinese in the United States: The work done by the Chinese kept them in or near large cities, and it kept them in a state of institutional dependency.

Whether the Chinese worked as laundrymen, domestics, cigarmakers, woolen mill workers, or as restaurateurs, they lived in cities. The city was where the jobs were to be had, and the city was where the traditional associations that ministered to the Chinese workers' needs were located. Even when he left the city to take up temporary work along a railroad line or in California's swamps, the Chinese laborer ultimately returned to his urban habitat. Unemployment or desire for a new job brought him back to the center of the job market.

> San Francisco is the heart and hive and home of all the Chinese upon this coast. Our Chinese quarter, as it is called, is their place really of residence. If they go to a washhouse in the vicinity, to a suburban manufactory, to gardening near the town, or if to build railroads in San Bernardino or on the Colorado, or to reclaim tule lands in the interior, their departure there is temporary, and their return here is certain; therefore the number in San Francisco depends upon seasons and the contract labor market.[48]

The Chinese returned to the city not only to seek labor but to renew his associations with fellow-Chinese and with the prefectural, clan, or secret societies on which he was dependent for his livelihood.[49] It was these associations, and especially the kongsis, which contracted labor and controlled supply and wages in the Chinese labor market.

The movement of Chinese labor from the mines, railroads, and "sweatshops" controlled by "white men" to the restaurants, stores, and "sweatshops" owned by the Chinese, did little to alter their dependence on immigrant associations. Indeed, it increased that dependency by broadening the opportunities for direct exploitation by the kongsis' mercantile elite.[50] A student of present-day Chinatowns in the United States has accurately described this dependence:

> Men who achieve economic success, either in Chinatown or elsewhere in the city's environs, reach prominence in the *hua ch'iao* ["overseas Chinese"] community, becoming active in the councils of the surname and regional associations and in the occupational guilds. With the increased participation of an employer in these groups, the worker's dependence upon him for social approval is intensified. The social necessity of conforming to local Chinese modes of economic behavior becomes all the more crucial as the employer acquires the status of lineage elder or quasi-governmental official. The process of upward social mobility for some thus has its effect upon those in the lower socioeconomic levels; clerks and other mercantile employees become enmeshed in job situations which discourage their joining unions. It is striking to note that, the existence of a highly developed trade union movement notwithstanding, the traditional Chinese guild, comprised of employers and employees, still plays a decisive role with respect to wages, hours, and conditions of work. The social bonds of genealogical relationship and locality ties, rather than class identification, provide the framework for the hua ch'iao economy.[51]

The Japanese

The end of the era of gold mining and major railroad bulding coincided with the exclusion of the Chinese laborers from the United States and the brief respite before the coming of Japanese. When significant numbers of the latter began arriving in the United States after 1890, the two occupations which had served the Chinese immigrants were no longer open. Like the Chinese before them, the Japanese adjusted their occupational lives and community organization to the available economic opportunities.

California and the West in 1890, and after, presented new opportunities for the employment of immigrants. For a brief transitional period Japanese replaced Chinese in some of the industries in which the latter had been employed: railroad work, mining, lumbering, and the canning of fish. Other industries in which the Chinese had played an important part—the sewing trades, cigar and cigarette manufacturing, and the manufacture of gunpowder—either declined, relocated, or refused to employ Japanese. The most advantageous situation for the Japanese occurred with the development of small-scale intensive agriculture, a development that the Japanese pioneered. In farming the Japanese were to prosper and, unlike the Chinese, become a largely rural people, attached to the land and concentrated along the Pacific coast.

From 1890 to 1909, much Japanese labor was employed in railroad work.[52] The Japanese were most extensively engaged in maintenance of way work and construction and less often in the railway shops and bridge and building construction. During late spring and early summer, Japanese railroad workers left their employ and worked as harvesters in the sugar beet fields or in fisheries. Despite a slight rise in their wages over the years, the Japanese left the railroads to take up work in agriculture.

Mining was more often than not closed to the Japanese not only because of the general anti-Oriental animus, but also because the Japanese, in certain instances, demanded higher wages and better working conditions. The combination of anti-Orientalism and antiunionism restricted employment in metalliferous mining and smelting in Arizona, Montana, Colorado, and Utah to native or foreign-born whites who were not affiliated with organized labor.

The Japanese were ineligible for employment in the mining of coke and coal in Washington and northern Colorado, but a few were employed in southern Colorado and New Mexico. The Immigration Commission discovered that the "prevalent race antipathy toward Asiatics in Washington has led to the refusal of employment in the mines to all Japanese, Chinese, or Hindus,"[53] while in northern Colorado; "discrimination to the extent of refusing employment has been constantly exercised toward Chinese, Japanese, and Negroes, and except in times of stress, toward Greeks." The anti-Oriental animus was shared by management and labor alike. "Another obstacle to the introduction of these races is their ineligibility for membership in the local union, because of the prejudice of the members of the union. . ."[54] In southern Colorado and New Mexico a few Japanese worked as "scabs" during the United Mine Workers' strike (1903-04); some continued working in the mines after the strike, but most left to secure work in agriculture.[55]

In Wyoming, the Japanese were the single most prevalent group among foreign-born laborers in the mining of coke and coal in 1908. The relatively unique history of labor relations in Wyoming accounts for both the unusually favorable attitude toward Japanese, and for the latter's subsequent withdrawal from the mines. Opened in 1869, the mines did not employ Japanese until 1900, when, during a labor shortage, the mine owners entered into correspondence with a Japanese contractor. Japanese continued to be employed there until 1907, when, hoping to circumvent their labor contract with the United Mine Workers, the mine owners sought to engage the Japanese, who were ineligible for union membership, at a lower wage. The Japanese persuaded union officials to let them join and secure an equal wage. "This diplomatic concession on the part of the miners," reported the Immigration Commission, "doubtless prevented the introduction of more Japanese. As it is, their numbers are decreasing rather than increasing."[56]

In the lumber mills of Oregon, Washington, and British Columbia, a large number of Japanese were employed at wages much lower than those paid other races for the same kind of work. However, because of racial antipathy the Japanese were not employed proportionate to their available numbers nor the demand. The Immigration Commission reported:

> Most of the mills, however, have not employed Japanese, and the prejudices against them have prevented them from being employed as extensively as they otherwise would have been. In some cases they have not been employed because of the race prejudices of the employer, but in numerous instances because of the attitude of the employees, who almost invariably dislike the Japanese. In one instance 50 Japanese brought in from Portland were not permitted to leave the train. In a second where they, at a lower wage, replaced Italians, the Japanese found it difficult to live in the community. Evidences of hostility have been found elsewhere, but in most place they have not been open. Yet the antagonism has been effective in preventing the Japanese from gaining entrance to some of the mills and from finding employment, other than the least remunerative, in most of the mills where they have been employed.[57]

Agitation against the Japanese in lumbering became quite strong between 1908 and 1914. Then, the demand for lumber during the first world war and the attendant labor shortage gave a greater impetus to the Japanese to enter the industry. The postwar job shortage again drove the Japanese out of the industry.

Along the northwestern coast of the United States and Canada, the fishing industry provided employment for Chinese and Japanese for longer than any other industry. In cannery and saltery work on the Columbia River, at Puget Sound, and in central Alaska, first Chinese and then Japanese constituted the bulk of the labor force. Beginning in 1885, at a small village, Steveston, in British Columbia, the Japanese undertook commercial fishing operations all along the Canadian Pacific Coast.[58] Japanese fisherman were persecuted by harsh legislation and by discriminatory practices,[59] but Oriental laborers in canneries and salteries went unmolested for the most part. The scarcity of labor, low pay, seasonal nature, and relative isolation of the latter industry no doubt contributed to its employment of the Pacific Coast's least favored minority—the Oriental.

In the three urban industries in which Chinese had predominated or been an important element—the manufacture of gunpowder, cigars and cigarettes, and garments—the Japanese were seldom if at all to be found.[60]

The bulk of the Japanese immigrants settled into the occupation that was, at first, least restricted to them and most appropriate to their skills and talents—agriculture.

California's agricultural revolution, and to a lesser extent that of Oregon and Washington as well, took the form of a shift into the production of fruit and produce. With the lack of opportunity in urban areas, and the decline in mining, railroading, and the other occupations that had provided the Chinese with a living, the new agriculture presented opportunities for those immigrants willing to turn their hands at intensive cultivation of small parcels of land.

In the "pioneer" era, the Japanese, like their Chinese predecessors, were less willing to engage in land investment and hardly ever offered the opportunity of doing so. In that period, a number of Japanese migratory agricultural labor gangs worked up and down the Pacific Coast, especially in California, under the direction of Japanese bosses. These gangs later formed into clubs with secretaries and relatively formalized procedures. They underbid their ethnic competitors and were fairly successful during the period around the turn of the century.[61] These gangs were an adaptation to the American scene of the *hokonin* system which had prevailed earlier in Japan.[62]

After the turn of the century, the original boss-gang system continued and facilitated the spread of Japanese tenancy, for landowners without Japanese tenants found it "increasingly difficult...to obtain desirable laborers of that race."[63]

In a certain sense the Japanese in California found themselves in a position nearly identical to that of their forefathers in Japan two centuries earlier. Some landholdings in California proved unprofitable as large-scale ventures much as had similarly large farms in Japan. Moreover, much of the potentially arable land needed to be drained, leveled, and reduced for cultivation. Some of this work had been done by the Chinese. Japanese gangs undertook these tasks successfully and then leased the land from the owner.[64] The Japanese shifted from extensive farming to the more profitable intensive cultivation of berries, fruits, and vegetables. Accepting inferior housing—often living in the crude "Asiatic bunkhouse"—and supplying the landowner with help at harvest-time, the Japanese provided relief for some of the agricultural problems of the day just as the hokonin in Japan had done earlier. Moreover, the Japanese paid very high rents, "such high rents, in fact, that leasing his land [gave] the owner a better return than farming it himself, allowance being made for the diminished risk."[65]

Tenancy increased rapidly even after 1913, when the first of California's Alien Land Laws was passed. This law was followed by even more restrictive measures in 1920 and 1923, including an amendment which presumed fraud prima facie when an alien, ineligible for citizenship, bought or leased land in the name of his citizen offspring. If these laws had been enacted earlier or strictly enforced, the Japanese might have been forced out of agriculture and into either urban areas or remigration. But evasion was not difficult, and the laws were unevenly enforced and unpopular to the public.[66] It was not, then, until the forced governmental removal of Japanese from the Pacific Coast in 1942, that the rural agricultural life of the Japanese was upset.

In conclusion, the movement of the Japanese out of the market of contract labor and into agriculture did much to loosen the traditional bonds of solidarity. As a farmer with a wife and children and a plot of ground to cultivate, the Japanese needed less and less that kind of aid from the kenjinkai that would have made him its dependent. He now worked on his own, utilized his family, and lived separate from his fellow countrymen. When his children went to the city to seek their fortune, they turned not to a kenjinkai, but to their own family for help and advice.

Rather than the association, it has been the family that has provided welfare and employment for members in need in both Japan and among the overseas Japanese.[67] The number of Japanese classified as "unpaid family farm laborers" or "unpaid family workers" reveals the extent of this practice.[68] Urban unemployment could be counteracted, by a position in the family store or by returning to the family farm. Among urban Issei the practice of sending their children as fruit pickers to the farms of close relatives or friends was not uncommon as recently as the 1950s and was, in many cases, looked upon as a vacation for the children and a custom. Through agriculture and through the establishment of families, the Japanese unloosened the institutional ties that the Chinese—detached from wife and family and without an independent means of livelihood—could not unbind.

PATTERNS OF LOCATION AND SETTLEMENT

The occupations of the Chinese and the Japanese affected their respective patterns of settlement, distribution, and concentration in the United States, in turn, affecting their respective relationships to immigrant associations. The Chinese have remained primarily an urban people,[69] concentrated in large cities that could support a Chinatown and accommodate the extra-territorial situation of the Chinese quarter.

Many Japanese, in contrast, after a brief stint as wage-laborers, settled in the rural hinterlands of the Pacific area. In the face of strong anti-Japanese prejudice, the Issei married, reared children, worked their plots. Isolated from fellow Japanese, not in need of institutional means for sexual gratification, and controlling their means of livelihood, the Japanese farmers found less and less reason to be obliged to immigrant associations. The Japanese were, moreover, too removed from centers of association control and too isolated to be mobilized in behalf of association activities; the Chinese, on the other hand, were concentrated in ghettos, subject to their associations' call.

Settlement, Distribution and Concentration[70]

Both the Chinese and the Japanese have settled predominantly in the Pacific and mountain states, but the regional rural concentration of the latter is greater than that of the former. The Chinese are to be found in the major cities of eastern and midwestern industrial states and in a few places in the South. The Japanese show a lower percentage of their population in urban areas than the Chinese. There is a proportionally greater settlement of the Chinese than Japanese in large cities. Not only are the Chinese a more urban people than the Japanese, but their urban distribution is spread much wider in the United States than that of the Japanese.

The patterns of regional concentration, and rural-urban distribution of the Chinese and Japanese clearly contrast with one another. The Chinese in the United States are urban; over 70 percent are found in cities. The Japanese are far more rural. The gradual increase in the urbanization of the Japanese; that is, the tendency of Nisei to seek opportunities in the city, began in the 1930s but was greatly accelerated by their incarceration and exclusion from the Pacific Coast in 1942.

Living in close physical and social contact with one another and with economic and social needs that could not be met except by resort to cooperation, the Chinatown Chinese turned to his mutual aid societies. If the Chinese had been dispersed evenly among the whole population, their needs might have been satisfied by institutions of the larger society. If the Chinese had been isolated from one another, some of their needs—for instance, the need for protection against hostile clan or secret society enemies—might have diminished considerably. As it was, however, the Chinese were neither evenly distributed among the larger population nor isolated from one another. Because of the indifference or hostility of the larger society, their personal and social problems did not become matters of widespread public concern. Urbanization and segregation threw the Chinese upon their own resources.

In large cities in the United States the needs of enfranchised immigrants have been recognized by political machines that have traded on these for political support. Manifestly a testimony of public corruption, the political machine is more important for ameliorating situations especially peculiar to immigrant life that are not met by society's legitimate institutions.[71] Had the Chinese had the vote they too might have been patronized by Democratic or Republican ward bosses who, in their desire for power, might have ministered quite readily to the Chinese's need for sexual gratification and jobs. But no ward boss was interested in aliens ineligible to citizenship and the vote. The Chinese were left to organize their own "ward" under their own political direction. In place of the political machine, there grew up in Chinatown a communal polity with its own laws, its own law enforcement, and its own special relations with the institutions of American civil society.

The Japanese were in quite a different position. Most of them lived in the country, isolated not only from the larger society and much of its general antipathy toward them,[72] but also from one another. They were self-supporting and had founded families. Unlike the Chinese, they were not in the position to maintain an active and separatist communal solidarity and not in nearly so much need for the mutual aid dispenses by *landsmannschaften.* The California truck farm did for the Japanese farmer what the rural small holding did for the French peasant. The isolation and independence of the latter, which closely parallel the condition of the former, have been described by Karl Marx:

> The small holding peasants form a vast mass, the members of which live in similar conditions but without entering into manifold relations with one another. Their mode of production isolates them from one another instead of bringing them into mutual intercourse...Their field of production, the small holding, admits of no division of labor in its cultivation, no application of science, and therefore no diversity of development, no variety of talent, no wealth of social relationships. Each individual peasant family is almost self-sufficient; it itself directly produces the major part of its consumption, and thus acquires its means of life more through exchange with nature than in intercourse with society...Insofar as millions of families live under economic conditions of existence that separate their mode of life, their interests, and their culture from those of the other classes and put them in hostile opposition to the latter, they form a class. Insofar as there is merely a local interconnection among these small holding peasants and the identity of their interests begets no community, no national bond, and no political organization among them, they do not form a class.[73]

Conclusion

The development of communalism among overseas Chinese and its failure to develop among overseas Japanese may be attributed to the specific interplay of each group's social endowments at the time of arrival with its experience as immigrants in the host society.

The Chinese moved into the industrializing sector of American society bearing the traits of a traditional people relatively untouched by modernizing developments. Their social organization in the New World bore the stamp of the lineage communities, guildlike associations, and secret societies that characterized society in nineteenth-century China.

The Japanese entered the American scene when their own country was in the midst of developing further a new social organization that had been given impetus two centuries earlier. Many of the traditional institutions of pre-Tokugawa Japanese society had disappeared by the time emigration began. A national consciousness had arisen, cutting through local and familial ties and weakening local social and political allegiances. In contrast to the Chinese, the Japanese were more susceptible to the kind of changes and adaptations that modernization entails. Japanese overseas organization was a piecemeal affair reflecting the rapid accommodation of the Japanese to the new society.

The experiences of the immigrants in the host country confirmed their respective modes of social organization and adjustment. Because of the self-defined status of sojourner among the Chinese, it wasn't necessary for them to be accompanied by wives. Frustrated in their original plan to make money fast and then return to their home villages, the overseas migrants did not lose hope of returning. Constrained within the circumscribed economic operations permitted them by a hostile society, and thrown upon their own social, political, and economic resources, the Chinese tended to become more and more obliged to the traditional associations that surveilled all that they did and provided for their needs.

Entering into small-scale agriculture, the Japanese migrants further disobliged themselves from their already attenuated immigrant associations. Agricultural investment, in turn, helped end their sojourner status, especially when the young and middle-aged bachelor farmers sent for wives from Japan. Had the Chinese become independent farmers perhaps they too would have married or sent for their wives from China.[74]

Dependent upon themselves and their families for satisfaction of their economic and personal needs, and isolated from one another on separate landholdings, the Japanese tended to disentangle their lives from traditional associations of mutual aid. As new needs arose, those most affected formed special *ad hoc* organizations to meet them. The same would not begin to occur among the Chinese until the sex-ratio was brought into balance, families reunited or established in the United States, and a significant second generation born in America and grown to maturity.

NOTES

1. The following case studies of Chinese village life are most helpful:
   Martin Yang, *A Chinese Village, Taitou, Shantung Province* (London: Kegan Paul, Rench, Trubner, 1948);
   C.K. Yang, *A Chinese Village in Communist Transition* (Cambridge, Mass.: Harvard U.P., 1959);
   C.K. Yang, *The Chinese Family in the Communist Revolution* (Cambridge, Mass.: Harvard U.P., 1959);
   Lin Yueh-hwa, *The Golden Wing, A Sociological Study of Chinese*

Familism (London: Kegan Paul, Trench, Trubner, 1948);
Hsiao-tung Fei, *China's Gentry, Essays in Rural-Urban Relations* (Chicago: U. of Chicago P., 1953);
Hsiao-tung Fei and Chih-I Chang, *Earthbound China: A Study of Rural Economy in Yunnan* (London: Rutledge and Kegan Paul, 1948);
Francis L.K. Hsu, *Under the Ancestors' Shadow* (London: Routledge and Kegan Paul, 1949).

2. Japanese traders had settles in Manila in the late sixteenth century. Iyeyasu desired to open commercial relations with New Spain (Mexico) and to that end dispatched ships there in 1609. No agreement with the Spanish government was possible however, because of mutual suspicions. Independent of Iyeyasu, Date Masamune, a southern daimyo who had flirted with Christianity and even been prevailed upon to send a Japanese delegation to Rome, sent an expedition to Mexico City in 1614. Hostilities toward the Japanese were strong, however, and nothing came of this venture. In 1620, the last of the Japanese returned from New Spain. See William Lytle Schurz, *The Manila Galleon* (New York: Dutton, 1939, 1951), pp. 99-128;
See also Charles E. Chapman, *A History of California: The Spanish Period* (New York: Macmillan, 1919), pp. 31-42.

3. Lineage is defined here as a unilateral consanguineous group agnatically descended from a common patrilineal ancestor. Lineages in China and Japan were exogamous units. Hence a lineage community was composed of "a lineage plus all the wives of the males of the lineage and minus the women who have married."
Maurice Freedman, *Chinese Family and Marriage in Singapore* (London: HMSO, 1957), p. 18.
For a thorough discussion of the lineage in southeastern China see
Freedman, *Lineage Organization in Southeastern China* (London: Athlone Press, 1958).
A discussion of the lineage community in Japan will be found in
Lafcadio Hearn, *Japan, An Interpretation* (Tokyo and Rutland, Vt.: Charles E. Tuttle, 1904, 1955), pp. 81-106.
In Japan the village god was called *Ujigami*, "god of the lineage." In at least one important respect the Japanese "lineage" (*uji*) is not strictly comparable with its Chinese counterpart (*tsu*). The original uji, it is surmised, was, like the Chinese tsu, a patrilineal unit, establihsed in patriarchal, patrilocal villages. However, unlike the lineages of Kwangtung and Fukien, the Japanese lineages later incorporated into themselves the hereditary servants, the males of which were often adopted as sons. See
George B. Sansom, *Japan, A Short Cultural History* (New York: Appleton, 1946), pp. 37-38.

4. [T]here was now an almost complete breakdown of allegiance, of the habit of submission to authority. It is visible throughout all grades of society, down to the lowest. The clan system collapses and is replaced by the family system, loyalty to the head of a clan is

> superseded by obedience to the head of a household and may even involve active hostility toward other members of the clan. There is a general feeling that the social order is disintegrating.

Sansom, *Japan*, p. 361, describing the consequences of the one hundred years' strife in Japan prior to the advent of Tokugawa. A recent work on the Tokugawa period illustrates the "family revolution" that had taken place in Japan:

> There were no clans or sibs, the lineage and nuclear family being the most important structural units. . . . The household might consist of several generations but was not usually of great size since it did not include collaterals. That is, the family of only one son, normally the eldest, would usually live with the parents, the younger sons establishing separate households as they married.

Robert N. Bellah, *Tokugawa Religion* (New York: Free Press, 1957), p. 46.

For a comprehensive analysis of Meiji and pre-Meiji kinship structure see

R.P. Dore, *City Life in Japan* (Berkeley: University of California Press, 1958), pp. 91-190.

5. Max Weber, *The Religion of India* (New York: Free Press, 1958), pp. 272-73;
   Reinhard Bendix, *Max Weber: An Intellectual Portrait* (New York: Doubleday, 1960), pp. 368-69.
   For a description of the fief at the time of Tokugawa see
   Bellah, *Tokugawa Religion*, pp. 43-44.
6. Sansom, *Japan*, pp. 440-70.
7. Weber, *Religion of China* (New York: Free Press, 1951), pp. 13-20.
8. Sansom, *Japan*, p. 356.
9. Thomas C. Smith, *Agrarian Origins of Modern Japan* (Stanford: Stanford U.P.), pp.67-86;
   Irene Taeuber, *The Population of Japan* (Princeton: Princeton University Press, 1958), pp. 25-27.
10. Smith, *Agrarian Origins of Modern Japan*, p. 68.
11. See Gideon Sjoberg, *The Preindustrial City* (New York: Free Press, 1960), pp. 62-63, 180-219;
    Weber, *The City* (New York: Free Press, 1958), pp. 91-106.
12. Sansom, *Japan*, pp. 356-58.
13. See the following novels:
    John Okada, *No No Boy* (Rutland and Tokyo: 1957);
    James Michener, *Hawaii* (New York: Random, 1959), pp. 599-804.
14. Clarence Glick, "The Transition from Familism to Nationalism Among the Chinese in Hawaii," *American Journal of Sociology*, March 1938, pp. 734-43;
    Lea Williams, *Overseas Chinese Nationalism*.
15. Hsieh Pao Chao, *The Government of China* (Baltimore, 1925), pp. 309-10, quoted in Freedman, *Lineage Organization in Southeastern China*, pp. 64-65.

16. For a discussion of the failure of pao-chia in China see
Freedman, *Lineage Organization in Southeastern China*, pp. 64-68;
Hsiao-tung Fei, *China's Gentry*, pp. 86-88;
Martin Yang, *A Chinese Village, Taitou, Shantung Province*, p. 150;
C.K. Yang, *A Chinese Village in Early Communist Transition*, pp. 104-6;
Weber, *Religion of China*, pp. 75-78, 86-95.
17. Bellah, *Tokugawa Religion*, pp. 42-46.
Hearn, *Japan*, p. 91n.
18. In Michener's fictional account of Chinese and Japanese life in Hawaii, these differences are nicely illustrated. Nyuk Tsin, the common-law widow of a Cantonese migrant, continues to remit money to her late husband's home village, despite the fact that she has never been there, and that his first wife has in all probability died. The Japanese migrant, Kamejiro, on the other hand, often sighs nostalgically for his home village, but devotes his charitable activities to donations for Japanese military strength.

The sense of national consciousness among the Japanese immigrants should not be interpreted too seriously. As a Nisei said to me about the attitude of the Issei (immigrants) during the Pacific War: "It was like a rooting section at a football game. The old folks cheered each Japanese success, but none of them would ever have dreamed of going out 'on the field' and helping them 'carry the ball.' "
19. Mary Coolidge, *Chinese Immigration* (New York: Henry Holt, 1909), p. 502;
Sixteenth Census of the United States, Summary, Race by Nativity and Sex, for the Uited States: 1850 to 1940, p. 19.
20. Coolidge, *Chinese Immigration*, pp. 17-20.
21. For comparative purposes it is instructive to note that an intensive study of one Chinatown street in Singapore in 1954-56 found "that over half the persons in the interviewed households were unmarried; 65% of the men and 45% of the women. 25% of the women residents were widows; only 26% were living in a simple family."
Barrington Kaye, *Upper Nankin Street, Singapore* (Singapore: University of Malaya Press, 1960), p. 167.
22. Interracial unions were uncommon among Chinese in the frontier days when the language and cultural barriers between whites and Chinese were severe and prejudice was strong. Most states have had antimiscegenation laws forbidding interracial marriage. California's antimiscegenation statute was not invalidated until October 1, 1948. On the low occurrence of interracial marriage among Chinese, see
Lee, *Chinese in the United States*, pp. 250-51.
On antimiscegenation laws see
E.C. McDonagh and E.S. Richards, *Ethnic Relations in the United States* (New York: Appleton, 1953), pp. 392-93.
23. See the discussion in
Dore, *City Life in Japan*, pp. 123-35, 144-52.
24. This was the case in nineteenth-century Malaya, where a severe imbal-

ance in the sex ratio also characterized Chinese society. For details of the Malayan situation see
Leon Comber, *Chinese Secret Societies in Malaya* (Locust Valley: J.J. Augustin, 1959), pp. 95.

25. Jacob A. Riis, *How the Other Half Lives* (New York: Sagamore Press, 1890, 1957), p. 76.
The same suggestion was made after the first experience with Chinese coolies in Hawaii.
R.S. Kuykendall, *Hawaiian Kingdom, 1854-1874* (Honolulu: University of Hawaii Press, 1953), vol. I, p. 329.
26. U.S. Congress, Senate, Joint Special Committee to Investigate Chinese Immigration, 44th Cong., 2d sess., February 27, 1877, S. Rept. 689, p. 17 (hereafter cited as Rept. 689).
Testimony of the Hon. Frank M. Pixley, representing the municipality of San Francisco.
27. Ibid.
28. U.S. Congress, Senate, Immigration Commission. Immigrants in Industry. *Japanese and Other Immigrant Races in the Pacific Coast and Rocky Mountain States*, 61st. Cong., 2d sess., 1911, S. Doc. 633, vol. III, pp. 409-19, 421-29, 439;
Stewart Culin, "China in America: A Study of the Social Life of Chinese in the Eastern Cities of the United States," Paper read before the American Association for the Advancement of Science, New York, 1887, Philadelphia, 1887;
Carle Wittke, *We Who Built America* (New York: Prentice-Hall, 1948), p. 460-61.
For the information on Chinese in the South see the Appendix to this book and the sources cited therein.
29. Ira B. Cross, *A History of the Labor Movement in California* (Berkeley: University of California Press, 1935), p. 79.
30. Samuel Gompers and Herman Gustadt, *Meat vs. Rice. American Manhood Against Asiatic Coolieism. Which Shall Survive?* Published by the American Federation of Labor, reprinted as Sen. Doc. 137, 1902.
31. The Naturalization Act of 1790, limited eligibility for citizenship to any alien who was a "free, white person." After the Civil War it was amended to include persons of African descent. The Chinese became eligible for naturalization by passage of Public Law 199, December 17, 1943.
32. Sen. Doc. 633, pp. 411-13.
33. Ibid., p. 439.
34. The author knows one person so employed and has seen one of these shops during its hours of operation.
35. Ibid., p. 425. Indemnities paid in case of death or injury were lower for Chinese than for Caucasians. "This indemnity is different for the Chinese and for the various 'white races.' For example, if a Chinese is killed, the indemnity is fixed at $175, whereas in the case of a fatal accident to a white employee the relatives receive from $300 to $500 according to their financial condition, and the extent to which they were dependent upon

the man killed." Ibid., p. 429.

36. Ibid., pp. 387-407.
37. "The enforcement of the Exclusion Act caught some 30,000 sojourners visiting China, whose return was denied because of their status as laborers and who were disqualified under the ten admissible classes established by this Act."
    Lee, *Chinese in the United States*, p. 22.
38. In California, in 1910, 16,087 or over fifty-one percent of the male Chinese in the state, were forty-five years old or older. *Thirteenth Census of the United States*. "Characteristics of the Population—California. Marital Condition of Persons 15 year of age and over," p. 161.
39. Lee, "Occupational Invasion, Succession, and Accommodation of the Chinese of Butte, Montana," *American Journal of Sociology*, July 1949, pp. 50-58.
40. Lee, "The Decline of Chinatowns in the United States," *American Journal of Sociology*, March 1949, pp. 422-32.
41. *Yick Wo v. Hopkins*, 118 U.S. 356 (1885). "Laundries operated by Chinese, at one time, were very numerous. In fact, Chicago in 1950, had 430 of them as against 167 restaurants, 21 groceries, 30 general merchandise stores, 10 food manufacturing concerns, and 11 gift shops."
    Lee, *Chinese in the United States*, p. 266.
42. Kingsley Davis, *Human Society* (New York: Macmillan, 1948, 1949), p. 369.
43. "White women did not settle there in large numbers until the turn of the century. The slogan, Go West, young man, was a literal one in that territory."
    Lee, *Chinese in the United States*, p. 13.
44. Ibid., p. 261.
45. Ibid., pp. 81, 121, 146, 208, 255, 267, 271, 353, 360-61, 370.
46. Ibid., p. 35. A Montana law, typical of its genre, read: "Every person engaged in the laundry business, other than steam laundry, shall pay a license fee of $10 per quarter. . . . Any person doing business without a license where a license is required by law is guilty of misdemeanor. The Penalty shall not exceed six months in jail or a fine of no more than $500, or both."
    Montana Rev. Codes, sec. 2776 and *Montana Session Laws*, sec. 8602, quoted in ibid., p. 267.
    For San Francisco ordinances on this matter see the Appendix.
47. Cf. *Soon Hing v. Crowley* 113 U.S. 703 with *Yick Wo v. Hopkins* 118 U.S. 356.
    The opposition to Chinese laundrymen was later transferred to the Japanese. In San Francisco an "Anti-Jap Laundry League" was formed in March 1908, by the San Francisco Laundry Drivers' Union.
    ten Broek, Barnhart, and Matson, *Prejudice, War, and the Constitution*, p. 36.
48. Testimony of the Hon. Frank M. Pixley, representing the Municipality of San Francisco, *Report 689*, p. 12.

49. A not dissimilar situation occurs when a peasant society is in an early stage of foreign capitalist industrialization. The laborers maintain their dependence on familistic institutions during the early stages of economic growth. In Indonesia the effect has been to create a rural proletariat when unemployment occurred in the cities. The jobless returned to their home villages in search of aid, thus transferring the relief problem to those least able, financially, to bear it—the impoverished families and friends of the workers. See

    J.D. Boeke, "The Village Community in Collision with Capitalism," *Class, Status, and Power*, eds. S.M. Lipset and B. Bendix (New York: Free Press, 1953), pp. 541-46.

    In the case of the overseas Chinese, the relief problem has been transferred to the clans and kongsis, and, less often, to the secret societies, which serve as substitutes for the aid provided to friends and kinsmen in the faraway village.
50. During the 1940s I saw the same waiter working an eight-hour shift in the morning at one restaurant in Chinatown, only to find him, the same night, working another shift at another restaurant. Waiters and others employed in Chinatown are notoriously underpaid. Unions have chosen not to organize workers in Chinatown.
51. Milton L. Barnett, "Kinship as a Factor Affecting Cantonese Economic Adaptation in the United States," *Human Organization*, Spring 1960, p. 46.
52. The following is based on materials in Sen. Doc. 633, pp. 13-50, and *passim.*
53. Ibid., p. 295.
54. Ibid., p. 256.
55. Ibid., pp. 259-60.
56. Ibid., p. 282.
57. Ibid., p. 347.
58. Young, Reid, and Carrothers, *Japanese Canadians*, p. 42.
59. No "Asiatics" were engaged in salmon fishing in the Columbia River-Puget Sound region in 1909.

    Sen. Doc. 633, p. 389.

    From 1922 to 1931, the Canadian government sought to reduce the number of Japanese fishermen by license quotas.

    Young, Reid, and Carrothers, *Japanese Canadians*, pp. 43-44.

    In 1943, California prohibited the issuance of fishing licenses to aliens ineligible for citizenship; that is, Japanese, but this law was declared unconstitutional.

    Takahashi v. Fish and Game Commission, 334 U.S. 410 (1948).
60. Sen. Doc 633, pp. 412-40.
61. Dorothy Swaine Thomas, Charles Kikuchi, and J. Sakoda, *The Salvage* (Berkeley: University of California Press, 1952), pp. 22-23.
62. The rise of cities and the rural disorganization accompanying the advent of the Tokugawa era had an important effect on the labor force in Japan. The cities attracted many of the rural farm workers. Agricultural labor

became scarce. Gradually the status of agricultural laborers changed from *fudai* ("hereditary servants who were frequently adopted into the uji") to hokonin ("persons employed under various types of long-term servitude"). The hokonin, in turn, gradually shortened their period of service, and increased their bargaining rights. The shortage of labor drove up its price and increased its mobility. Bands of hokonin, under a headman, roamed the countryside selling their services to the highest bidder. Large-scale agriculture became increasingly unprofitable. Landowners, unwilling to sell their property, but unable to farm it, began to lease portions to hokonin. The tenants profited in the deal because they employed their own families, engaged in nonagricultural home industry as a sideline, and took advantage of advances in agriculture—seed selection, commercial fertilizers, "and many other innovations [that] required a patience and devotion to the minutiae of cultivation that the nuclear family could provide but the large, unwieldy, and socially heterogeneous labor force could not."

Smith, *Agrarian Origins of Modern Japan*, pp. 124-38, quotation on p. 129.

In this sense, then, the Japanese experience in California was a recapitulation of an earlier experience in Japan.

63. Millis, *Japanese Problem*, p. 141, quoted in Thomas, Kikuchi, and Sato, *Salvage*, p. 23.
64. The following is from Thomas, Kikuchi, and Sakoda, *Salvage*, p. 23.
65. Millis, *Japanese Problem*, p. 141, quoted in Thomas, Kikuchi, and Sakoda, *Salvage*, p. 23.
66. Thomas, Kikuchi, and Sakoda, *Salvage*, pp. 23-25;
Iyenaga and Sakoda, *California Problem*, pp. 138-40;
Kawakami, *Japanese Question*, pp. 237-51.

That clause which presumed prima facie intent to violoate the Alien Land Law when an ineligible alien purchased land in the name of a citizen offspring was declared in violation of the Fourteenth Amendment of the United States Constitution in *Oyama et al. v. California*, 332 U.S. 631 (1948).

The entire Alien Land Law was invalidated in a later case before the California Supreme Court. *Sei Fujii v. State of California*, 242 P. 2nd 617.

For a critical discussion of the Alien Land Law and the Oyama case, see Jacobus ten Broek, Edward Barnhart, and Floyd Matson, *Prejudice, War, and the Constitution* (Berkeley: University of California Press, 1954), pp. 50-57, 304-7.

67. Irene Taeuber, "Family, Migration, and Industrialization in Japan," *American Sociological Review*, April 1951, pp. 149-57.
68. In Los Angeles County, 1940, the census reported that 1,746 Japanese of a total of 17,005 employed were unpaid family farm laborers; of these 605 were native-born males, 432 native-born females. In a 20-percent sample of employed Japanese in Los Angeles in 1941, 576 unpaid family workers were listed: 161 in clerical work and sales; 36 operatives and

kindred workers; 79 service workers; 297 farm and nursery workers; and 3 nonfarm laborers. (The sample utilized a universe of 3,500; the percent unpaid family workers was 16.5).
Bloom and Riemer, *Removal and Return*, pp. 13, 19.

69. The urbanization of the Chinese has also been noted in Singapore:

> When the Chinese went to Singapore they were in search of a livelihood. They found it in the growing of gambier and pepper, in the practice of labor and crafts which were necessary for building up and maintenance of the new settlement, and in various forms of trade. For the most part, these activities kept [the] Chinese in the town, but some of them established clearings in the wild countryside which was remote from British authority in the early period. When the Chinese population later increased by leaps and bounds and the growing of pepper and gambier ceased to play an important part in Singapore's economy (as it began to do in the sixties), the role of the agriculturalist in Singapore Chinese society declined. Trade, the pursuit of crafts, and the performance of unskilled labor characterized a largely urban economy.

Maurice Freedman, "Immigrants and Associations: Chinese in Nineteenth Century Singapore," *Comparative Studies in Society and History*, October 1960, p. 27.

70. Data for this section were obtained from the Reports of the United States census, 1850-1950 (decennial reports). Originally this portion of the paper appeared in slightly different form in my unpublished manuscript, "Factors Affecting the Location of Chinese and Japanese in the United States: A Socio-demographic Study."

71. Robert K. Merton, "Manifest and Latent Functions," *Social Theory and Social Structure* (New York: Free Press, 1957), pp. 71-82;
D.W. Brogan, *Politics in America* (New York: Doubleday-Anchor, 1960), pp. 104-48;
Martin Meyerson and Edward C. Banfield, *Politics, Planning, and the Public Interest* (New York: Free Press, 1955), pp. 61-120.

72. The Chinese as urban dweller, distinct and congregated together, were the victims of numerous race riots. The Japanese were persecuted by harsh laws and vitriolic invective, but rarely by riots, which are always more difficult to arouse in the country than in the city.

73. Karl Marx, *The Eighteenth Brumaire of Louis Napoleon* (Moscow: Foreign Language Publishing House, 1852), quoted in Marx and Friedrich Engels, *Basic Writings on Politics and Philosophy*, ed. Lewis S. Feuer (New York: Doubleday-Anchor, 1959), pp. 338-39.

74. The evidence on Chinese patterns of marriage in nineteenth-century Thailand suggests this possibility:

> The great majority of the mining and plantation laborers did not marry so long as they remained in that occupational status. The same could be said of urban wage earners, though apparently a somewhat larger minority did marry in Siam. On the other hand, Chinese who settled down on the land as farmers or plantation owners almost always got married.

G. William Skinner, *Chinese Society in Thailand: An Analytical History* (Ithaca: Cornell U.P., 1957), p. 127.

Chinese Social Organization in the United States | *III*

Community Institutions ||6

|| CLANS

Introduction

Overseas kinship organization is based on the principle of "clan" organization; that is, on the basis of common surnames.[1] Clans are an imperfect re-creation of the exoamous lineage communities common to southeastern China. The lineage could reckon its consanguinity through the family histories and control its purity through enforced exogamy and patrilocal residence, but overseas, or away from the isolated village, the Chinese had to be quite careful lest situations arise in which the prohibition against endogamy be placed in jeopardy.

Not only did village custom support the rules against marriage within the patrilineal agnatic unit, but also the imperial penal code:

> Whenever any persons having the same family name intermarry, the parties and the contractor of the marriage shall each receive 60 blows, and the marriage being null and void, the man and woman shall be separated, and the marriage presents forfeited to government.[2]

Surname exogamy still prevails today even among relatively assimilated Americans of Chinese ancestry[3] and is one of the major reasons cited for migration away from small Chinatowns by marriageable males.[4]

Surname associations penetrated the overseas Chinese communities in two different but related ways. First, clans were formed by persons coming from the same single-lineage community in China who thus formed what was at once both a territorial and a surname association. Second, the religious importance of separate agnatic units in the homeland, together with the immigrants' need for mutual aid and cooperation, provided any surname grouping with a natural qualification for formalization. In reality, overseas clans were often gross exaggerations of the agnation inherent in the single lineage village. Members were enrolled, in many cases, on the basis of surname alone, not on the basis of place of origin, so that the kinship net of the overseas Chinese was flung far wider than it was in China. Moreover, just as similar surnames had often been the basis of linkages wider than the original patrilineal group in China, so among the overseas Chinese formations occurred through the recognition of "similarities" in the linguistic construction of surnames.

Chinese Clanship in the United States

The Chinese merchants who first pioneered California informed their relatives in China about the lucrative opportunities they found in the New World.[5] The first clans were formed about the merchant's store. The family store served as the basic focal point around which Chinese social life revolved. From the store sprang not only the clan, but the kongsi, although, as has been indicated, these institutions are older than the stores from which they arose.[6]

Clans vary in size and in distribution throughout the United States. The largest clans are the Chans, the Lees, and the Wongs. However, because of disproportional distribution the Yees predominate in Pittsburgh, the Moys in Chicago, and the Gees in Oakland.[7] In Sacramento the Fongs are most numerous; in Santa Barbara the Ginns and Halls;[8] in Boston, the Lis.[9]

A romanized version of a Chinese surname sometimes obscures the fact that the same Occidental term might stand for two quite different Chinese surnames. There are two Wong clans with two quite different Chinese radicals forming the spelling of the surname. The Wong Wun Shan Clan is composed of those Chinese whose surname in English is pronounced Wong and means "yellow;" the Wong Kong Har Clan from those Chinese whose surname in Englsh is also pronounced Wong and means "kingly" or "regal." (The latter is spelled with a radical which includes three horizontal brush strokes. They are sometimes called the *Sam Wah;* that is, "three-stroke," Wongs.)[10]

Within each clan subclans called fongs may be found. These are organized according to village, prefecture, or province or origin, or by dialect. The power of any clan in the political structure of Chinatown is a function of its size and its hereditary-charismatic prestige. One of the Wong clans of New York has twenty fongs, thus giving it a strong political position. A similar clan structure is found in southeastern China.[11]

Moreover, clans not only segmented into smaller units, but also combined into larger groupings. The creation of transfamilial organizations took place for one of four reasons: permanent sworn ancestral brotherhood; traditional friendship, based, perhaps, on intermarriage of the remote ancestors; neighboring home districts in China having produced a lasting fraternal relationship; and a similarity in the radical symbol of the surname.[12]

The *Four Brothers Association* provides an illustration of the sworn brotherhood. It joined the Lin, Kwan, Chang, and Chao families ca. A.D. 200, when their forbears signed the Peach Garden Oath in order to save the Han Dynasty.[13]

> This alliance was sworn during the civil wars that desolated the Chinese empire between the overthrow of the Han dynasty and the establshment of the eastern Tsin.... It was in the year 184, that the Western Chinese revolted against the Emperor.... As is generally the case in China the Emperor was too weak to subdue these rebels. He issued a proclamation, calling upon all the valiant of the empire to enlist and fight against the insurgents.
>
> Two men, Liu-pi and Chang-fi, having read this proclamation, went to a tavern to speak about it.
>
> Liu-pi, himself, was an offspring of the reigning dynasty of Han. Whilst sitting there, a certain Kwan-yu joined them. Animated by a common spirit, these three men sought to devise the means of restoring peace to the land.
>
> At the proposal of Chang-fi, they came the next day in the peach-garden behind his house; and being assembled under the blooming peach-trees, they sacrificed a black ox and a white horse, and having offered incense, they knelt down and swore the oath of fraternity. Liu-pi was named "first brother" of the league. Having enlisted volunteers, they succeeded... in restoring peace to their country.[14]

Traditional friendship is illustrated by the agreements that united the Chan, Hu, and Yuan clans and that of the Wongs and Engs. The neighboring clans of Tsai, Wu, and Chow formed the San Teh Society, and those of the Louie, Fong, and Fang, the Su Yuen tong. A common radical signifying the surname bound together the Tom, Tan, Hsu, and Hsieh clans, while different spellings in English obscure the common clan relationship of the Dear, Jear, Dere, Dea and Jay groups.[15] Through such combinations the larger and more powerful clan associations were able to dominate and often direct the territorial associations (see *infra*) in the overseas Chinese community.

While suprafamily organizations provide greater chances for power in the community, the fongs serve local needs for fellowship and mutal aid.

> To provide for closer fellowship, it is quite common for a familial group to organize smaller "clubs" with membership open to persons with a common family name and from the same village or district in Canton. These "clubs" are not always organized constitutionally and are, more or less, throwbacks to the old system of family store groups. However, because of their number, they represent an important factor in the control of the individual. They play a vital part in the lives of the Chinese because it is to these clubs that the individual looks for assistance, social life, and social wefare when he is unemployed or otherwise in need.[16]

The elders of the family associated controlled social, economic, and protective matters for their fellow members.

> Just as the family village is governed by elders, the control of the family association is vested in the hands of the older generation. Elections are held to choose officers to perform the routine work of running the organization with candidates chosen from the rank and file. However, the important affairs involving the welfare of the family are entrusted to the elders. To them falls the responsibility of protecting the honor of the family name, answering complaints lodged by other groups, and meeting some of the social and economic problems of the members. Since San Francisco's Chinatown is the largest Chinese settlement outside of China, the responsibility falls heavily on the shoulders of the elders of the local unit. When the problems threaten to cause an open break with another group, the local council frequently calls in the more important elders from other sections of the country for consultation.[17]

The power of the elders, sustained by hereditary and customary authority, went almost unchecked in the Chinese community in America. "The influence of the clan is strongly felt among the Chinese in this country. Those of the same family name are often able to trace their relationship, although it may be many times removed, and in disputes they usually side together."[18]

> The decisions reached by the elders of a family association are adhered to faithfully by all members of the particular family. In a few instances the decisions have meant open warfare with the complainants. In recent years actual warfare has been rare, since the elders are reluctant to admit that they have failed to reach a compromise and force is the only alternative.[19]

An example may show the form in which familial authority was exercised. As has been noted earlier, the early Chinese immigrant population was chiefly male and was composed of absentee husbands or single men who regarded themselves as "sojourners" in America, seeking to earn money for the support of families at home in China. In some instances the overseas migrant became a prodigal and failed to carry out his filial obligations. In one such instance the boy's mother wrote to him:

> I hear that you, ____, my son, are acting the prodigal. . . . For many months there has arrived no letter, nor money. My supplies are exhausted. I am old; too infirm to work; too lame to beg. Your father in the mines of the mountains suffers from a crushed foot. He is weak, and unable to accumulate money. Hereafter, my son, change your course; be industrious and frugal, and remit to me your earnings; and within the year let me welcome home both your father and yourself. Heed my words and reform, lest persisting in rebellion, you will hasten my dissolution, and you, descending to the regions of darkness, will see me nevermore.[20]

However, the young migrant's mother did not cease her efforts with this letter, She wrote to an older relative, in America, to whom she had given the boy in custodial care.

> . . . I hear that my son is playing the prodigal, being idle, or spending his earnings for unnecessary articles of clothing and in other forms of self-indulgence. I authorize you, his near relative and senior in years, to strenuously admonish him. If moderate chastisement fails, then call to your aid one or more of the brothers [relatives] and sorely beat him, not pitying his body.[21]

Such a method of control usually was effective. Reverend A.W. Loomis remarks, "The docility of these youths, their respect for age, and the cheerfulness with which they usually submit to the control of those of superior age, stand out in strong relief as compared with Young America."[22] "The family associations are in a position to exercise a great deal of control over their members," reported the Chinese Chamber of Commerce: "The riffraff element is held in check while the interests of its weaker members are protected by a solidarity that is common only to a Chinese community."[23]

For purposes of meeting and handling clan affairs, a Chinatown building was set aside and held in trust by the elders.

> Most family organizations, regardless of whether they are single units or combined family associations, have buildings or headquarters which provide a meeting place for members. The larger family buildings also have living quarters which are rented to members of the organization. Unlike American fraternal orders, most Chinese association property is held in trust by individuals.[24]

As Chinatown clans were established around the merchants' stores, family monopolies over certain trades developed. These monopolies are supported by custom and by the strength of the kinship association. Generally they are not violated and persist in Chinatowns.[25]

> In modern Chinatown...not only are a large number of stores controlled by families, but there is also a definite family group of certain types of businesses as well as occupations. For example, the Dear family (also spelled Jear, Dere, Dea, and Jay) operates fruit and candy stores; while the Yees and Lees own the better restaurants and supply most of the family cooks.[26]

Chinese clans in the United States organized on grounds of presumed kinship for immigrant association and mutual aid. However, Chinese clans were not the only grouping transplanted from China. Locality and dialect also united certain Chinese with one another and separated these from others. Secret societies united "pariahs," rebels, and those ideologically dedicated to the overthrow of the Ch'ing Dynasty.

"TERRITORIAL" OR DIALECT ASSOCIATIONS

Introduction

Overseas Chinese are organized not only by surname, but also by place of origin and dialect. Membership in the clan and kongsi associations sometimes cut across one another, although this was not always the case. A surname association might enroll all persons of the same name regardless of territorial origin or dialect. Or it might enroll only those for whom surname, territory, and dialect were coextensive. In the former case, the clan might segment into fongs along territorial or linguistic lines. A kongsi, on the other hand, might admit only those coming from a single lineage community. Or it might enroll all those speaking the same dialect, or coming from a particular locality, (village, district, prefecture, or province), regardless of surname.

It might very well be asked why, if the Chinese were organized into clans according to principles of presumed agnation, they were also organized into kongsis. Other analysts of overseas Chinese society are themselves not certain of the answer to this question.[27] However, the conditions of Chinese life at home and abroad provide some suggestions for solving this problem. First, it must be emphasized that the overseas Chinese were immigrants in a strange land racially and culturally distinct from the indigenous inhabitants. When immigrants are thrown together in an alien setting they are likely to divide into units expressive of the solidarity of homeland ties. In the Chinese case landsmannschaften were constructed in accordance with "blood," linguistic, village, country, prefectural, and provincial ties. The various criteria of association serve as status markers for persons who otherwise would be undifferentiated members of a racial mass. Outside of Chinatown, the Cantonese immigrant received categorical treatment as just one more "Chinaman"; within the confines of the ghetto he was a man from a specific locality, speaking a local dialect, and belonging to a particular clan.[28]

Second, kongsis have their specific origin in Chinese cities which, as I have explained previously, were "governed" less by the civic authority than by the voluntary associations of the citizenry. The overseas territorial and dialect organizations are re-creations of the hui kuan and kongsis established earlier in Chinese cities by rural students, merchants, and artisans.

From the early sixteenth century on, the custom arose for various provinces, large prefectures, sometimes even counties, to establish hostelries in Peking for students preparing themselves for the metropolitan and imperial examinations.[29] These hostelries were called hui kuan, a term frequently applied to territorial, dialect, and various other associations of overseas Chinese, and etymologically derived from *hui-shih* ("metropolitan examination"). The hui kuan of the southeastern Chinese appear to have been the earliest and most numerous established in the capital, while the peoples of the northern provinces established hui kuan later and less frequently. As early as the Cheng-te period (1506-21) the hostel of Fuchou Prefecture in Fukien accommodated not only academic candidates, but also local officials in need of temporary lodging in the nation's capital. Before the end of the Ming period (1368-1644), all prefectures of Fukien save one had established hostelries in Peking. From 1644 to 1760, Fukien local histories indicate that migrants from at least eight different counties in Fukien had founded separate hostelries in the capital. Kiangsi Province was represented by several prefectural and even a few county hostelries in the national capital during the Ming period. Shansi, a northern province, did not have a hostelry in Peking until late in the seventeenth century.

Side by side with the student hostelries in the national capital and other urban centers stood the various merchant guilds and artisan associations organized along territorial and dialect lines.[30] Also variously referred to as hui kuan or kongsi, these were formed for mutual aid and protection by tradesmen and merchants hailing from the same territory or speaking the same dialect.

Nineteenth-century China was divided into eighteen provinces (Shang), each province being subdivided into prefectures (Fu), and each prefecture being subdivided into districts of three classes according to fiscal importance, known as Yun (first class), Chau (second class), and Teng (third class). The word kuan, as found in hui kuan, is the obsolete term for prefecture, but is colloquially translated as "the part of the country" from which a man hails, and it has come to be used in this more general sense to describe overseas Chinese dialect and territorial units.[31] They organized for self-defense against the sectional prejudices to which settlers from different localities were subject and regulated affairs and settled disputes among their own members. A typical example of the fear of sectional jealousies is manifested in the preamble of the Ning-po Guild at Wen-chou.

> For a century no province has been without Ning-poese residents. Ning-po is a maritime region. those of its people who cannot find employment as agriculturists resort to other places for trade. Here at Wen-chou we find ourselves isolated; mountains and sea separate us from Ning-po, and when in trade we excite envy on

> the part of Wenchowese, and suffer insult and injury, we have no adequate redress. Mercantile firms, each caring only for itself, experience disgrace and loss—the natural outcome of isolated and individual resistance. It is this which imposes on us the duty of establishing a guild.[32]

The guild of Cantonese merchants established in Pei-hai, expressed a similar sentiment in the preamble to its charter:

> The people [of Pei-hai] are very covetous, and of a licentious nature, showing little respect for the laws; while cases of robbery and theft are innumerable, to the great annoyance of our merchants; and when trouble arises between our trades and local merchants there is no way of dealing with the latter.
>
> It is hoped that the rules we have adopted will lead to uniformity of action and unanimity of feeling among our members, who are bound by ties of townsmanship, and in this way secure ourselves against gradual degeneration, while it will teach those outside the guild that being of one mind to oppose wrong, unscrupulous merchants and bad characters will seek to avoid us, and so avert their own discomfiture.[33]

Guilds acted to protect themselves against the depredations of rival merchants, from secret societies, and from the local authorities. In their struggles with the latter, the guilds were not above appealing for redress to Peking, as is evidenced by the successful appeal of the Ning-po Guild against the seizure of its junks.[34]

Guild revenues were derived from proportional assessments on its merchant members, and on import duties from its trader members.

Guild self-regulation[35] required the selection of officers who included in their duties

Inspecting and assessing members' books for fiscal purposes
Allocating and withholding credit
Managing the storage of goods
Establishing and enforcing a uniform system of weights and measures
Fixing a tariff on all goods sold
Providing a protection force or insurance for fire
Regulating the times during which goods might be sold
Policing the civil, business, and criminal behavior of members
Arbitrating internal disputes
Offenders and malefactors were fined, expelled from the guild, or,

in extreme cases, sentenced to death. In some cases an offender's store was boycotted.

Modeled on the merchant guilds were the associations of artisans and certain retail traders found in many Chinese cities.[36] These associations functioned to preserve trade secrets among their members, to protect their compatriots against sectional rivalries, and to regulate internal matters. Among the more prominent of these associations were the Ning-po fishmongers' union and the several kongsi in Wenchow: carpenters', copper-wire-drawers', silk-weavers', millers', gold-beaters', barbers', and postal companies'. Other artisan guilds of umbrella makers, pewterers, tailors, dyers, and needle-makers were generally to be found.

Some of these associations; for instance, the gold-beaters' association at Wen-chou, were organized to preserve a particular trade and its art for members of a lineage. Others restricted members along the lines of locality or dialect.

The self-regulation of the artisans included limiting the hours of work, setting the number and criteria for apprentices, boycotting the establishments of recalcitrant members, arbitrating internal disputes, and punishing miscreants. With respect to the latter, the penalties extended from fines to death to torture. Among the more ferocious and ghastly versions of torture was being bitten to death by fellow guild members. A gold-beaters' union passed such a sentence on a member who violated the prohibition against employing more than one apprentice at a time. "To make sure that none shirked their duty on that occasion, no one was allowed to quit the shop whose bloody lips and gums did not attest to his fidelity. The murderer who took the first bite was discovered and beheaded."[37]

The importance and power of these associations in China is to be seen in terms of the underdeveloped system of centralized civil and criminal law in China at this time:

> Individuals can easily find redress in the courts of law in Europe, but in China this is not the case, the individual not being recognized by law except a community becomes responsible for him. Thus it is when the natural community of the clan or village is found not to answer the purpose, Chinamen are forced into communities of a more artificial nature. Without external pressure the Chinese are as inadhesive to one another as other people animated by selfish motives generally are. Lawsuits before mandarins are moreover very expensive. The mandarins, as a rule, understand better how to relieve their clients' pockets than to help them to justice in questions of commercial law and

custom. It is a common practice among the people to bring all cases of civil law before their elders or into the public hall. These have a kind of local jurisdiction, allowed by the Government, not consisting only in the power to adjust matters, but also in the power to inflict fines, imprisonment, and corporal punishment. Their testimony is, besides, commonly decisive in criminal cases before the mandarin. The decisions arrived at by the headmen of these corporations are, however, not guided by a written law, but by local custom, which differs materially in different parts of China, even in different districts of the same prefecture.[38]

Kongsis in the United States

The Chinese immigrants to the United States came almost exclusively from twenty-four of the eighty districts in Kwangtung Province. Of these, the greatest number appear to have emigrated from two dialect areas in Kong Chow Prefecture: Sam Yup (literally "three districts"), composed of the districts of Shun Tak (Shun Tih), Namhoi (Nan Hae), and Pun Yui (Canton City); and Sz Yup (literally "four districts"), composed of the districts of Toyshan, Hoi Ping, Yan Ping, and Sun Wui.

To the peoples of Kwangtung, each language is also an indicator of the status and sophistication of the speaker. "The people of the different districts vary somewhat in speech and manners; those of the Sam Yup approximate in both language and customs to the inhabitants of the city of Canton, while the Sz Yup people, who largely outnumber the others, exhibit many local peculiarities, and often speak a patois almost unintelligible to those who come from nearer the capital."[39] "The Sz Yup people, who are in the majority, are not so well educated as those from the Sam Yup, and seem more susceptible to foreign influences. The professed converts to Christianity are chiefly among them, and they comprise almost the entire membership of the secret society that has for its object the overthrow of the present Chinese dynasty."[40]

In twentieth-century San Francisco the distinctions among language groupings have been slightly blurred by intermarriage across dialect lines and as groups learn each other's languages. When I asked an American of immigrant Chinese parentage to designate his language grouping he held up four fingers signifying Sz Yup. Many San Francisco Chinese can converse in both Sam Yup and Sz Yup, and most understand both. Other dialects—Heungshan and Hakka—can also be heard in San Francisco, though less frequently then either Sam Yup or Sz Yup. "Mandarin"—the designation given to the language of

Peking and the northern provinces—is rarely heard. Descendants of the Sam Yup-speaking migrants are still proud of their cultural "superiority" over the "rustic" Sz Yup speakers. When, in addressing a convention of American-Chinese students at the University of California, I casually remarked that at one time the Sam Yup people had considered the Sz Yup people to be "hillbillies," the students roared with understanding laughter—many pointed with humorously accusing fingers at their Sz Yup-speaking friends. I have often heard Sam Yup-speaking American-Chinese poke fun at the inferior cultural inheritance of Sz Yup-speaking companions.

The Chinese merchant "pioneers"—in the manner of rural migrants living in a city in China—established kongsis for their landsmänner and assisted the latter in their emigration from China. From an early letter of two kongsi leaders to the governor of California, it is possible to obtain a glimpse of the mercantile character and employee assistance offered to fellow countrymen by the newly established kongsis:

> One of the subscribers of this letter is now employed as a clerk in an American store, because of the services he can render them as a broker in business with his countrymen; he has sometimes sold $10,000 a day of Chinese goods. Chy Lung, who arrived a few days since with some $10,000 in China goods, has sold out, and returns for another cargo in the *Challenge.* Fei Chaong, who brought in a cargo about a month ago, has sold out, and also returns in the *Challenge.* So does the partner of Sam Wa of this city, Tuk-Shaong, for the same purpose—for more selling cargoes. A great many others send for goods by the *Challenge,* and all the other ships, which you speak of as being expected, will bring cargoes of Chinese goods as well as Chinamen. Nor does this by any means give you an idea of the trade of the Chinamen. They not only freight your ships, but they have bought many of them, and will buy more;...
>
> The ship *Challenge,* of which you speak in your message as bringing over more than five hundred Chinamen, did not bring over one who was under "cooly" contract to labor. Hab-wa, who came in her [as] agent for the charterers, one of the signers of this letter, states to your Excellency that they were all passengers, and are going to work in the mines for themselves.[41]

Merchandising was the base around which konsis were established. Traditional Chinese ideology has not awarded great esteem to the merchant in China,[42] but overseas this class of Chinese soon came to be the recognized power elite in the Chinese community. In the absence of the traditional Mandarin-scholar-cum-land-owning-gentry class, most of whose members did not emigrate, the wealthy merchant enjoyed high prestige among the aspiring farmers, artisans, storekeepers, and laborers. The fact that wealth is closely related to success and social position among Americans helped to legitimate the merchants' claim to community-wide authority in Chinatown.

The mercantile establishment was the hub of all Chinatown activities:

> The store is the center around which life in a Chinese colony revolves...In a short time this place becomes the resort of all the Chinese in the colony, many of whom may have a small money interest in the concern. They have provisions and clothes to buy; news of the outside world and of their own homes may be learned here; and, besides, there is a couch provided for opium smoking, which the immigrant, with newly acquired money to spend, readily practices as the first dissipation at hand. In time the shopkeeper, knowing the advantage of increasing the attractions of his place, may procure a tolerably skillful cook and open a restaurant in an upper story of his building; but at first this will only be kept open on Sundays and holidays.
>
> Other opportunities for making money will not be lost sight of. The cellar will be fitted up with bunks for opium smoking, and tables covered with matting for the convenience of those who desire to play dominoes; and the profit on the opium consumed and the portion of the winnings set aside for the use of the tables soon constitute a more important source of revenue than the store itself.
>
> Thus many interests beside those of the dealer in clothes and provisions grow up under the roof of the little shop. Often a doctor, some poor and broken-down student, dispenses medicines from a supply ranged along one side of the store; the itinerant barber, an indispensable personage, makes it a place of call; letters for the colony are directed in care of the store; public notices are written on tablets of red paper and posted beside the door; Chinese newspapers, both of San Francisco and the native ports, are received; and here, too, interpreters are to be found, who conduct negotiations and adjust differences with the outside world.[44]

The first territorial association known to have been formed in America was the Kong Chow Society, organized in San Francisco in 1851, two years after the first Chinese began to come to California. It was not, strictly speaking, a *district association* since the membership was open to all Chinese from 6 of the 72 districts of Kwangtung: Yan Ping, Hoi Ping, Sun-Ning (Sinning, Toyshan), Sun Wui, Hok Shan, and Sz-Wui.[45] "Although no figures have ever been available, it is probable that of the 12,000 Chinese in California in 1851, close to 10,000 of them came from the Kong Chow region."[46]

The second territorial association was formed in the same year from the remaining 2,000 Chinese on the Pacific Coast. The Sam Yup Association, composed of immigrants from the three districts northeast of Kong Chow, established offices on Clay Steet above Powell in San Francisco, and in Sacramento.[47]

The third organization grew out of disputes between the various territorial representatives in the Kong Chow Association. Failure at settlement of these matters resulted in the withdrawal of four of the districts, namely the Yan Ping, Hoi Ping, Sun-Ning (Toyshan, Sinning), and part of the Sun Wui, who formed the Sz Yup Associations.[48]

The fourth and fifth organizations were formed in 1852. The Yeong Wo Association included the people from Heungshan (Chungshan), most of whom had migrated only as far as Hawaii, and later the Tung Gwoon Jung Shing, and Bok Law peoples. That the origin of this organization is not strictly territorial is evidenced by the term Yeong Wo, which does not designate a territory, but means Masculine Concord, perhaps indicative of all the male emigration from South China.[49] The Hip Kat Association was formed in 1852, and was based on ethnic rather than territorial background. The Hip Kat was composed solely of the Hakka people from the Bow On, Chak Kai, Tung Gwoon, and Chu Mui districts. The Hakka were not native to Kwangtung, but a migratory people, speaking a dialect quite unlike Cantonese, who had come into the province from the north. They were generally despised by Cantonese—the closest comparable term for them in Western purlance being *gypsy*, a term still used in reference to their descendants in American Chinatowns. The word *Hakka* means "stranger families."[50] A Hakka-Punti (Cantonese) War took place (1854-68), and is indicative of the hostility between the two groups.[51] In 1856, the Hip Kat changed its name to Yan Wo (Yan On), a term meaning Association of Human Concord.[52]

Destined to become the most powerful association, the Ning Yeung, or Association of Masculine Tranquility, arose out of a dispute within the Sz Yup Association. In 1854, the entire membership from the Sun-Ning (Toyshan) district withdrew from the Sz Yup. The Sun-

Ning had been its largest constituency, and their withdrawal rendered the Sz Yup so ineffective that it was not represented in the later consolidation of the district associations. "The formation of the Ning Yeung left the Sze Yap in control of the people from Hoi Ping, Yan Ping, and part of Sun Wui districts, who were in the minority as far as number was concerned. Henceforth, the Sze Yap group was to wield no power or influence, at least none that the Ning Yeung could not nullify."[53]

In 1862, the Sz Yup suffered another setback. The majority of its membership from Hoi Ping and Yan Ping withdrew and formed the Hop Wo, Association of United Harmony. At about the same time, the Yee Clan from Toyshan District and the Ong Clan from Hoi Ping District, withdrew from the Ning Yeung Association and joined the Hop Wo group.

In the late 1890s, the Shew Hing Association was formed by immigrants from that region in Kwangtung. Later, the Shew Hing Association added peoples from Yang Kong, and Yang Chun, two districts considerably distant from the Shew Hing Region. The Shew Hing also absorbed the abortive Yin-Hoi District Assocation, originally formed by disgruntled Hop Wo members from Hoi Ping and Yan Ping. Still later the Shew Hing Association became the representative of even more districts by absorbing the peoples of Sam-shui, Tsing Yuen, and Sz-Wui, three districts northwest of the Shew Hing Region.[54] The organizations were not essentially territorial in origin and were not stable.

There is some evidence from the organizational history of the associations to indicate that clan and district feuds were the source of much internal dissent and group defections. Clan disputes were sometimes carried from the Chinese mainland to America:

> By 1854, certain clan organizations had also been formed in San Francisco alongside the district associations. With a motley population of Cantonese from a score of districts in Kwang-tung and bearing over half a hundred clan names, disputes between members of different clans or districts naturally arose inside the community. The disputes were sometimes over individual rights and sometimes over commercial transactions. And sometimes as in the case of the famous "Chinese War" in Weaverville in 1854, it was over just a trivial minor quarrel. Sometimes these differences were adjusted by the ruling elders of the district or family associations to which the parties concerned belonged, but more often than not, a third or neutral organization was called in to settle matters.[55]

In the first decade of Chinese immigration to America violent disputes broke out among all the associations. Similar in cause to those that occurred in south China, some were continuations of ancient clan feuds, othere stirred up by ethnic differences, commercial rivalries, and geomantic occurrences. As a result of these eruptions, as well as the growing anti-Chinese sentiment in California, and the formation of two secret societies—the Kwong Duck and Hip Yee tongs—in San Francisco, the leaders of five of the district associations agreed to form a new organization composed of the representatives of their five associations, called the *Chung Wah Kung Saw* [Kongsi] (Meeting Hall of the Chinese People), and known in America as the "Chinese Six Companies." This occurred sometime in the late 1850s.[56] In New York City, the Chung Wah Kung Saw was established in 1884, composed of the Ning Yeung, Lun Ning Yeung, and Lun Sing associations. The latter is made up of six associations which, together with the Ning Yeung, compose the community-wide association in San Francisco.[57] In smaller cities where Chinatowns were established, such elaborate hierarchic organizations did not arise. Instead, smaller Chinatowns developed organizational and community control through four clans that were united into functional equivalents of the consolidated district associations.[58]

Through the establishment of the supra-district association, the Chinese achieved a national organization connecting each urban colony with all the others. As the Chinese moved East after 1880, they established district associations and Chung Wah Kongsi in the larger cities. An examination of the names, structure, and organization of these territorial associations reveals that they are branches of the original clans or kongsis established in San Francisco.[59] Moreover, in times of stress, these associations called on one another for financial help and advice. When difficulties became very severe, the Chinese imperial government might be asked to become the supreme arbiter or mediator.

Membership and Structure of the Territorial and Supraterritorial Associations

Chinese immigrants to America were members of the district organization representing the dialect or area from which they came. Membership, said to be "voluntary," was in fact obtained by association agents, who met each arriving ship and enrolled every Chinese passenger in the appropriate organizations.[60]

Whether all Chinese arriving in America were enrolled as members of territorial associations is difficult to ascertain. This question has been shrouded in secrecy or clouded by confusion because of its political significance during the latter part of the nineteenth century. Those groups that sought to exclude Chinese from America attempted to prove that most Chinese immigrants were "coolies," involuntary "contract laborers," undesirable because of their servile condition.[61] To demonstrate the validity of their propositions, they argued that the Chinese were unwilling members of the district associations, organizations which, they asserted, controlled the importation of the Chinese to America. Conversely, those who sought to prevent the restriction of Chinese immigration, or who, after restriction, sought to show the folly of that legislation, asserted that membership in the kongsis was voluntary.[62]

The "companies," themselves, were unwilling to disclose their membership. They did so occasionally, but only for purposes of contradicting exaggerated estimates of the number of Chinese in America. However, since they did argue that their membership was equivalent to the number of Chinese in America, it is safe to assume that they did enroll all Chinese immigrants, or believed that they did.

There are other pressing reasons to assume that the vast majority of Chinese immigrants were enrolled in their respective district associations. The Chinese were enrolled as they debarked from the ships, but they would probably have joined the associations anyway. Only through the associations of clan and district could a Chinese find a secure place in the new, strange country. Not speaking English, not conversant with American law, customs, or usages, and in no position to learn them, the Chinese immigrant did as his brethren in China who migrated from the country to the strange city: he enrolled in that association which represented his home, village, or lineage. Especially for the Chinese immigrant to America, there was an economic advantage in being enrolled with his clan and district association. Most Chinese were *assisted immigrants,* owing passage fare in the form of an indenture. Among other things, the association was a loan and credit agency; as such, it was vitally interested in the name, occupation, and whereabouts of its clients and debtors. Lastly, note that the association was a benevolent, protective, and mutual aid society, ministering to those needs of the Chinese immigrant about which the dominant society neither inquired nor cared. With the almost immediate advent of anti-Chinese agitation in California, the Chinese would understandably turn to those institutions which could shelter him and stand between him and the hostile outside world.

Each of the district associations maintained a "hall" in San Francisco, and if its members were concentrated for any length of time in another area, a second hall was established there. In 1868, the headquarters of the Sam Yup Company were in a hall on Clay Street above Powell in San Francisco, another building on Sacramento Street, and the association rented offices for its commercial transactions on Commercial Street. The Kong Chow Association built a hall in 1854, at a cost of $40,000. Yeung Wo men met at a beautiful house on the southwestern slope of Telegraph Hill, but in 1868, were building a new hall on Sacramento Street. They also had houses in Sacramento and Stockton. The Ning Yeung company owned a three-story brick edifice on Broadway, between Kearney and Dupont (Grant Avenue). The Hop Wo, only eight years in existence by 1868, rented a building on Commercial Street. In 1865, the house of the Hakka people of the Yan Wo Association burned to the ground. They then purchased a building on Dupont Street between Washington and Jackson.[63] The offices of what Reverend A.W. Loomis called the "Congress of the six companies"; that is, of the Chung Wah Kongsi, were located at 709 Commercial Street in 1868.[64] In New York City, the "Chinese Public Hall" was located on Mott Street,[65]

> ...the heart of the Chinese community...and very appropriately, at its center are the rooms of the Chinese Masonic Lodge, or benevolent social club, an organization which illustrates a peculiar phase of Chinese civilization and really, to a greater extent, represents law as well as social enjoyment and charity to the Americanized Celestial.[66]

The economic and commercial significance of the district associations is exhibited in the expense and ornateness that went into their construction. The Kong Chow house cost $40,000 to build in 1854. The Yeung Wo ui-kun was a marvelous structure:

> Upon the southern side of Telegraph Hill, which shields on the north the harbor of San Francisco from the ocean winds which rush through the Golden Gate, a large frame structure stands conspicuous, which is evidently of Chinese architecture, yet different in its appearance from the Chinese dwellings in the city. The front is painted light blue, ...A pair of lions, carved in wood, guard the wide doorway. Above and on either side of it are guilded tablets, with upon each an inscription of several large Chinese characters. This building has often been referred to as a temple. But its object is not religious. It is an ui-kun (pronounced ooy-koon), or Company House. The large tablet over the door tells, if English alphabetic letters be employed for the Chinese characters, the name of the company: Yeung Wo, Ui-kun. The two

perpendicular inscriptions on either side are poetical lines. They read:

Tseung kwong ham man li sui hi p'o t'ung you
May the prosperous light fill a thousand leagues.
May the auspicious air pervade mankind.[67]

The inside of the Company House testified to its pervasive influence:

> Upon entering the house by the side door, an uncovered area, in accordance with the Chinese custom, is seen in the middle, from which rooms open toward the front and rear, and stairs ascend on either side to the second story. The smaller apartments below are occupied by the managers and servants of the Company. The largest room or hall is pasted over with sheets of red paper covered with writing. These contain a record of the names and residence of every member of the Company, and the amount of his subscription to the general fund. The upper story and the attic, with the outbuildings on the upper side, are, it may be, filled with lodgers, nearly all of whom are staying but temporarily, on a visit from the mines, or on their way to or from China. A few sick persons be on their pallets around, and a group here and there discuss [over] a bowl of rice, or smoke and chat together. In the rear is the kichen. All is quiet, orderly, and neat.[68]

Similarly, the New York City ui-kun was, apparently, devoted to benevolence and fellowship.

> It is to a certain extent Masonic in its methods, and it is therefore difficult for an American to get a very thorough insight of its government. What is apparent on the surface is an earnest of the beneficient character of its work. It furnished, in the first place, a pleasant meeting room, in which to while away a leisure hour. Chinese games are played. The Chinese orchestra practices here; and the poetical contests, which are a feature of Chinese amusements are held in its large meeting rooms. . . .[69]

The governmental structure of the territorial associations appears to have been nominally democratic. The "New Rules of the Yeung Wo Ui-kun," translated into English and published in 1868, but adopted in 1854, require the association to

> . . . elect three managers; one to attend to the internal affairs, one

> to attend to the business with Americans, and one to be the treasurer; and these shall mutually assist one another.
>
> A faithful servant shall be hired as a house servant and porter.
>
> A committee of four shall be elected as counselors, who shall be allowed five dollars a month for refreshments.[70]

Other officers of significance were the collectors appointed to secure money owed to the companies and a secretary. Officers were expected to be honest, but, after one association official secretly sold the company house and escaped to China with the proceeds, the rules were changed to specifically require an honest administration.

> The monthly accounts of the company shall be counted till the last Sunday of the month, on which day the committee shall audit and publish them by a placard.
>
> The treasurer shall never retain more than four hundred dollars in his own hands at one time; and his deposits in the treasury, and payments from it, shall be under the supervision of the committee of four. The treasury shall have four different padlocks, and each of the committee shall have one key. The treasurer must always be present when money is taken out.
>
> Shoud the committee employ collectors who have not been duly elected by the company, they shall be held responsible for them. The accounts of the company shall be closed with each month, that there be no private or wasteful employment of its funds; and in cases of fraud a meeting shall be called and the offender expelled. When inadvertent mistakes are made in accounts, the committee shall state them to be so on oath, and the corrrection shall then be entered. Managers or committeemen whose accounts are not clear shall be censured. None but the managers shall have common access to the account books. Payments in behalf of the company shall, when made at their house, be endorsed by the committee, but in the interior they may be made by the proper manager alone. . . . Managers who may be remiss in attending at the office shall be mulcted to twice the amount of their salary for the time lost.[71]

The Sz Yup Association also attempted to ensure the honesty of its elections and officials.

> The agents of the company are elected. At the election all the districts must have a voice. If from any one no members are present, it must be heard from. The agents must be men of tried

> honesty, and are required to furnish security before they enter upon their office. Their election is for the term of six months, of the expiration of which they must give notice and call a new election. But if they be found faithful to their duties, they are eligible to reelection.[72]

Officers sometimes were paid a low salary, but in other instances received nothing. In the Sz Yup Association

> the officers...are a secretary and treasurer, at a salary from eighty to one hundred dollars [per month], and a servant and messenger, whose salary is about forty dollars. Besides these salaried officers, each company has a sort of advisory committee of about half a dozen men of acknowledged wisdom and integrity, who are consulted in all affairs of importance.[73]

However, the low salary was more than compensated for by the prestige, power, and opportunities that election meant to a Chinese merchant.[74]

The political structure of the Chung Wah Kongsi, the supradistrict organization, was also nominally democratic but only within the elaborate framework of the district structure. Although all Chinese were represented by the Chung Wah Kongsi, not every Chinese was permitted to elect the officers of this communal "government." Instead, elections were carried out by the officers and leaders of the several district associations. In New York the elections were carried out by the Ning Yeung and the Lung Sing associations according to the following rules:

> The four officers—president, Chinese secretary, English secretary, and office boy—are elected alternately by the Ning Young and the Lun Sing Associations. For instance, if the president and the Chinese secretary are to be elected by the Ning Young Association, the English secretary and the office boy must be chosen by the Lun Sing Association, and vice versa.[75]

Election and postelection activities in early New York City have been described by the American ethnologist, Stewart Culin.

> In New York City the merchants support a guild hall, entitled the *Chung Wa Kung Sho*, or Chinese Public Hall, which is in charge of a person of approved character, who is elected to the office annually, This custodian has been described in our newpapers as

> the "Mayor of Chinatown." He really has no executive powers, but quarrels are laid before him for settlement, and he acts as a peacemaker in the Chinese community. He receives a salary of $30 per month and the profits on the incense and candles sold to worshippers in the guild hall. The election for this office is held just before the Chinese New Year, when the new manager is driven in a carriage to each of the Chinese shops. His deputy precedes him on foot, with a bundle of red paper visiting cards about a foot in length. Two of these, one bearing the name and the other the official title of the new manager, are handed to each store-keeper.[76]

The government of the San Francisco Chung Wah Kongsi was organized during the first decade of Chinese immigration to the United States. The supreme organ representing Chinese interests in America, it had original jurisdiction in matters affecting the Chinese immigrant population as a whole, and appellate jurisdiction over matters referred by family or district organizations.

The administration of the San Francisco Chung Wah Kongsi consisted of a board of presidents, a board of directors, a permanent secretary, and a sergeant at arms.

The board of presidents, composed of the presidents of each of the separate member district associations, served as the supreme executive of the organization. The Six Companies revised its constitution in 1930, but the board of presidents remained the executive body. With the exception of the president of the Yan Wo association, which represents such a small proportion of the Chinese in America, each president serves as chairman of this board. However, another rule required that the president of the Ning Yeung Association, representing forty-six percent of the total membership of the seven district groups, must serve as chairman of the board every other term. A term consists of two months; hence, the Ning Yeung president serves as chairman six months out of the year.[78]

According to Hoy, the presidents of the district associations during the first half-century of Chinese immigration were "usually the pick of the scholarly men from the various districts. Since scholars were a rarity among the California Chinese, the district associations, in most instances, had to import scholars from the native hearths for their presidents."[79] However, the merchant class among the Chinese in America had come to replace the scholars by the turn of the century.[80]

These officers can be differentiated according to their ability to speak English. Most nineteenth-century Chinese were not able to speak English and often unable to read Chinese. The few who were more knowledgeable in Chinese probably achieved leadership positions. At the turn of the century, leadership had passed into the hands of China-born persons possessing derivative citizenship in the United States, that is, persons whose fathers claimed to have been in San Francisco before the San Francisco fire of 1906 and whose claims to United States citizenship could not be challenged in the absence of the naturalization records destroyed in the conflagration. This group knew more English and more Chinese than the preceding generation. By the second world war the leaders were drawn from the third generation, knew more spoken and written English than their fathers or grandfathers, but had only verbal fluency in Chinese. In most cases their eduction had not gone beyond high school.[81]

The district association often found themselves in conflict with the secret societies of Chinatown. As a result of their rivalry, a partially successful attempt was made to exclude secret society members from the presidency of the district associations.

> In the early years of the Six Companies there was an unwritten law that no member of a fighting Tong may become president of the organization, or a member of the board of presidents. This unwritten law was adhered to throughout the history of the organization, except for one period in the eighties when the fighting Tongs, then at the height of their power, succeeded in breaking this rule by conniving with the district associations. This rule remained broken for about a quarter of a century before the district association gained it back. Today this unwritten law is still in effect.[82]

The difficulties involved in holding the office of president, or serving on the board of presidents, were sometimes so great that the offices went begging. In some instances officials of the Chinese government or distinguished visiting scholars were prevailed upon to accept these positions.

> In the early years only learned and reputable gentlemen were elected to office, quite often against their wishes, for there was a heavy burden to shoulder, with little or no compensation. For instance, it is generally known among the Chinese that the Reverend Lu Two died of a heart attack as president of the Association, while trying to patch up a Tong war. He had already done a great deal to improve the general condition of his countrymen. The task, however, was thankless. Then came an interval when no one would accept the presidency. Finally the people had

> to plead with the late Dr. Chan Fuan-Chang, at the time a student at Columbia University, to accept the honor. Such a distinguished man as K.S. Fung, before he became Vice-Consul in New York, was English secretary to the Association for years.[83]

Elections to these offices were troubled by corruption. Candidates often vied with one another in buying the votes of important Chinatown merchants. In one election in New York City in the mid 1920s, votes were allegedly being sold for fifty dollars and, after these irregularities had been exposed, the winning candidate reimbursed his opponent.[84] In the same election a dark horse candidate for the office of English secretary, discovering that his defeat was certain, advised his supporters to sell his votes at whatever the market would bear. The result was election of an English secretary who needed an English interpreter.[85]

The board of directors of the Chung Wah Kongsi, which must be distinguished from its board of presidents, was elected according to a system of proportional representation.

> In apportioning delegates to the Chinese Six Companies to serve as members of its board of directors, each district company is allowed one representative, per 500 members in its roster. . . .

The executive secretary of the Chung Wah Kongsi, called Tung See, acts as liaison officer and business agent for the association. In New York City there were two Tung See, an English and a Chinese secretary. The office rotated among the different district associations annually. The Yan Wo Association is excluded because of its small membership, while the Ning Yeung is permitted to select one of its members for this office every other year.[86]

|| SECRET SOCIETIES

Introduction

The third principal type of association found among overseas Chinese is the secret society. Like clans and kongsis, the secret societies found in Chinese settlements in Southeast Asia and North America are overseas versions of an institution that originated in China.[87]

Kwangtung and Fukien provinces have been the locus of operations for secret societies since the time of the Sung Dynasty (960-1279) and perhaps for even longer.[88] It is not entirely clear why secret societies flourished in an area also noted for its high degree of lineage solidarity and for interlineage feuds. One plausible suggestion is that two distinct alignments of conflict cut across one another in southeastern China.[89] In some instances lineages were ranged against lineages in age-old "blood" feuds or in disputes over property, women, or other matters; in other instances lineages, or segments of them, and pariahs, outcasts, criminals, and rebels were united in common hostility to the state. The latter combination required that a basis for association be established beyond agnation. Secret societies grew up in response to the demands for an organization that could represent resistance to the state by people ordinarily divided by blood, local, and linguistic ties.[90] The rebellious associations did not succeed in ending the older traditional conflicts. Rather, the interlineage feuds counterbalanced the rebellions against the state led by the secret societies. Indeed, as one British officer observed, southeastern China was sometimes paralyzed into inaction by the cross-pressures imposed by its dual structure of conflict:

> All the neighboring country was in a state of chronic anarchy; the villages, towns, and hamlets were all walled, and each seemed prepared to fight with its neighbor. There were villages, certainly not a quarter of a mile distanct from each other, both surrounded with distinct walls about sixteen to twenty feet high. . . .
>
> Strange as it may appear, this desperate state of clannish anarchy has proved to be the sole safety of this part of China from worse anarchy at the hands of the rebels. The people were so given to quarreling that they would not agree to fight.[91]

The Triad Society: Its Origins and Activities

The most important of the many Chinese secret societies, and the one most often associated with rebellious and rapacious activities in southeastern China and overseas, is the Triad Society, or the Heaven-and-Earth League, or Hung League.[92] Its origins are shrouded in myth and mystery. According to the most widely accepted account, the society is said to have been organized by Buddhist monks whose monastery had been burned by order of Ch'ing Emperor Yung-Ching (1723-36), even though monks from that monastery had been instrumental in former Emperor Khang-hsi's (1661-1722) suppression of the Eleuth Revolt. The five surviving monks gathered a band of rebellious peasants and supporters of the Ming pretender around them and pledged themselves to "overthrow the Ch'ing and restore the Ming."

The hastily organized band of revolutionaries fought one battle against imperial tropps to a pyrrhic victory in 1734, and then decentralized into five major and five minor lodges in Fukien, Kwangtung, Yunnan, Hunan, Hupeh, and Chekiang provinces.[93] In 1841, the censor of Hukwang (that is, Hunan and Hupeh provinces) memorialized the emperor that the head lodge of the Triad Society was at Fukien and the second at Kwangtung.[94]

For the most part, the Triad Society took advantage of the sporadic peasant revolts which arose in southeastern China from 1787 until the close of the nineteenth century to increase its own wealth or enhance its own power.[95] At times, chapters of this secret society were employed by wealthy landlords to prevent the enserfed peasantry from translating their accumulated grievances into armed violence.[96] In the Yao Revolt of Kwangsi, Kwangtung, and Hunan peasants in 1832, the Triad Society fought at first for, and then against, the rebels and even acted as a mediator between the rebels and the government.[97] In the Taiping Rebellion, a true revolution aiming at a fundamental reconstruction of Chinese society, the Triad Society allied temporarily with Hung Hsiu-ch'uan, the proto-Christian revolutionary leader, but later deserted his ranks, made war upon his armies, and took advantage of the chaotic conditions to capture and govern for several months both Amoy and Shanghai.[98]

Though it continued to profess its anti-Manchu ideology and its intention to restore the former Ming rulers, the Triad Society appears to have demeaned itself by the nineteenth century. It was proscribed alike by the imperial government and the Taiping revolutionaries. The Imperial Penal Code imposed its ban on all associations of persons unrelated by blood or marriage and specifically designated the Triad Society as beyond the pale:

> All persons who, without being related or connected by intermarriage, establish a brotherhood or other association among themselves, by the ceremonial of tasting blood and burning incense, shall be guilty of an intent to commit the crime of rebellion. . . . The punishment of the brotherhod associated by the initiation with blood, which exists in the province of Fo-kien, shall be conformable to the aforementioned regulations. . . . All those vagabonds and disorderly persons who have been known to assemble together, and to commit robberies, and other acts of violence, under the particular designation of *Tien-tee-whee*, or The association of Heaven and Earth shall, immediately after seizure and conviction, suffer death by being beheaded.[99]

The leader of the Taiping Godworshippers, Hung Hsiu-ch'uan, denounced the Triad Society for its anachronistic devotion to the Ming cause as well as for its vulgarity and impiety:

> Though I never entered the Triad Society I have often heard it said that their object is to subvert the Tsing and restore the Ming dynasty. Such an expression was very proper in the time of Kang-he when this Society was at first formed, but now, after the lapse of two hundred years, we may still speak of subverting the Tsing, but we cannot properly speak of restoring the Ming. At all events when our native mountains and rivers are recovered a new dynasty must be established. How could we at present arouse the energies of men by speaking of restoring the Ming dynasty? There are several evil practices connected with the Triad Society, which I detest. If any new member enter the Society, he must worship the devil and utter 36 oaths; a sword is placed upon his neck, and he is forced to contribute money for the use of the Society. Their real object has now become mean and unworthy. If we preach the true doctrine, and rely upon the powerful help of God, a few of us will equal a multitude of others. I do not even think that Dun pin, Woo ke, Kung-ming, and others famous in history for their military skill and tactics, are deserving much estimation—how much less these bands of the Triad Society?[100]

Membership in Secret Societies

By their very nature, Chinese secret societies are hidden from public gaze; hence, little accurate information is available on the social sources of their membership. Moreover, what information there is comes either from opponents of the societies or from the dramatic and colorful, but often inaccurate, accounts by romantic chroniclers of the Chinese scene. Nevertheless, keeping in mind the shortcomings of the data, some suggestions can be made about the social composition of the secret societies. In general these societies drew their members from

1. Impoverished peasantry
2. Criminals and outcasts
3. Expellees from clans
4. Disappointed office seekers
5. Rebels and revolutionaries
6. Persons hungering after adventure and excitement

In times of relative prosperity and when rebellious activity was at a low ebb, the secret societies were composed of "rural poverty-stricken peasants and urban unemployed workers and scoundrels."[101] But in periods of widespread distress, agricultural depression, and general unemployment and dissatisfaction, the ranks of the societies would be swelled by those moved to action by disappointment and resentment. "It is known that the [Triad] Society includes among its members persons in almost every rank of official and private life throughout the provinces..."[102] "All classes are permitted to join; and amongst the Triad Society there are at present mandarins of low degree, police runners, soldiers, merchants, brothel-keepers, gamblers, and needy characters of every description..."[103]

In addition to the impoverished peasantry, two other classes seem to have been especially attracted to the secret societies: ostracized clansmen and disappointed office seekers.

The clan rules of the lineage communities in southeastern China forbade membership in, or aid to, secret societies.[104] But among the punishments meted out for violators of the clan rules was expulsion from the clan itself. Such an expulsion might take one of four forms: excision from the ancestral record, expunction from the genealogy, exclusion from the clan group, and expulsion from the lineage community. All acts forbidden by clan rules—and these numbered in the hundreds—carried the potential penalty of expulsion.[105] Ostracism from the lineage community left the expellee bereft of kin and sources of aid, easy prey for robber gangs or cruel exactions by corrupt officials. It is not unlikely that such persons would join secret societies for protection and for revenge. One part of the ritual of the Triad Society gives us indirect evidence in support of this contention. The initiate is required to renounce all relations save those of the brotherhood:

> "Have you a father?" asks the catechist.
> "No!" the novice must reply.
> "Have you any sisters?"
> "No!"
> "Brothers?"
> "Only my brothers the Patriots."[106]

Furthermore, the ritually created brothers undertook many of the obligations of agnatic kinship.[107] A member promised not to marry, not to have sex relations with the widow of a fellow member; the widow of a ritual brother, like the widow of an agnate, was forbidden to marry or cohabit with members of the oath-bound fraternity. While the application of agnatic incest rules to oath-bound brotherhoods might have been designed to protect members' wives and daughters against the importunities of fellow members, it also re-created a fictive clan in place of the one to which an expellee had once belonged.

Frustrated office seekers, that is, those who failed to find a position in the imperial service, or, worse, who failed the qualifying examinations, frequently blamed their inability to obtain office or advancement in rank on the corruption of the examination system. One recent study suggests that the examination system was far less corrupt than its accusers claimed it to be,[108] but that during the Ming-Ch'ing periods the number of lower officers (Sheng-yuan) was inflated to a far greater extent than the number of higher offices. ". . . [T]he inflated number of Sheng-yuan resulted in a glut at the higher-level examinations and engendered an increasing amount of social frustration. . ."[109] Unsuccessful candidates sometimes took out their frustrations by writing book length satires on the examination system.[110] In other instances, the complaints, often irresponsible, led to the dismissal or imprisonment of examiners.[111] In still other cases, the disappointed candidates became demagogues inciting the peasantry to riot and revolt.[112] In support of the contention that the secret societies attracted these disappointed office seekers, it is to be noted that the first recruits of the revolutionary Godworshippers were village schoolteachers, that is, persons who had failed the higher examinations, and that Hung Hsiu-ch'uan himself had failed the imperial examinations three times.[113]

Secret societies also attracted to their membership those who found the legitimate avenues to wealth or power blocked or too slow to suit their ambitions.[114] Most of the gambling, robbery, and prostitution of China and overseas Chinese colonies were under the direct or indirect control of secret societies. A career in a secret society promised at the minimum a brief, exciting life of local glory—for the local peasantry revered their bandits as Robin Hoods[115]—and at the most the establishment of a new dynasty:

> A man, originally a mere thief, burglar, or highwayman, whose sole object was the indiscriminate plunder of all who were unable to guard against him, finds it possible in the state of general apathy to public order produced by continued oppression, to connect himself with a few fellow thieves, &c. and at their head to evade all efforts of the local authorities to put him down. As his band increases, he openly defies these authorities, pillages the local customhouses and treasuries, levies a tax on passing merchandise and a blackmail from the wealthier residents, but refrains from plundering anyone outright, and while, by exempt-

> ing the great bulk of the population from all exactions, he prevents the rise of a general ill feeling toward him, he, as the scourge of the oppressors, gains the latent or conscious sympathy of all classes. Now, these captains of bandits, whatever their origin, do not, it is true, while their followers amount merely to a few hundreds, choose to make themselves ridiculous or to rouse the general government to more serious efforts against them, by issuing dynastic manifestos or assuming the state of royalty. But when they began to count their followers by thousands, forming a regularly governed force they declare openly against the hitherto reigning sovereign, whom they denounce as a usurper. And from the very first, when merely at the head of a small band, no Chinese, acquainted with the history of his country, can refuse to see in such a man a possible, if not probable, founder of a dynasty. More than one Chinese dynasty has been founded by men like this; the Ming dynasty which preceded the present was so founded; and—what is really very important as an historical example—the greatest of all native Chinese dynasties, that of Han, was so founded.[116]

A recent study by a noted Sinologist asserts that, in medieval China, the formation of a new dynasty might take place through foreign conquest, through the intrigues of the gentry families, or through the success of a gangster-led peasant rebellion.[117] The latter was not at all uncommon. The form by which such a dynastic change could come about may be presented schematically:

> ***Stage 1***—For reasons which were not in all cases exactly the same, the economic conditions of the farmers in a certain, comparatively broad region became intolerably bad. Here and there small groups of despairing farmers left their villages and went into the mountains. They became "bandits." They lived in the mountains by robbing passersby and rich landlords. Normally the contacts with the village were upheld and a kind of symbiosis developed: the gang in the mountains received a certain sum from the nearest landlords and its food supply from the village, and as compensation the gang protected the village from the neighboring gang.
>
> ***Stage 2***—The gang increased its numbers and therefore had to extend its area of activity, coming into contact with the neighboring gangs. A fight between the gangs started, ending with the supremacy of one strong gang under a capable leader for the whole area.

> ***Stage 3***—The victorious gang increased again by incorporating the conquered gangs. Symbiosis was then impossible as there was only one large gang in the area. The landlords became alarmed and refused to pay. The gang was therefore forced to attack the nearest city. The government representative, informed by the landlords, took military precautions. The attack of the gang against the city may have ended with defeat, so that the large gang disintegrated and the play and counterplay of small gangs started anew. The attack may have also ended with a siege of the city; the government forces may not have been willing to fight for the government, but rather had sympathies for the gang. In such a situation the representatives of the government, the rich landlords and other gentry members in the city, had to make up their minds: either fight to the last, with death as the natural outcome when defeated; or surrender, in which case their lives would be spared, but they would be outlawed as "supporters of bandits." They could not back out from this choice.
>
> ***Stage 4***—The gang leader, after conquest of the city, had to conquer other cities in order to get supplies. He also had to defend himself against the now irritated government and its armies. Normally in such a situation he lacked experience and therefore had to ask gentry members who had surrendered to him to give advice. Upon advice the gang leader was induced to adopt the behavior and ways of the gentry, make himself a "general," "prince," or even "emperor,"—and a new dynasty came into being. If the gang leader really became an exponent of traditional gentry policy, the gentry were ready to collaborate with him unconditionally. If, however, the leader continued to behave as he did in the early part of his career—squeezing the rich, treating them as enemies or slaves, thinking only of the profit of his gang, and not of the administrators—he soon ran into difficulties. These became the greater, the more territory he conquered: he and his gang could not be everywhere, or control everything; they had simply to rely on the old gentry for lack of trained personnel.[118]

The remarkable successes of a few highly touted bandits probably served as encouragement to adventurers and disgruntled office seekers to try to emulate their achievements. In the ninth century A.D., the disappointed scholar Huang Ch'ao, took over the leadership of an agrarian revolt, coordinated the various rival gangs into a formidable peasant army, and eventualy crowned himself emperor (880 A.D.). His success was short-lived, however. He was beset by dissension from within his ranks and attack from without. Eventually he fled the capital. Other rebels fought over his seat of power.[119]

The founder of the Ming Dynasty began life as the son of an impoverished peasant, turned to religion as a Buddhist novice, and later jointed a band of vagabonds and bandits. His "Red army" was at first a proletarian rebel force.

Other celebrated bandits, though not quite so successful as Emperor Chu Yuan-Chang, could also serve as attractive models. Ma Wei-hsing, who had been a bandit during his young manhood, and who had been so poor and illiterate that he did not even know his parents' names, eventually rose to the rank of brigade general in the imperial troops. Chang Chia-hsiang had been a robber before becoming provincial governor. Lo Ssu-Chu, "a highwayman, repeated jailbreaker, and even a onetime cannibal," rose to great prominence during the campaign against the White Lotus Sect—another secret society—in the years 1796-1802. Liu Ming-ch'uan had been a salt smuggler before becoming governor of Formosa and Fukien.[120] Koxinga (Cheng Ch'eng-kung), Ming general and allegedly a member of the Triad Society, expelled the Dutch from Formosa, ruled over that island for several years, and sent his raiding fleet of junks as far as the Philippine Islands.[121]

Chinese Secret Societies in the United States

The first Chinese secret society in the United States was formed in 1852, in San Francisco, by a disaffected member of the small Mock Clan.[122] At this time the power elite of San Francisco's Chinatown was composed of five of the largest clans: Wong, Chin, Lee, Yee, and the Four Brothers. Of these, the Wong and Four Brothers clans were the most powerful. The members of these clans controlled the Chung Wah Kongsi, dispensing civil and criminal justice through the tribunals held by that organization. Resenting the inequities imposed by the more powerful clans, the small clans sought to organize along interfamily lines to break the power of the larger clans. When this stratgem failed, the smaller clans attempted to go outside Chinatown and use the American courts for settlement of their disputes. Here again, however, they were thwarted, for the larger clans exercised sufficient control over the court-appointed Chinese interpreters to ensure a poor representation of the rebellious clan. Mock Wah, upon the advice of a Chinese student, organized a fraternal order based neither on clan nor territorial lines.[123] He named the organization the *Kwong Duck Tong,* meaning "a broadening of the humane side of man." A fraternal oath bound the brothers to mutual protection and they dedicated themselves to wiping out clan despotism "by the judicious use of violence."[124]

There can be little doublt that the disputes arising within the various clan and "territorial" associations were causes for secret society formation. As has been pointed out, the early fifties marked a period of extreme social disorganization between and within the kongsis. It is from the ranks of the Sz Yup, who broke away from the Kong Chow Kongsi and ultimately were divided among the Nin Yeung, Sz Yup, Hop Wo, Shew Hing, and Yin Hoi associations,[125] that the vast majority of tong recruits came. The Sz Yup were emigrants from a folkish, rural, superstitious, and unsophisticated background that contrasted sharply with the Sam Yup peoples, who had come from around Canton.[126] These differences bred dissent.

It is unclear which secret society was formed next in San Francisco. William Hoy, Otis Gibson, and H.H. Bancroft speak of the Hip Yee (or Hip Ye) Tong's existence as early as 1852. Stewart Culin points out that the "Hip I T'ong" was the name of a branch of the "I Hing", that is, the Triad Society in America. On the other hand, Eng Ying Gong and Bruce Grant designate the next secret society formed after the Kwong Duck as the Hip Sing Tong, started as a national body by Num Sing Bark, "a radical." Culin believes that the Hip I should be distinguished from the Hip Shin T'ong, the latter being known only for its vice activities. Mary Coolidge argues that tong organization in the United States did not occur until after 1863,[127] and fierce rivalry rather than allegiance marked the relations between tong chapters. Presumably her point of view rests on her assumption that tongs were established by renegade members of the Triad Society who had fled from China following the defeat of the Tai Ping rebels. Apparently she also assumes a direct relationship between the Tai Ping Rebellion and the Triad Society. According to Professor C.N. Reynolds,[128] the Kwong Duck, Hip Yee, and Don Sung tongs were all rival chapters of the Triad Society established by members fleeing from the Tai Ping Rebellion. Originally the three groups were united as the Sam Hop Tong and later were known as the Gee Kung Tong. The Kwong Duck Tong, according to Reynolds, was the "mother tong" from which the others sprang.[129] At any rate, the Hip Sing Tong began with fifty members and still exists today.[130]

In the same year that the Hip Sing group organized, still another secret society was formed. Members of the Yee Clan, under the leadership of Yee Low Dai, having failed to win a property dispute adjudicated before the tribunal of the Six Companies, founded the Suey Sing Tong, forcibly took over the piece of property, and then, in order to shame the vanquished, gave the property to their district association.[131] The Suey Sing Tong was marked by fierce internal strife. At length, its left and right wing factions withdrew, forming respectively, the San Suey Ying and Suey On tongs. Still later, in a struggle with the Yee Clan, the On Yick group broke away; in 1910, the On Yick Tong, small though it was, became the victor in a bloody battle with a "fong" of the Yee family association.[132]

The period from 1864 to 1892, appears to have been the time of the greatest number of tong formations.[133] Tongs spread to every major Chinese colony in the United States, and through the examination of their documents by Culin, definite evidence is available linking some of them to the Triad Society.[134] According to Culin, chapters of the Triad Society were instituted in San Francisco during and after the Tai Ping Rebellion. The head chapter was called the Chi Kung T'ong and subsidiary chapters were also establshed.[135] In San Francisco the subsidiary chapter was called Hip I T'ong. Actually, however, the national secret society in America was popularly known as the *I Hing*, or Patriotic Rising, but the chapters in different cities all had different names in accordance with the desired secrecy of the organization. In Chicago and St. Louis the organization was known as the Hung Shun T'ong.[136] In New York City, the name was the Lun I T'ong; in Philadelphia it was known first as the Hung Sung T'ong, later as the Sun I T'ong. According to Culin, a rival organization in Philadelphia, the Hip Shin T'ong, was not a branch of the Triad Society, but drew all its members from members of the latter. So significant was the I Hing in Philadelphia's Chinatown that Chinese there were distinguishable in accordance with membership or non-membership in the Sun I T'ong.

In New York City the Triad Society chapter, variously known as the Lun I T'ong or Chee Kung T'ong, reigned supreme in its control over gambling and other forms of vice until the appearance of the On Leong T'ong in 1899, under the leadership of Tom Lee. The On Leong group wrested control from the Chee Kung and grew to be the most powerful secret society on the East Coast. In the 1930s, the organization changed its name to the On Leong Merchant Association.[137]

Tong organizations flourished in the latter three decades of the nineteenth century, but the number of tongs in America began to decline during the third and fourth decades of the twentieth century. C.N. Reynolds, who compliled a list of tongs from newspaper reports in California for two five-year periods (1912-1917 and 1919-1923) listed twenty tongs, although he suggests that some similar spellings might indicate the same organization.[138] In 1923, Nora Sterry claimed that only the Hop Sing and Bing Kung tongs operated in Los Angeles, while four others were to be found in other parts of the United States.[139] On the other hand, Leong Gor Yun counted fifty tongs in western America between 1917 and 1923.[140] Many secret societies disbanded, were wiped out, went bankrupt in tong "wars," or were absorbed into other tongs. According to Rose Hum Lee there were six tongs in the United States in 1960: Chee Kung, Hip Sing, Bing Kung, On Leong, Ying On and Sui Ying.[141] In 1960, Burton H. Wolfe, an investigative reporter, asserted that there were six tongs in San Francisco. In addition to the Hip Sing, Bing Kung, On Leong, and Chee Kung tongs, the Hop Sing and Suey Sing are listed, while the Ying On and Sui Ying are omitted.[142]

The surviving secret societies appear to have established geographical spheres of influence in the United States, in some instances marking defeat of all rival tongs in the area. In other Chinatowns, powerful secret societies still vie with one another for power.

The Chee Kung Tong occupies a special place in relation to the rest of the American tongs. It seems to have preserved its political and ideological character, despite the fact that is has been linked with vice and criminal activities. Culin at first doubted the reports which linked "I Hing" activity with the gambling and vice practices of the Hip Shin Tong.[143] A few years later he was, however, less sanguine with respect to the objects of Triad branches in America:

> It is not altogether sure that the I Hing itself has not degenerated into a mere blackmailing organization, as its lodge in New York City, the Lun I T'ong, is known to levy a monthly assessment of seventy-five cents on each lottery, and *fan t'an* table. The *Kung Sho*, or Public Hall, in New York City, however, which was founded by Chinese merchants, and furnished at their expense, is supported by a similar contribution of fifty cents per month, so that the amount paid to the Lun I T'ong may be regarded by the gamblers as a reasonable compensation for friendly offices.[144]

Gong and Grant, in a similar fashion, point out the universality of the Chee Kung Tong and further note that it included in its membership persons who were simultaneously members of other rival tongs.[145] Writing in 1936, Leong Gor Yun observed that

> the Gee Kung Tong (the Chinese Freemasons), being more political in nature, is definitely out of the Tong war picture in this country, but off and on, in Cuba and Canada, it still engages in bitter conflicts with the Kuomintang (The Nationalist Party). It is doubtful whether this Tong will ever recover its vitality in the United States, since a majority of its members are old, and its membership line is never clearly drawn.[146]

Reynolds also comments that "the Chee or Gee Kung Tong, or Chinese Freemasons of the World, is not a society of the same stamp as the Hip Sing Tong or the Bing Kong Tong, and the same might be said of the Sam Yip Tong."[147]

Despite the dynastic ideology of the Chee Kung Tong, it is not clear that its members were particularly interested in the politics of their Chinese homeland. Indeed, Culin noticed a great variance between the political beliefs of the society, and the real interests of its members, whose social background and economic position left little time for political activity.

> It is among the latter class [that is, the Sz' Yup] who largely outnumber the others that the order of the I Hing is recruited. A simpleminded people, usually from remote agricultural districts, they have passed their early life in extreme ignorance and poverty. When they come to America they are not unwilling to join a powerful society of their countrymen, through which they are promised protection against the oppression of their own people and the terrors of a foreign land. Little thought of sedition or opposition to Tartar domination fills the mind of the average emigrant; he is only anxious to obtain the small sum of money regarded by him as a fortune, and return home to pass the rest of his life peacefully with his children around him.[148]

Culin further observed that, while the lower-class, rural, Sz Yup people, who made up the bulk of I Hing membership, were less interested in politics than in their immediate, personal economic situation, the middle-class merchant element supported the imperial government in China and was loath to join anti-Manchu secret societies. He suggested, however, that continued exposure to American political institutions might influence the merchant class to favor a more democratic regime in China, so that "the I Hing, nursing the spirit of discontent, may someday play no unimportant part in the revolution, political and social, which contact with foreign civilizations must inevitably bring about in China.[149]

To a certain extent, Culin's prognostication became fact. Although evidence is scanty, there is reason to believe that Dr. Sun Yat Sen obtained support for his revolutionary activity in China from American as well as other overseas Chinese. Sun himself wrote that "the overseas Chinese were the mother of the Chinese revolution."[150] American Chinese laborers willlingly helped finance the revolution of Sun and the Chinese Freemasons, that is, the Chee Kung Tong, pledged him their support.[151] But in 1927, when Chiang Kai-shek "betrayed the revolution, and so caused a split in the Kuomintang at home and abroad,"[152] the Chee Kung Society withdrew its support of Chiang's government. In Cuba and Canada the Chee Kung Tong engaged in bitter conflicts with Kuomintang elements.[153]

Membership in Chinese Secret Societies in the United States

Unlike the district associations, the secret societies have never made their membership public. Their very secrecy would, of course, forbid this. It is, therefore, impossible to gauge the exact membership. However, from information about tong activities, it is safe to say that membership was large enough and strong enough to cause the kongsis to see in the tongs a dangerous rival for power in Chinatown.

Moreover, the tongs recruited their adherents from the largest single linguistic-territorial group among the Chinese emigrants: the people of the Sz Yup. These people were the poorest, least-educated, most folkish, and most disaffected of the Chinese arriving in America. Their district association became fragmented shortly after arrival, and after numerous internal and interdistrict disputes, was refused membership in the federation of the Chinese district associations, the Chung Wah Kongsi.

Sz Yup disaffection with other Chinatown kongsis is certainly a factor in swelling the secret societies' ranks with its people. In south China and in southeastern Asia, secret societies recruited among the alienated, the aggrieved, and the angered. As Maurice Freedman has suggested, there is a dual structure of conflict that affects lineage and clan solidarity, village-state relations, and the activities and membership of the secret societies in south China.[154]

The dual structure of conflict was also a feature of overseas Chinese social organization. That the founders and charter members of the Chinatown tongs were in some way socially or personally marginal to the rest of Chinese society is indicated in their biographies.[155] A number were unsuccessful businessmen in Chinatown. Wong du King joined the Bing Kung Tong in Los Angeles only after failing in business there. Mock Wah, the founder of the Kwong Duck Tong, was from a small clan unable to secure a fair hearing before the Chung Wah Kongsi tribunal, dominated by the larger clans. His only chance for effective countervailing power was to organize a society based neither on clan nor territorial background. Num Sing Bark, who established the Hip Sing Tong, was an alienated intellectual who had turned to storekeeping in Chinatown. Formerly a scholar and teacher in China, he blamed his failure on the tyrannical domination of the clans over business in Chinatown. Yee Low Dai, a leader of the powerful Yee clan, had a falling-out with his fellow kongsi members over a piece of property. Unable to secure a beneficial hearing before the Chung Wah Kongsi, he formed the Suey Sing Tong with members of his own clan and won his dispute by force. Gaut Sing Dock, born in San Francisco and educated in China by his merchant-father, became a tong assassin after witnessing the ease with which members of more powerful clans cheated the small Hong Clan out of its business. Unable to collect the outstanding debts owed to his father, and unable to pay off his father's obligations, Gaut Sing Dock joined the Hip Sing Tong as a gunman in 1896. Later he affiliated with the Hip Ying, Hop Sing, and five other secret societies. He was eventually killed in New York by Yee Toy, a rival gunman, in 1911. His secret society career had lasted fifteen years.

Other secret society members apparently suffered from melancholia because of the absence of women in their lives. One fine example is Hong Ah Kay, notorious gunman for the Suey Sing Tong. Educated in China with money provided by his merchant-father in San Francisco, Hong watched helplessly as the family business was taken over by members of a more powerful clan. Unable to obtain redress before the Six Companies' Tribunal, Hong's father fell ill and died; Hong Ah Kay's attempts to revive his father's business failed. Shortly thereafter he suffered another, more emotional setback. Hong fell in love with a Chinese prostitute, held in bonded servitude by a tong. The woman, realizing the hopelessness of their situation, and fearing for Hong's life should their affair continue, committed suicide. Completely distraught after these two traumatic events, Hong joined the Suey Sing Tong, in which he became well-known for both his marksmanship and his melancholia. In the feud between the Suey Sing Tong and the Wong Clan, Hong is alleged to have assassinated seven Wongs. He was arrested, and after an abortive attempt at escape, convicted of murder and hanged.

Two leaders of various chapters were disaffected intellectuals. Kung Ah Get of the San Jose chapter of the Hip Sing Tong was a self-educated, though illiterate, orator of considerable eloquence. Ton Back Woo, another Hip Sing leader, was an erstwhile military student in China who had passed only the first of his examinations before emigrating to New York City. After a successful career in secret society circles he returned to China.

The American chapters of Chinese secret societies seem to have recruited their members from the same classes as did their counterparts in China and Southeast Asia. The alienated, disaffected, rebellious, and adventure-seekers in Chinatown were attracted to the secret societies. But, unlike the situation in mainland China, a tong bandit could not hope to become an emperor. He might, however, participate from afar in uprisings, rebellions, and revolutions in China. The first Chinese Republic was founded with the financial assistance of overseas Chinese tongs.

Membership in Chinese secret societies was not always voluntary. One of the earliest descriptions of a Triad initiation ritual in the Straits Settlements reports in gruesome detail the torture and eventual execution of a Chinese who refused to join the society.[156] Secret societies have been accused of participating in smuggling of Chinese from Formosa, Hong Kong, and mainland China into the United States and Canada. Once landed, it is alleged that the illegal immigrant is obliged to serve the societies or persons who arranged his entry.[157]

Moreover, although membership in a secret society *often* meant that one had disavowed membership in one's kongsi or renounced allegiance to one's clan, it did not *necessarily* mean so. It appears that the alignments of conflict in Chinatown between clans, kongsis, and tongs were not stable and shifted frequently. At one time a man might fight together with his clan brothers against another clan. At another time the same man might align himself with his secret society against a kongsi or with his kongsi against another clan, kongsi, or secret society. A member of the Yee Clan who was also president of the Hip Sing Tong is said to have shot to death his tong brother for murdering his clan brother. In the course of the trial of a "ring" smuggling heroin into the United States it was disclosed that one of the accused, an official of the Hip Sing Tong, had also served as an officer of the Chung Wah Kongsi.[158] In New York's Nassau County, when "the leader of Chinatown," a respected businessman, court interpreter, and occasional secret agent fo the federal government, was indicted and unsuccessfuly tried for smuggling aliens, it was revealed that he had served as a peacemaker between the Hip Sing and On Leong tongs during the 1930s.[159]

The interrelationships between clans, kongsis, and secret societies are complex but fraught with conflict. In the next chapter I shall attempt to weave together this web of conflict and group relations in order to describe the communal process that facilitated a disharmonious solidarity in Chinatown.

NOTES

1. Maurice Freedman, *Lineage Organization in Southeastern China* (London: University of London, Athlone Press, London School of Economics, Monographs on Social Anthropology, no. 18, 1958), pp. 2-8;
   Freedman, *Chinese Family and Marriage in Singapore* (London: Her Majesty's Stationery Office, Colonial Research Studies, no. 20, 1957), pp. 15-20, 68-99;
   Freedman, "Migrants and Associations: Chinese in Nineteenth-Century Singapore,";
   Ju-K'ang T'ien, *The Chinese in Sarawak* (London: London School of Economics Monographs on Social Anthropology, 1953), pp. 21-34.
2. Sir George Thomas Staunton, *Tsa Tsing Leu Lee: Being the Fundamental Laws, and a Selection from the Supplementary Penal Code of China* (London, 1810), p. 114. quoted in Freedman, *Lineage Organization*, p. 4n.
3. Information from interviews.
4. Rose Hum Lee, "The Decline of Chinatowns in the United States," *American Journal of Sociology*, March 1949, pp. 422-32.
5. The early Chinese settlement was made up largely of familial groups. Unlike modern Chinatown where each family group is represented by a family organization, the social and economic activities of a familial group were centered first around a merchandise store. These businesses were the forerunners of the family association. Persons arriving from China were met at the waterfront by representatives of their respective stores. Living accommodations were furnished to the newcomers until they were sent for by relatives living elsewhere or placed in private industry.

   San Francisco Chinese Chamber of Commerce, *San Francisco's Chinatown, History, Function, and Importance of Social Organization*, (San Francisco, 1953), pp. 2-3.
6. Stewart Culin, "China in America: A Study of the Social Life of the Chinese in the Eastern Cities of the United States," A paper read before the American Association for the Advancement of Science, Section of Anthropology, at the thirty-sixth meeting, New York, 1887, (Philadelphia, 1887), p. 10.
7. Ibid.
8. S.F. Chinese Chamber of Commerce, *Chinatown*, p. 3.
9. Mary Chapman, "Notes on the Chinese in Boston," *Journal of American Folk-Lore*, October/December 1892, p. 324.
10. Interview materials. See also Yun, *Chinatown Inside Out*, pp. 55.

11.el does not mention the "fourth brother," Chao.

15. Yun, *Chinatown Inside Out*, p. 59;
    S.F. Chinese Chamber of Commerce, *Chinatown*, p. 3.
16. S.F. Chinese Chamber of Commerce, *Chinatown*, p. 3.
17. Ibid., pp. 3-4.
18. Culin, "Customs of the Chinese in America," *Journal of American Folk-*

Lore, III; 10, July/September 1890, p. 192.

19. S.F. Chinese Chamber of Commerce, *Chinatown*, p. 4.
20. Translated by Reverend A.W. Loomis, "The Old East in the New West," *Overland Monthly*, I (October 1868), p. 362.
21. Ibid., p. 362.
22. Ibid.
23. S.F. Chinese Chamber of Commerce, *Chinatown*, p. 4.
24. Ibid., p. 3.
25. Interview with Gilbert Woo, editor, the *Chinese Pacific Weekly*, San Francisco.
26. S.F. Chinese Chamber of Commerce, *Chinatown*, p. 3.
27. Freedman, "Immigrants and Associations," pp. 39-41.
28. Ibid., p. 43.
29. Ping-ti Ho, *Aspects of Social Mobility in China, 1368-1911*, mimeographed (New York: Columbia U.P., forthcoming, pp. 226-227.
30. D.J. Macgowan, "Chinese Guilds or Chambers of Commerce and Trades Unions," *Journal of the Royal Asiatic Society, North China Branch*, August 1886, pp. 133-92.
31. Wynne, *Triad and Tabut*, pp. 260.
32. Macgowan, "Chinese Guilds," p. 136.
33. Ibid.
34. Ibid., pp. 137-38.
35. Ibid., pp. 139-45.
36. Ibid., pp. 170-78.
37. Ibid., pp. 182-83.
38. Remarks of Reverend Ernest Faber, "Proceedings," *Journal of the Royal Asiatic Society, North China Branch*, December 1886, p. 253. Compare the similar attitudes toward, and processes of, litigation in Chinese villages described in
    Martin Yang, *A Chinese Village, Taitou, Shantung Province* (London: Kegan Paul, Trench, Trubner, 1948), pp. 165-72;
    C.K. Yang, *A Chinese Village in Early Communist Transition* (Cambridge: Technology Press, 1959), pp. 97-98;
    Hui-chen Wang Liu, *The Traditional Chines Clan Rules* (Locust Valley: J.J. Augustin, 1959), pp. 36-46, 154-58.
39. Culin, *The Religous Ceremonies of the Chinese in the Eastern Cities of the United States*, An essay read before the Numismatic and Antiquarian Society of Philadelphia, April 1, 1886 (Privately printed, Philadelphia, 1887), p. 3.
40. Culin, "Customs of the Chinese in America," p. 192. See also
    Ball, *Things Chinese*, p. 207;
    Wynne, *Triad and Tabut*, pp. 260-64.
    For fruther differences between the Sam Yup and Sz Yup groupings in America see the section of this paper on "Debt, Labor, Mercantile, and Judicial Control."
41. "Letter of the Chinamen to His Excellency, Governor Bigler. San Francisco, Thursday, April 29, 1852," *op. cit.*, pp. 32-34.

42. In traditonal Chinese thinking the status hierarchy is ranked in descending order: (1) scholars, (2) farmers, (3) artisans and laborers, and (4) merchants. Actually merchants had been acquiring higher status in China since the sixteenth century. See Ho, "Social Mobility in China," *Comparative Studies in Society and History*, June 1959, pp. 330-59.
43. See Milton L. Barnett, "Kinship as a Factor Affecting Cantonese Economic Adaptation in the United States," *Human Organization*, Spring 1960;
Willmott, *Chinese of Semarang*, pp. 116-19;
Skinner, *Leadership and Power*, pp. 1, 6-7, 10-12, 172-76.
44. Culin, "China in America," pp. 10-12.
45. William Hoy, *The Chinese Six Companies*, (San Francisco: Chinese Consolidated Benevolent Association, 1942), p. 2;
Allan Warrington, "The Formation and Organization of the Chinese Companies: 1849-1854."
46. Hoy, *Chinese Six Companies*, p. 2.
47. Ibid., p. 2;
Loomis, "The Six Chinese Companies," *Overland Monthly*, September 1868, p. 224.
48. Hoy, *Chinese Six Companies*, p. 3.
49. Ibid., pp. 4-5, 17.
50. Hoy, *Chinese Six Companies*, pp. 4-5;
Loomis, "The Old East," p. 225.
51. Freedman, *Lineage Organization in Southeastern China*, p. 116n.
52. Hoy, *Chinese Six Companies*, p. 5.
53. Ibid., p. 6.
54. Ibid., pp. 12-14.
55. Ibid., p. 8; see also
S.F. Chinese Chamber of Commerce, *Chinatown*, p. 5.
56. Hoy, *Chinese Six Companies*, pp. 28, 59-62.
57. Yun, *Chinatown Inside Out*, pp. 6-9.
58. Lee, "Decline of Chinatowns in the United States," p. 156.
59. But see Culin: "Complete autonomy exists in all the Chinese communities in the East. The Six Companies exercise no authority whatever, and there is little intercourse or sympathy with the consular and diplomatic representatives of the Chinese government." But in the same article Culin points out, "In New York City the merchants support a guild hall, entitled the *Chung Wa Kung Sho*, or 'Chinese Public Hall'. . . ." Apparently Culin did not realize that the term *Six Companies* was the American appelation for Chung Wah Kung Saw. "Customs of the Chinese in America," pp. 193-94. Moreover, according to Leong Gor Yun, the New York group registered with the Peking government in 1884. *Chinatown Inside Out*, p. 28.
60. Testimony of E.J. Lewis. *Chinese Immigration: Its Social, Moral, and Political Effects*, report to the California State Senate of Its Special Committee on Chinese Immigration (Sacramento: 1876, 1878), p. 109 (hereafter referred to as *Chinese Immigration*).

61. U.S. Congress, Senate, Joint Special Committee to Investigate Chinese Immigration, 44th Cong., 2d sess., February 27, 1877, S. Rept. 689 (hereafter referred to as Sen. Doc. 689), pp. 83-109.
62. For the argument see Mary Coolidge, *Chinese Immigration,* (New York: Henry Holt, 1909), pp. 41-55, and *passim;*
Otis Gibson, *The Chinese in America,* (Cincinnati: Hitchcock and Walden, 1877), pp. 13-24, 45-62, 333-44;
Loomis, "Six Chinese Companies," pp. 221;
William B. Farwell, *The Chinese at Home and Abroad,* (San Francisco: A.L. Bancroft, 1885);
Sen Doc. 689, p. 17, 93.
63. Loomis, "Six Chinese Companies," pp. 224-25.
64. Ibid.
65. Culin, "Customs of the Chinese in America," p. 193.
66. Allan Forman, "Celestial Gothan," *The Arena* VII (1893), pp. 620-21. These curious comparisons and designations of Chinese institutions are typical of nineteenth-century American writings on the subject.
67. Speer, "Democracy of the Chinese," *Harper's Monthly,* vol. XXXVII, no. 222, November 1868, pp. 844-45.
68. Ibid.
69. Forman, "Celestial Gotham," p. 621.
70. "New Rules of the Yeung Wo Ui-kun," trans. Speer, *op. cit.,* pp. 845-46. The Sz Yup company also employed three executives. "Sze Yap Company," *loc. cit.*
71. "New Rules of the Yeung Wo Ui-kun," trans. Speer, pp. 846.
72. "Sze Yap," in Speer, p. 847.
73. Ibid., pp. 53-65.
74. Leong Gor Yun, *Chinatown Inside Out,* pp. 53-65.
75. Ibid., p. 33.
76. Culin, "Customs of the Chinese in America," p. 193.
77. Hoy, *Chinese Six Companies,* pp. 10-11.
78. Ibid., pp. 10-11, 27-29.
79. Ibid., p. 11.
80. Ibid., p. 12. See also
Leong Gor Yun, *Chinatown Inside Out,* pp. 28-29.
81. This classification was obtained from a letter in the author's private file from Professor Lee of Roosevelt University.
82. Hoy, *Chinese Six Companies,* p. 11.
83. Leong Gor Yun, *Chinatown Inside Out,* pp. 28-29.
84. Ibid., p. 33.
85. Ibid., p. 35.
86. Hoy, *Chinese Six Companies,* pp. 29-30.
87. A common but erroneous belief is that secret societies are an autochthonous product of Chinese life in America. For this view see "The Why and Wherefore of Chinese Tongs," *Current Opinion,* November 1922, pp. 621-22. For the relationship between mainland and Malayan secret societies see

Leon Comber, *Chinese Secret Societies in Malaya: A Survey of the Triad Society from 1800 to 1900,* (Locust Valley: J.J. Augustin, 1959), pp. 1-31.

88. Eberhard, *History of China,* pp. 60-61.
89. Freedman, *Lineage Organization in Southeastern China,* pp. 114-25.
90. A similar situation can be discerned in thirteenth- and fourteenth-century Europe. On the one hand, manors in their entirety—lord or abbot, serfs, villeins, (or free village peasants) and bondsmen—were ranged against one another in age-old feuds, or disputes over property or other matters. On the other hand, the freeman, villeins, and bondsmen of different manors forsook their oaths of loyalty and service on occasion and rose up in "class" revolts against the nobility. In the latter conflicts the "looser elements of society" often joined in. The revolts of the poor were, however, too sporadic and disorganized to check or balance the power of the nobles. See G.G. Coulton, *Medieval Village, Manor, and Monastery* (New York: Harper "Torchbooks," 1925, 1960), pp. 121-39, 345-67.
91. John Scarth, *Twelve Years in China* (Edinburgh, 1860), pp. 66-67, 52-53, quoted in Freedman, *Lineage Organization in Southeastern China,* pp. 8, 124.
92. These are but some of its many names. It is known in Malaya and China as the Three United Society, the Three Dots Society, Pure Water Society, Pair of Daggers Society, Small Dagger Society, Big Sword Society, and Copper Coins Society. Comber, *Chinese Secret Societies in Malaya,* p. 1. In the United States it is called the Chee Kung Tong, the I Hing Society, and the Chinese Freemasons.
   Culin, "The I Hing, or 'Patriotic Rising,' A Secret Society Among Chinese in America," *Proceedings of the Numismatic and Antiquarian Society of Philadelphia,* November 3, 1887, pp. 51-58;
   Culin, "Chinese Secret Societies in the United States," *Journal of American Folk-Lore* III, (Janaury-March 1890), 39-45.
93. Such at any rate is the account in captured Triad documents (translated by Schlegel, *Thian Ti Hwui,* pp. 1-20, and accepted by most authorities). See
   Comber, *Chinese Secret Societies in Malaya,* pp. 1-32;
   Victor Purcell, *The Chinese in Southeast Asia* (London: Oxford, 1951), p. 29;
   Freedman, *Lineage Organization in Southeastern China,* pp. 121-22.
   However, it is certain that the society, or one like it existed before the originating date, 1734. Schlegel himself, in different parts of his monumental work, dates the founding of the society in A.D. 845 as a result of the persecution of Buddhist monks, but claims it to be the Eastern branch of world freemasonry, originating in antiquity. Culin, who translated Triad documents captured in Philadelphia, doubted its relationship to freemasonry and showed that this branch of the society derived its existence from a tale, "The Story of the Banks of a River," and dated its establishment sometime in the eleventh century A.D. "The I Hing," pp. 56-57. Secret societies were known to exist in the Han

Dynasty (206 B.C.-A.D. 23). The half-Chinese pirate, Koxinga (1624-62) is said to have been a member of the Triad Society, thus dating its existence before 1734. Comber, *Chinese Secret Societies in Malaya*, p. 44.

94. Freedman, *Lineage Organization in Southeastern China*, pp. 119-20.
95. Among the most important of these are the revolt of the Formosan branch of the Triad Society against the local government in 1787; the rebellion in Sun I Prefecture, Kiangsi Province, in 1809; the rebellion against the governments of Kwangtung and Kiangsi in 1817; the Yao Revolt in Kwangsi, Kwangtung, and Hunan provinces in 1832; and the Tai P'ing Rebellion in Kwangtung and, later, much of south China from 1850 to 1864; and the uprising in the Yu Forest, Kwangsi Province, in 1898. Comber, *Chinese Secret Societies in Malaya*, pp. 19-31.
96. John K. Fairbanks, *The United States and China* (Cambridge, Mass.: Harvard U.P., 1958), p. 329.
97. Ultimately the Triad Society rejoined the rebels only to be deserted by them after an especially lucrative raid and left to face the severe counter attack of the government forces alone. Comber, *Secret Societies in Malaya*, p. 22.
98. See Meadows, *Chinese and Their Rebellions*, pp. 151-52;
Comber, *Chinese Secret Societies in Malaya*, pp. 22-28;
Teng Ssu-yu, *New Light on the History of the Tai Ping Rebellion* (Cambridge, Mass.: Harvard U.P., 1950), p. 28;
G. Hughes, "The Small Knife Rebels (An Unpublished Chapter of Amoy History)," *The China Review*, vol. I, no. 4, 1872-1873;
Wynne, *Triad and Tabut*, pp. 62-63;
Freedman, *Lineage Organization in Southeastern China*, p. 122.
99. Staunton, *Tsa Tsing Leu Lee*, pp. 546.
100. Meadows, *Chinese and Their Rebellions*, pp. 152-53.
101. Teng Ssu-yu, *History of the Tai Ping Rebellion*, p. 28.
102. "Oath Taken by Members of the Triad Society and Notices of Its Origin," *The Chinese Repository*, vol. XVIII, no. 6, 1849, p. 36, cited in Freedman, *Lineage Organization in Southeastern China*, p. 121.
103. C. Gutzlaff, "On the Secret Triad Society of China, Chiefly from Papers Belonging to the Society Found at Hong Kong," *Journal of the Royal Asiatic Society of Great Britain and Ireland* VIII (1846); 364, cited in Freedman, *Lineage Organization in Southeastern China*.
104. Liu, *Traditional Chinese Clan Rules*, p. 175.
105. Ibid., p. 217-63.
106. Stewart Culin, "The I Hing, or 'Patriotic Rising,' A Secret Society Among the Chinese in America," *Procedures of the Numismatic and Antiquarian Society of Philadelphia for the Years 1887-1889*, November 3, 1887, p. 55.
107. Freedman, *Lineage Organization on Southeastern China*, p. 123.
108. Ho, *Social Mobility in China*, pp. 209-11.
109. Ibid., p. 200.
110. See, e.g., Wu Ching-tzu, *The Scholars* (Peking: Foreign Langauge Publishing House, ca. 1751, 1957), and esp. the Forward by Wu Tsu-

hsiang, pp. 9-25.

111. Ho, *Social Mobility in China*, pp. 210-11.
112. Meadows, *Chinese and Their Rebellions*, pp. 27-28.
113. Ibid., pp. 117-18;
Flavia Anderson, *The Rebel Emperor* (London: Gollancz, 1959).
114.
> In general, then, there was available within the actual confines of Nanching social life one channel to wealth and prominence, namely, banditry, racketeering, or illegal traffic such as opium and gambling. But this channel was open only to a daring and lucky few, and only in times of disturbance when the revolutionary process had weakened the forces of government and law.

Yang, *Chinese Village*, p. 126.

115. See Yung-teh Chow, "Life Histories: the Gangster, Captain Yang," in *China's Gentry*, ed Hsiao-tung Fei (Chicago: U. of Chicago, 1953), pp. 242-268.
116. Meadows, *Chinese and Their Rebellions*, pp. 117-18.
117. Wolfram Eberhard, *Conquerors and Rulers: Social Forces in Medieval China* (Leiden: E.J. Brill, 1952), pp. 52-64.
118. Ibid., pp. 62-63.
119. Ibid., pp. 55-61.
120. For these examples see Ho, *Social Mobility in China*, pp. 235-36.
121. See Comber, *Chinese Secret Societies in Malaya*, pp. 44-45;
Victor Purcell, *The Chinese in Southeast Asia*, (London: Oxford University Press, 1951);
Ho, *Studies on the Population of China*, pp. 163-64;
C.P. Fitzgerald, *China: A Short Cultural History* (London: Cresset Press, 1935), pp. 486-87;
Schlegel, *Thian Ti Hwui*, p. 4.
122. This account is from Eng Ying Gong and Bruce Grant, *Tong War!* (New York: Nicholas L. Brown, 1930), pp. 25-59; See also
Coolidge, *Chinese Immigration*, p. 407.
123. It is interesting to point out that Gong and Grant consistently deny that the tongs originated in China. In fact, the authors of this romantic, journalistic, and dubious "history" of tongs in America claim that the tong idea was copied from California vigilance committee organization. Gong was the retired president of the Hip Sing Tong. Grant was a police reporter for an unnamed New York newspaper. For purposes of this study attempts have been made wherever possible to cross-reference the data from this source.
124. Gong and Grant, *Tong War!*, p. 28.
125. From an interview with a well-informed Chinese immigrant, Q.L. Lang, I am informed that one source of friction among the Sz Yup was the status differences between those Sz Yup from Toyshan, and those from Sun Wui. The former district was very poor, depended entirely on imports for survival, and its people lived on salt fish. Sun Wui, on the other hand, was an agricultural district, producing rice, melons, vegetables, and the "best tangerines in China." Local pride among the Sun Wui

people caused them to look down upon the poverty-stricken people from Toyshan.

126. Culin, "Religious Ceremonies of the Chinese," p. 3;
Culin, "Customs of the Chinese in America," p. 192;
Culin, "The 'I Hing'," p. 54. See footnote 134.

127. Hoy, *The Chinese Six Companies*, pp. 8-9;
Gibson, *Chinese in America*, pp. 136-39;
Bancroft, "Mongolianism in America" in his *Essays and Miscellany* (San Francisco: History Co., 1890), p. 356;
Culin, "The 'I Hing'," pp. 53-55;
Culin, "Chinese Secret Societies in the United States," p. 42;
Coolidge, *Chinese Immigrants*, p. 407;
Gong and Grant, *Tong War!*, pp. 29-30.

128. C.N. Reynolds, "The Chinese Tongs," *American Journal of Sociology*, March 1935, pp. 612-23.

129. Reynolds cites a Chinese manuscript for his authority on the subject: Cheh Yeh Long, "The Chinese Social Organism" (translated from Japanese into Chinese by Chu Chia Tsing), pp. 279-94. The names Sam Hop, Gee Kung, Ghi Hin, and so forth, which are found in America, are similar to those that appear in Southeast Asis as branches of the Triad Society. See
Wynne, *Triad and Tabut*, pp. 67;
Comber, *Chinese Secret Societies in Malaya*, pp. 291-93.

130. Gong and Grant, *Tong War!*, pp. 29-30.

131. Ibid., pp. 31-32.

132. Ibid., pp. 34, 194-202. The fong was the Yee Mor Kai Tong.

133. Reports of the Industrial Commission on Immigration. *Chinese and Japanese Labor in the Mountain and Pacific States*, vol. 15, part IV, 1901, p. 762.

134. I have repeatedly cited the works of Culin in this paper. His ethnological reports rank with the work of Schlegel in the Dutch East Indies. Cognizant of Schlegel's pioneering efforts in clarifying the nature of Chinese secret societies, Culin examined secret society documents captured in Philadelphia and compared them with the documents Schlegel had examined in Batavia. Culin definitely established the Triad origins of the Chinese secret societies in America. Unfortunately, because of their obscurity, few writers on the Chinese have examined his work. In addition to those already cited, see
Culin, *The Gambling Games of the Chinese in America*, Publications of the University of Pennsylvania, Series in Philology, Literature, and Archaeology, vol. I, no. 4, 1891;
"Chinese Games with Dice and Dominoes," *Report of the U.S. National Museum, Smithsonian Institution*, 1893, pp. 489-537.

135. The following is from Culin, "The 'I Hing'," pp. 51-58; Culin, "Chinese Secret Societies in the Unied States," pp. 39-43. "I Hing" was one of the five branches of the Triad Society set up in southeastern China after 1734.

136. The designation Hung Shun T'ong is a clear indication of Triad relationship. *Hung Shun T'ong* means Hall of Obedience to Hung. In Malaya Comber and other authorities found branches of the Triad Society also called Hall of Obedience to Hung. Culin, "Chinese Secret Societies in Malaya," p. 275.
In Malaya and in the United States many other names were used to camouflage the secret society's real object. In Philadelphia, the Hung Shun T'ong was incorporated in accordance with American law as the Roselyn Beneficial Association on July 7, 1888. Culin, "Chinese Secret Societies in the United States," pp. 39-40.
137. Robert Wells Ritchie, "The Wars of the Tongs," *Harper's Weekly*, August 27, 1910, pp. 8-10;
Leong Gor Yun, *Chinatown Inside Out*, pp. 66-84;
Gong and Grant, *Tong War!*, pp. 147-69;
Burton H. Wolfe, "Chinatown U.S.A.: The Unassimilated People," *The California Liberal*, February 1960, pp. 1, 3-5.
138. Reynolds, "Chinese Tongs," p. 620.
139. Nora Sterry, "Social Attitudes of Chinese Immigrants," *Journal of Applied Sociology*, July/August 1923, pp. 325-33. This estimate is probably low.
140. Leong Gor Yun, *Chinatown Inside Out*, p. 71.
141. Lee, *Chinese in the United States*, pp. 161-72.
142. Wolfe, "Chinatown U.S.A.," p. 4.
143. Culin, "The 'I Hing'," p. 53'
Culin, "Chinese Secret Societies in the United States," p. 42.
144. Culin, "The Gambling Games of the Chinese in America," p. 14.
145. Gong and Grant, *Tong War!*, pp. 149-50.
146. Leong Gor Yun, *Chinatown Inside Out*, pp. 72-73.
147. Reynolds, "Chinese Tongs," p. 620.
148. Culin, "The 'I Hing'," p. 54.
149. Ibid., p. 58.
150. Quoted in Leong Gor Yun, *Chinatown Inside Out*, p. 136.
151. Ibid, p. 138. See also
Comber, *Chinese Secret Societies in Malaya*, pp. 30-31, 270.
152. Leong Gor Yun, *Chinatown Inside Out*, p. 142.
153. Ibid., pp. 72-73.
154. Freedman, *Lineage Organization*, pp. 114-40.
155. I have here undertaken to generalize without much data. The brief life histories from which the following observations are drawn are taken from Gong and Grant, *Tong War!* previously cited. Gong's and Grant's thumbnail biographies are scattered throughout their book, and they draw no conclusions from them. The life history method is, of course, not unusual in sociological analysis. It has been employed extensively in the studies of the Japanese Americans during World War II. See
Dorothy Swaine Thomas and Richard Nishimoto, *The Spoilage* (Berkeley: University of California Press, 1952);
Leonard Broom and John Kitsuse, *The Managed Casualty* (Berkeley:

University of California Press, 1956).

156. Munshi Abdullah bin Abdul Kadir, *Hikayat Abdullan bin Abdul Kadir Munshi (The Story of Abdullah)* (Singapore: Methodist Publishing House, 1907), pp. 220-28, summarized in Comber, *Chinese Secret Societies in Malaya*, pp. 53-56.

157. Department of Justice *Press Release*, December 27, 1959, 5 pp., (mimeographed);
San Francisco *Examiner*, December 31, 1957, p. 5;
Vancouver *Sun*, May 24, 1960, p. 1; May 25, 1960, pp. 1, 32; May 26, 1960, p. 1; May 27, 1960, p. 1; May 30, 1960, p. 1; June 1, 1960, p. 4, 50; June 2, 1960, p. 37; June 3, 1960, p. 1; June 10, 1960, p. 1;
Toronto *Globe and Mail*, May 27, 1960; June 20, 1960, p. 1; June 11, 1960, p. 1; June 23, 1960, p. 1; July 7, 1960, pp. 1-2; July 16, 1960, p. 1; November 3, 1960, p. 1;
Toronto *Star*, July 4, 1960;
"The Chinese Racket," *Newsweek*, June 6, 1960, p. 63;
Lee, *The Chinese in the United States*, pp. 300-7;
Wolfe, "Chinatown, U.S.A.," *The California Liberal*, February 1960, pp. 1, 3-5;
New York Times, June 30, 1959, July 3, 1959, June 5, 1960, p. 68.

158. San Francisco *Chronicle*, January 13, 1959, April 30, 1959;
Portland *Oregonian*, January 15, 23, 24, 1959, February 3, 1959.

159. *New York Times*, June 30, 1959, July 7, 1959, June 5, 1960;
"Surprise Chapter in L.I. Man's Indictment," *Newsday*, June 30, 1959.

Power in Chinatown ‖7

‖ INTRODUCTION

The scope of community power is dependent on the extent to which the separate aspects of social life are coordinated under the control of a single ruler, group of rulers, institution, or group of institutions. In some cases, the holders of power are constrained to confine their authority to only those matters which are purely "political"; in others, power is stretched to include control over economic as well as political matters; in still others, the scope of domination is extended over such a wide range of matters that few if any activities can be said to be in the "private" sphere.

The power possessed by any person, group, or institution ultimately depends on the force which can be brought to bear in its support. Power is usually legitimated; that is, a consensus is established wherein ruler and ruled come to acknowledge the rightfulness of their respective positions. Nevertheless, rulers employ sanctions against malefactors and recalcitrants; often rulership coincides with a monoply or near monopoly on available means of coercion.

In what follows I describe the scope of Chinatown's institutions of domination and the available means of coercion in that community.

THE SCOPE OF COMMUNITY POWER

Within overseas Chinese colonies few activities of importance were left to operate outside the sphere of control of the central community institutions. Conflicts between associations frequently served to extend the domination of associations over a wider range of activities. In the course of their struggles each of the rival associations sought to bring more and more community activities under its aegis.[1] A Chinese kongsi might fall out with one of the tongs. As each sought to subvert, dominate, or destroy the other, more and more of the economic and community activities of one would be taken over or imitated by the other. So, for example, some kongsis began to operate houses of prostitution and gambling, and tongs to provide mutual aid for members.

MODES OF SANCTION AND COERCION

In Chinese as well as other ethnic communities, offices carry with them the power to invoke sanctions against the recalcitrant. The Amish minister can with his *nod*, bring about the dreaded *Meidung*—cutting off a miscreant from communication with any member of his congregation, family, friends, or neighbors.[2] The leaders of the Polish-American community ostracize their uncooperative members and expel the harmful ones, sometimes giving them over to the municipal police.[3] In both the European Jewish ghetto before the Emancipation and in traditional China are to be found the penultimate punishment of expulsion from the group, sometimes accompanied by false prosecution in the imperial courts, and the ultimate punishment of death.[4] In Chinatown the councils of the clans and above them those of the kongsis, and also those of the tongs, meted out punishments according to traditional ideas of justice. Civil suits were adjudicated; criminals were punished by expulsion, beatings, or death. In the United States American courts were used occasionally, to falsely prosecute enemies or to take blood vengeance.[5]

In Chinatown two major associations vied with one another for domination of the overseas Chinese community: the kongsis and the tongs. Clans vied for power within each and in their own commercial ventures. Control over immigration and its attendant matters—housing, employment, credit, remigration, burial and disposal of the dead—ensured kongsi authority over virtually the whole of the immigrant's sojourn. The secret societies catered to his recreational interests and sex needs and also provided an avenue for expressing antidynastic political sentiments and resentment against Chinatown's clan-kongsi power elite.

Both the kongsis and secret societies employed mercenaries to keep the peace, or, in times of open "warfare," to kill the enemy. Kongsi and tong executives also acted as war councils. Conflict was not a random affair in Chinatown. Like immigration, debt, and sex, it too was institutionalized.

INSTITUTIONALIZATION OF CHINATOWN ACTIVITIES

The California "Coolie Trade"[6]

Chinese immigration to the United States resulted from two simultaneous events: the collapse of the economy in southeastern China and the discovery of gold in California.

Except for the instances in which contract agricultural labor was brought to California in 1854, and forcibly introduced to the Arkansas and Mississippi valleys in 1869, the Chinese came to the United States through an indenture system, known as the credit-ticket system.

> Under the credit-ticket system Chinese brokers paid the expenses of the coolie emigration. Until the debt so incurred by the coolie was paid off, the broker had a lien on his services—a lien that might or might not be sold to a bona fide employer of labor... [T]he credit-ticket system...made possible the large emigration of Southern Chinese...which commenced during the fifties of last century and continued until it was gradually restricted or prohibited by the legislatures of [the United States, Canada, and Australia].[7]

From the only Chinese labor contract to America yet discovered, it appears that in 1849 American merchantmen negotiated with the *hongs* ("trading corporations") that operated at Canton and Shanghai to bring workers to California.

Agreement
Between
The English Merchant & Chinaman

The Tseang Sing Hong having hired the American Ship called the *Ah-mah-san* for voyaging purposes, the mechanics and labor-

> ers, of their own free will, will put to sea, the ship to proceed to Ka-la-fo-ne-a (California), and the port of Fuh-lan-sze-ko (San Francisco), in search of employment for the said mechanics and laborers. From the time of leaving Shanghae, the expenses of provisions and vessel are all to be defrayed by the head of the Tseang Sing Hong. On arrival it is expected that the foreign merchant will search out and recommend employment for the said laborers, and the money he advances on their account, shall be returned when the employment becomes settled. The one hundred and twenty-five dollars passage money, as agreed by us, are to be paid to the head of the said Hong, who will make arrangements with the employers of the coolies, that a moiety of their wages shall be deducted monthly until the debt is absorbed: after which they will receive their wages in full every month.
>
> The above is what we agree to, and there must be no different words; and as evidence, we enter into this contract, a copy of which, each party is to have.
>
> Done in the...moon of the 29th year of Taou Kwang (1849).[8]

The very first Chinese immigrants to California were not laborers, but merchants, who served as "headmen" for laborers coming soon after. As early as 1852, one of the two merchants who designated themselves as spokesmen for all the California Chinese was also a charterer of immigrant ships from China.[9]

An impoverished Chinese who desired to emigrate had to borrow the passage money. If fortunate, he might obtain an interest-free loan from his family. More than likely, however, he would borrow the money, at usurious rates, from brokers in the coastal cities. When he arrived in San Francisco, he would apply for more credit from the Chinatown traders. As the Chinese merchants explained to the governor of California:

> We will tell you how it is that the Chinese poor come to California. Some have borrowed the small amount necessary, to be returned with unusual interest, on account of the risk; some have been furnished with money without interest by their friends and relations, and some again, but much the smaller portion, have received advances in money, to be returned out of the profits of the adventure. The usual apportionment of the profits is about three tenths to the lender of the money, and rarely, if ever, any more. These arrangements, made at home, seldom bring them farther than San Francisco, and here the Chinese traders furnish them the means of getting to the mines. A great deal of money is

> thus lent at a nominal or very low interest, which to the credit of our countrymen, we are able to say, is almost invariably repaid.[10]

Putting together the credit methods described in the contract and in the letter written by the Chinese merchants, we have the essence of the credit-ticket system. The poverty-stricken Chinese emigrant secured passage money from a hong agent or broker, who in turn arranged for the return of the loan and interest through deductions from the wages of the borrower. It was of course necessary for the broker to have his client under surveillance and control in America. The kongsis acted for him in this capacity.

As pointed out earlier, the kongsis and the clan associations grew up around mercantile establishments in Chinatown. The Chinese letter to the governor of California, already referred to, was signed by two wealthy merchants, "For the Chinamen in California," indicating the ascendancy of a mercantile elite within the Chinese colony. The circumstances surrounding the indebted immigrants suggest that the credit-tickets were purchased by or consigned over to the kongsis, and that, dependent upon economic conditions in California, the kongsis raised or lowered the number of tickets they would accept, thus regulating the number of Chinese who could come to California.

Every immigrant ship was met by agents of the Chung Wah Kongsi, or, before its federation, by agents of the various independent kongsis. Each immigrant was interviewed, identified by district of origin, and taken to the appropriate ui-kun or "district house." On returning to the city in search of work, or to China, the remigrant also stopped at his ui-kun.

> The company building or Ui-Kun serves the purpose of the caravansary of eastern countries in olden times. To them the emigrants resort on landing from the ships, some servant of each Ui-Kun going off to meet and to give the necessary instructions to those on board who have come from the districts which are represented in his particular company. In the caravansary he is furnished a room in which to spread his mat in Oriental style, with water and facilities for cooking. This arrangement saves him much expense, and also protects him from those who otherwise might take advantage of his ignorance of the country, and its ways of doing business. Parties returning from the inland towns to embark for home often choose the company house instead of the boardinghouses; so also of parties who having finished one job of work in the country, return to look around for another.[11]

The Chung Wah Kongsi was accused of controlling Chinese emigration through its representatives in Hong Kong or Canton, and by restricting the flow of Chinese goods into Chinatown.

> [The Six Chinese Companies] deal with individuals through what is called the hospital at Canton where all their emigrants go, and they are recognized as an authority in relation to California matters. When. . .agitation was first started to arrest the influx of Chinese to this state, many of these intelligent members of the Chinese Six Companies agreed with intelligent Americans upon the necessity of preventing the Chinese from coming in the condition of public opinion at that time, and, as I understand, they telegraphed and communicated back to the hospital at Hong Kong, and from that radiated the information in various places that they sought to send them. The result was that it did prevent, to a very large degree, the incoming of these Chinese. They not only did that, but they went further. They not only wrote and recommended them not to come, but they recommended to their consignors in China, saying, "Do not send us any goods upon which there is more than a certain number of Chinese to come," as they feared, perhaps, that their goods would not be safe, or at all events it was a very effective mode of preventing the Chinese from coming to the extent that they were coming then.[12]

The Six Companies, in a statement addressed to the people of the United States, asserted that they had been unsuccessful in their attempt to restrict the immigration of Chinese.

> It is said that the six Chinese Companies buy and import Chinamen into this country. How can such things be said? Our six companies have, year after year, sent letters discouraging our people from coming to this country, but the people have not believed us, and have continued to come. the necessary expense of these poor newcomers is a constant drain upon the resources of those already settled here, so that the Chinese residents of this coutnry are also opposed to this Chinese emigration. But the capitalists of this honorable country are constantly calling for Chinese cheap labor.[13]

Apparently the demands for Chinese labor on the Pacific Coast and elsewhere strained the charitable and credit resources of the Chung Wah Kongsi. At times they too, wished to limit or restrict Chinese immigration but for different reasons than the American exclusionists.

Kongsi influence on immigration matters is evident in their contractual relationship with the steamship lines that carried passengers between China and America. The Chinese Six Companies had an arrangement with the Pacific Mail Steamship Company and with the Oriental Lines such that no Chinese would be permitted to return to China without presenting to the captain a voucher showing he had paid all his outstanding debts as well as a "departure fee" to the kongsis:

> A person proposing to return to China has been required, a certain number of days previous to sailing, to report his name to the Company to which he belongs, whereupon the books are searched to see whether all his dues are paid; also to see whether a person bearing his name has been reported to the Company as indebted to other parties. Notice is also sent to officers of the other Companies, and if the individual has been reported to them as indebted to any of their members, means are taken to prevent his leaving the country until he shall have made some satisfactory arragnement with his creditors.[14]
>
> The only power which the Companies claim, or which they try to exercise over the people, is the power to prevent any Chinaman from returning to China without a permit bearing the stamp of the Companies. The revenues of the Companies are derived mostly from these permits. But this power they could never exercise without the aid or partnership of the "Pacific Mail Steamship Company" and other steamship companies engaged in this carrying traffic. The Chinese Companies have shown more commercial shrewdness in this matter than the Americans have shown commercial ability.[15]

The "departure fee" required by the Chung Wah Kongsi survived long after the free immigration period, and despite the California legislation (1880) making it a misdemeanor for the steamship companies to require a debt voucher from retuning Chinese. When San Francisco's chief of police posted notice of the new state law in Chinatown, officers of the Six Companies responded with a notice of their own: if a Chinese did not pay his debts he would be sued in an American court. The chief of police arrested the printers of the latter notice and charged them with conspiracy to extort money. "As a result," Mary Coolidge reported in 1909, "the Six Companies were compelled to give up the agreement with the Steamship Company." Professor Coolidge could not find "any evidence that the Six Companies extorted money or went farther than *to make it very difficult* for a man to leave the country without paying his debts."[16] However, the practice of collecting a departure fee did not disappear after the legislation of 1880. As late as 1936, the Chinese in New York were bound by the revised bylaws of the Chung Wah Kongsi, one of which read:

> All Chinese who live in the district under the jurisdiction of this Association must each pay a port duty of $3 on leaving for China.
>
> Any store, organization, restaurant, laundry, or person that buys train and steamship tickets for anybody must report the case to the Association, so that the Association can collect the port duty in due time. Otherwise the Association must hold the store (organization, restaurant, laundry, or person) responsible and demand a $10 fine.
>
> Whoever leaves New York City for China without paying the port duty is to be stopped at any port or railway station and fined $30.
>
> The office boy of the Association must frequent the stores in Chinatown to see if any person is to leave for China, so that the port duty can be duly collected.[17]

In San Francisco, in 1942, the "departure fee" was still an important source of income for the Chung Wah Kongsi.

> The second source of Six Companies income consists of stipulated fees paid to it by all Chinese individuals over eighteen years of age who are on the point of making a trip to China. Only the indigent Chinese and those under eighteen are exempted from such payment. It is known as a departure fee, and is paid to the Six Companies in lieu of regular membership dues. The small amount of departure fee paid by each Chinese is not only used for the operations of the Six Companies, but portions of it are given for the support of the Six Companies-sponsored community native language school, the Chinese Hospital, and the Chinese Peace Society.[18]

In some instances Chinese laborers defied levies imposed by the Six Companies. As might be expected, specific complaints against the fee system were lodged, more often by debtors than creditors.

> The propriety and equity of this arrangement is commented on in quite a different strain by different parties. Creditors like it; bankrupts, and those disposed to be dishonest, speak against it.

> There is also a class who have become dissatisfied with the management of one or more of the companies, and who feel it a hardship to have to pay all their assessments....
>
> ...There are Chinamen in the country who profess to believe that their people would be as well cared for were there no Ui Kuns. These persons complain that the funds of some of the societies have not always been used in a legitimate way: they argue that the monthly expenses consumed in rents, salaries of officers, and taxes of common property call for too heavy an assessment upon the immigrant; and that the heavy arrears keep many from returning to their families who otherwise would long have had their eyes delighted with sight of home and native land.[19]

In 1874, several Chinese Christians who had withdrawn from the Six Companies discovered that their remigration to China was blocked because the Pacific Mail Stemship Company would honor no ticket unless the purchaser presented a debt-clearance voucher for the Six Companies, or paid nearly ten times the established price of the ticket. Only after white missionaries brought the matter to the attention of Congress did the steamship company allow the Christian Chinese to return to China, requiring them to present a character endorsement from the missionaries, and a stamped document from the Chinese Young Men's Christian Association.[20] The Chinese Young Men's Christian Association protested the kongsi control over remigration in a resolution sent to the Six Companies:

> We...respectfully represent to the Six Chinese Companies that we have formed ourselves into a Society...and we desire henceforth that whatever connection we may have been supposed to have with either or all of the Six Companies may cease; and we hereby release said Companies, individually and collectively, from all obligation to provide for, defend, or protect us in any way whatever, and in consequence of such release we ask to be excepted in any and all assessments, taxes, or charges of whatever kind which may be levied on other Chinese by these Societies.
>
> If any of our number is held to any of the Societies, by debts legitmately incurred, each individual will pay such indebtedness, and we ask to be left free to make our own negotiations for return to China without the interference or restraint of the Six Companies.[21]

That the Chung Wah Kongsi regarded their credit control over the passenger trade from China as essential to their authority in Chinatown is revealed in their desperate attempts to prevent any debtors from absconding. In 1876, the far-reaching measures which the companies would undertake were presented in the testimony of a sea captain involved in the China trade:

> All sailing vessels to China have conditions in their charters to take no Chinese but those supplied by the Companies. When loading a ship at Puget Sound for Hong Kong several years ago, I had many Chinese, some coming from hundreds of miles.... On inquiry I found they were escapees from these Companies' clutches. Many of them came to the ship at night to get passage, fearing that the Companies' agents might be on their track. The Companies' agents there, discovering that the escapees would probably go with me, came and chartered the whole passenger-capacity of my large ship at a much higher rate than offering here at San Francisco, and on conditions that I should take no other Chinese passengers than those furnished by them. They paid several thousand dollars to me in advance on the charter, and engaged to send several hundred, but on the day of sailing, no passengers, no charterers, were to be seen. Then I shipped the escapees as part of my crew, and took them to China; that is, such as had not been driven away or intimidated. I found that the whole Chinese part of my crew had been bribed by the Companies' agent there to intimidate and drive those men away. On the long voyage following, close and frequent examination of the escapees proved to me that they were not fugitives from justice, but from the Six Companies. All coolies returning to China complain of the extortions, deception, and arbitrary conduct of the Companies here. So ignorant do they remain of our laws, and so much do they rely on the power of the Companies, that they, when in China, more fearlessly...invest their own money got here in bringing back coolies, knowing like themselves that fearing persecution and by intimidation through ignorance they can enforce their contracts when made.[22]

The economic and political control of the kongsis over their indebted members remained so long as the credit-ticket system operated. Attempts to restrict the coming of Chinese laborers had little effect until federal exclusion was achieved in 1882. California's restrictive legislation was struck down by the courts as an unwarranted usurpation of federal power. The state's discriminatory legislation did not deter the Chinese from coming to California, thought it often violated the American Constitution. The federal government obtained few results from its petitions to the emperor of China to halt the coolie trade. Ultimately the United States Congress imposed a restriction on the coming of Chinese laborers, but even this did not close every door to immigration.[23]

Labor, Mercantile, and Judicial Control

Debt, Levies, and Charity

Many Chinese immigrants were in debt when they arrived, with their kongsi holding the credit-ticket. In addition to this initial debt, they were subject to special occupational taxes and fees and the vicissitudes of the cost of living in America. Borrowing from the kongsi was often a necessity. The kongsi collected an admission and a departure fee, assessed its members "voluntarily" on occasion, and, though ostensibly a benevolent association, did not offer services without charge. The officers of the kongsi were not above graft; kongsi corruption was a common complaint. Confronted by low wages and mounting debts, the immigrant watched his goal of returning to China recede into an ever-lengthening future.[24]

The most severe taxation imposed on the early Chinese immigrants was the California Foreign Miners' Tax[25] which, in one form or another, was collected from 1850 until 1870. Although designed to apply to all alien miners, the tax was particularly applied to the Chinese. In 1853, the Six Companies pointed out that the tax burden on the individual was so onerous that the various kongsis advanced the money to indigent Chinese.[26] Moreover, Chinese miners, unable to speak English or protect themselves, were often repeatedly taxed by the collectors, who derived their income from a portion of the collection.[27] The exactions were so severe that the Chung Wah Kongsi complained to the United States Congress:

> From the proceeds of a hard day's toil, after the pay for food and clothes very little remains. It is hard for them to be prepared to meet the collector when he comes for the license-money. If such a one turns his thoughts back to the time when he came here, perhaps he remembers that then he borrowed the money for his passage and expenses from his kindred and friends, or perhaps he sold all his property to obtain it; and how bitter those thoughts are! In the course of four years, out of each ten men that have come over scarcely more than one or two get back again. Among

> those who cannot do so, the purse is often empty; and the trials of many of them are worthy of deep compassion. Thus it is evident that the gold mines are truly of little advantage to the Chinese. Yet the legislature questions whether it shall not increase the license; that is, increase trouble upon trouble! It is pressing us to death. If it is your will that Chinese shall not dig the gold of your honorable country, then fix a limit as to time, say, for instance, three years, within which every man of them shall provides means to return to his own country. Thus we shall not perish in a foreign land. Thus mutual kindly sentiments shall be restored again.[28]

The author of this remonstrance was a San Francisco Chinese merchant. It is significant that, having recited the difficulties which arose from the miners' tax, he did not ask that the tax be rescinded, but, instead, that Chinese laborers be permited to make their attempts at gold-mining for only a fixed number of years and then be expelled from the country. Without presuming to know the motivation behind this request, it may be suggested that its anticipated results would be the insurance of kongsi control over the laborers. Few laborers could earn the required money in the time allotted and would remain thus, economically dependent upon the kongsis for passage money and for other expenses. The remonstrance goes on to urge not the relaxation of the tax collection, but rather more regularized patterns of collection with severe penalties for refusal to pay.

> Now we ask, first, that, in the collection of the licenses, each district shall be allotted to a certain man; that the boundaries of it shall be clearly defined; that other collectors shall not be allowed to come within them; that the day of each month when the collector will receive the license-money shall be previously published by placards; that on the payment of the four dollars he shall give the miner a written receipt as evidence, to prevent his being compelled to pay the money again; and that in the cases of those who are unable to pay, firstly, some extension of time; at the third demand, if neither they nor their security are ready to pay, then their property may be seized for the amount. There are none of us who would not gladly submit to such regulations as these. They would be just to both parties. And your losses from the miners running away or hiding their money would cease.[29]

The tax-collecting reforms proposed by the Chinese merchants did little to protect the individual miner, but they did ensure that the lending agency, that is, the kongsi, would not be doubly taxed by unscrupulous collectors. Moreover, it gave additional economic power to the kongsi since, by refusing a loan request, it could force a miner off his claim. The proposal that a miner be allowed only three years to make his fortune, when coupled with the severe penalties requested for nonpayment of taxes, suggests that the kongsis had only a limited interest in protecting the interests of the immigrant.

An immigrant's membership in a kongsi was virtually assured by his enrollment at dockside, but compared with his earning capacity, the initial registration fee was high. The kongsi held the immigrant's credit-ticket, and through its control of contracted labor, could deduct portions of the debt owed from his wages. Finally, the kongsi assessed its members for the costs of "wars" in which the kongsi was involved, and for expenses incurred in representing Chinese interests in the courts and legislature. For example, the Sam Yup-Yan Wo war cost the associations $40,000 and $20,000, respectively, a sum raised by a direct levy on all members.[30]

An entrance fee was collected from every Chinese eligible for membership in the kongsi. If he did not join, he lost his right to be heard in the settlement of disputes with other Chinese, to be represented in American court matters by the kongsi's attorneys,[31] and to be eligible for any of the kongsi's credit, benevolent, judicial, or social services. In short, he suffered a kind of communal "civil death." The rules of the Yeung Wo Kongsi, adopted in 1854, are emphatic on this point:

> People of the three districts of Heung-shan, Tung-yuen, and Tsang-ching are required to report themselves at the company's room; otherwise, the company will exercise no care for them in their concerns.
>
> The entrance fee shall be ten dollars; if not paid within six months, interest will be expected. These fees may be paid to collectors sent for the purpose into the Northern and Southern mines, in the fourth and tenth month of each year. No fees will be required of those proved to be invalids, or from transient persons. Receipts from payment of fees must be entered on the books and bear the company's seal. Disputes will not be settled between persons who have not paid the entrance fee. Members proposing to return to China must make the fact known to the agents, when their accounts will be examined, and measures will be taken to prevent it, if the entrance fee or other debts remain unpaid. Strangers to the agents of the company must obtain security in persons who will be responsible for their character and debts.

> Members leaving clandestinely shall be liable to a fine of fifty dollars; and the security for a debt for helping one thus to abscond shall be fined one hundred dollars.[32]

In addition to its regular charges, kongsis assessed members for special purposes and charged them for services rendered. In order to appeal the Geary Act to the United States Supreme Court, the Chung Wah Kongsi

> sent their emissaries through the length and breadth of the land proclaiming to the ignorant Chinese laborers that the enactment was in contravention of treaty stipulations, and they they intended to prove its illegality in the Courts of the United States. They raised a large sum of money—$200,000 it is estimated—for that purpose, by calling for pecuniary aid, or rather imposing a forced contribution of one dollar per head upon coolies and laborers, while merchants and other classes subscribed sums varying from that amount up to twenty dollars.[33]

> The six companies collect and remit to China the savings of the Chinese, aggregating from $20,000 to $100,000 by each steamer. This amount is made up of thousands of small sums from $2 to $100, which are sent by the poor class of Chinamen to their parents or friends, either as presents or to aid them in coming to this country. . . . The companies also carry thousands of American and European manufactured goods, sent as presents to the "old folks at home."[34]

Not only were Chinese laborers dependent upon the kongsis for credit and loans, but also for the intelligence and political resources that the kongsis alone could muster in defense of Chinese interests. As in other political associations, kongsi leadership entrenched itself because of its technical competence and contacts with institutions in white society. As anti-Chinese agitation increased, the gulf between the special lore of leadership and the routine tasks of proletarian labor widened; the leadership cadre became indispensable to the mass of Chinese immigrants.[35]

The kongsis also arrogated to themselves the right to collect debts owed by one Chinese to another. The rules of the Yeung Wo Association provided elaborate arrangements and safeguards for creditors and debtors.

> Claims for debts, to avoid mistakes, must particularize the true

> name, surname, town, and department of the debtor. The manager of the company shall give the claimant an acknowledgement, which shall be returned again when the money is paid. No claim can be presented for less than ten dollars. Claims presented through the company must, when afterward paid, bear the receipt of the company; else the debtor will not be allowed to return to China. Persons making false claims against an individual shall recompense him for any expenses to which he shall be put in consequence thereof. Accounts must be acknowledged by the debtor to be correct before collection. A person appointed as a collector must give a receipt for the account. A creditor in returning to China must name an agent who will receive the payment of any sums due to him. Accounts sent from China for collection may be accepted by the company. The manager will not pay over collections except upon the presentation of the paper of acknowledgement he has previously given. Part payments must bear the receipt of the company. In cases of dispute over debt, the debtor may return to China if a representative from his district is willing to become his security. Debtors shall not be hindered returning to China on their pleading poverty or chronic sickness. In losses occasioned by oversight of the agent he shall be held responsible for the amount, unless he declare them upon oath to have been not fraudulent. Claims for debt, if unpaid, must be again put on record at the expiration of three years. Claims presented by a member of another company, and when recorded, shall be subject to a fee of twenty-five cents.[36]

Spokesmen for the Six Companies justified such arrangements by claiming that their elaborate registration records gave them an unusual advantage for detecting an absconding debtor while their awesome authority in the Chinese community could compel any debtor to pay up:

> Sometimes a Chinaman owes another Chinaman money, and both live in other places than San Francisco. If the debtor tries to go back to China without paying his debt, the creditor writes to the Six Companies about it. When the debtor comes to pay his dues to the Six Companies the officers of the Six Companies will tell him he should pay his debt before he goes. If the debtor is unwilling to pay, the Six Companies retain him by the help of the American courts. We should clearly see why the creditor depends on the Six Companies to collect debts for him....
>
> The...Chinese custom of loaning money is very different from

> that of the American. A Chinaman often loans considerable money to one of his friends to help him to start business, not only without security, but even without a written word from the borrower. The creditor loans his money out, taking only the word of the borrower for it. The American law makes no provision to compel a man to pay his debts without any proof that he is a debtor. Therefore it is necessary for the Chinese creditor to depend largely on the Six Companies to collect his debts, if debtors become unfaithful to their promises.[37]

So effective were the resources and "muscle" of the kongsi elite that the annual repayment of loans on New Year's eve created a spectacular display of harassing debt collectors and sudden bankruptcies:

> ...It is a little singular, certainly, that the Chinese, who are not an overcharitable...or forgiving race, should enjoin the forgiveness of all debts at the beginning of the New Year.
>
> It is an amusing spectacle in Chinatown to see the creditor mercilessly hunting down the debtor during the few weeks that remain. No one is exempt from this necessity, for in order to pay his own debts he must in turn collect what is due to him. The debtor who cannot fulfill his obligations by New Year goes into bankruptcy by the operations of a custom stronger than law. He undoubtedly earns the contempt of his fellow men, but at least he is free from their persecution. His debts are forgiven with quite as much sincerity as could be expected under the circumstances.[38]

The joyous celebration ushering in the New Year was marred by the desperate search for the debtors and the equally desperate attempts of the latter to avoid their creditors.

> The business is closely watched and the books carefully written up and often examined, and an account of stock is taken. Collectors are early sent to any doubtul parties;...while accounts of long standing are taken again from the file and fresh efforts are made to press some drops of pay from the oldest and least hopeful subjects....San Francisco merchants increase their collecting force, who traverse the State, and who visit Oregon and Nevada, and penetrate the snow regions of Montana; nor are they deterred by any obstacles when there is before them a prospect of securing the settlement of an account....Express Companies

> find the Chinese department of their business very brisk about these days, occasioned by the quantities of letters going out and the amount of treasure coming in....
>
> It is not uncommon for those who have no means for meeting their liabilities to secrete themselves until the old year has fully expired and the New Year has come in, for during the New Year's congratulations and merrymakings no duns are tolerated.[39]

Although the kongsis were effectively organized for the collection of debts, they were not nearly so well organized for, nor interested in, the dispensation of charity. Despite the fact that their appellation in English was The Chinese Consolidated Benevolent Association, the Chung Wah Kongsi distributed its benevolence sparingly.

The rules of the Yeung Wo Association provided:

> Invalids that cannot labor, are poor, and without relatives, may be returned to China at the expense of the Company for their passage-money; but provisions and fuel and other expenses must be obtained by subscriptions. Coffins may be furnished for the poor, but of such a careful record shall be kept.[40]

Charitable aid to the indigent was dispensed less by the kongsis than by clans and friends. When, however, clan or other sources of aid were unavailable the kongsi provided help financed by levies on the membership.

> Some of the companies have had regulations for relieving the indigent sick and disabled. Such cases, however, are generally provided for by private contributions, the relatives and townsmen of the unfortunate individual voluntarily assuming the care of their relative or neighbor. Scarce a day passes without the recurrence of such cases. No people give more in charity than do the Chinese. They help their sick friends, pay their rent, their nurses, their doctor's bills, the expenses of their funerals, if they die; and many poor men have their passage paid back to China when it becomes apparent that they cannot recover health in this country. If, however, the unfortunate individual has no friends to care for him, the company to which he belongs will attend to these duties, making an assessment for the expense, unless there are especial funds for the purpose.[41]

At the height of the American depression the Chinese Unemployed Alliance of Greater New York wrote to the Chung Wah Kongsi for aid to those out of work and destitute. The reply from the president of the Chinese Charitable and Benevolent Assocation reveals the extent of its interest in aid to the indigent:

> Sirs:
>
> In reply to your letter dated January 22, and the one presented on February 1, by your delegates with reference to apportionment of relief funds and aid to your organization, we hereby inform you that after considering every detail, we are of the opinion that unemployment relief, though much needed, must be carefully undertaken. To bestow largely and relieve the needy was highly esteemed by the old sages.
>
> At our meeting on February 8, we again deliberated on this subject, and resolved that unemployment relief should be carried on by various organizations independently and voluntarily. Hence, we cannot accept your request for relief and notify you accordingly to this effect.[42]

The proper ceremonial and burial of the dead in China was one of the most important obligations laid upon the Chinese. The kongsis directly or indirectly assumed this duty, levying a required fee for the voluntary service. With money raised from levies the New York kongsis bought a few graveyards in Brooklyn and on Staten Island. However, the cost of a grave was $25 for anyone "who has paid all his dues when living." Those who had defaulted on debts were charged $45. The charge for shipping the bones to China was $30 in 1936.[43]

Expenses involved in carrying out death rituals occasionally kept a religious Chinese laborer in debt to his kongsi. Because ancestral honor was so powerful an idea, money was set aside in advance to provide proper care for a corpse and for its eventual burial in China. As Reverend Loomis observed:

> Partly because of the Chinaman's love for his native land, and the desire that his last resting place shall be where the ashes of his kindred lie, but principally in order that his bones may receive from his relatives and descendants the attentions [he deserves] so much solicitude is exhibited that the remains of those who die abroad may be returned for final interment in the ancient tombs. Consequently a large portion of the Chinese in California have secured this object by the prepayment of a special

> sum to their Ui-Kun, or to some independent association, which guarantees to find the body wherever it may be buried, and at the proper time to send it to his friends. The reception of the body, or the ashes, and its reinterment in China, involve a considerable expense. Also there must be religious ceremonies to lure home the spirit, as well as the care in bringing home the body, so that, as we see, it must cost a large amount for a Chinaman to die and to get finally laid down where "the weary may be at rest."[44]

The kongsis should not be regarded as *charitable* and *benevolent associations* in the usual meaning of those terms. Rather, they were the embodiment of oligarchical merchant-clan leadership. Their public benevolent activities—such as contributing a large sum of money to the relief of victims of flood disasters—served to detour public interest away from their political and economic role inside Chinatown. Through collection of debt, levy of assessments, and bureaucratization of benevolence, the Chung Wah Kongsi exercised considerable control over the mass of overseas Chinese.[45]

Kongsi Judicial Activity

The social and political power of the kongsis received added impetus through their judicial system. Not only did the kongsis hold the credit-lien on the services of the debtor, control the sources for credit and loans, operate the benevolent and charitable services of Chinatown, and politically represent the Chinese to the American public, but they also dispensed civil and criminal justice according to codes designed by and for the merchant leaders. The latter sat as a court to settle grievances among the Chinese. In addition, the kongsis took advantage of the unequal standing the Chinese had in American courts after 1854. Attorneys to represent the Chinese could only be obtained through the good offices of the kongsis.[46] If a Chinese refused to abide by the decision of the kongsis, he could be left undefended to the mercy of the American courts.

Kongsi spokesmen denied that Chinatown was governed under its own legal system, but they admitted the existence of a traditonal legal apparatus within the secret societies and acknowledged that kongsi merchants settled intra-community disputes in lieu of scholars and elders, who exercised this authority in China:

> [T]he Americans have an idea that the Six Companies have their own court to try their own subjects. The Six Companies have no more power to have a court of their own than the

> President of the United States to compel the people to call him emperor. There is, however, a society, Jee Kong Tong, which is the secret society of the Chinese. Its aim is to overthrow the present dynasty of China. This secret society does have a sort of government of its own, but it has nothing to do with the Six Companies. . . .The Six Companies have power only to advise their people to do things, but not compel. Occasionally they hold meetings to settle disputes and debts, in the same way as the clan organizations in China. Instead of having the titled scholars and elders decide cases, the merchants and the prominent Chinese take their places. If the plaintiff and the defendant do not agree with their arbitration, the case must be settled by American law.[47]

The kongsi judiciary was the heart of its control system. In every city where a Chinatown sprang up, the arbitration boards of the kongsis, headed by the president of the Chung Wah Kongsi (known to Americans as the mayor of Chinatown), were in evidence.

> Home customs and traditions govern the life and regulate the conduct of most of these people. . . .[T]heir own code. . .rests for its enforcement upon the public sentiment of their little communities. . .In Philadelphia the merchants occasionally meet to discuss some question affecting the welfare of the colony, and a bundle of slips of bamboo is kept for the purpose of calling such meetings together. The object for which the meeting is called, with the time and place, is written upon the smooth side of the tablets, one of which is sent to each shop, and serves as the credential to its representative. These tablets are said to be used in voting.[48]

Acting as a judicial body, the kongsi council had extensive power over civil and criminal matters. It determined the scope of its jurisdiction, the relationship it would have with American courts, and the type of punishment to be meted out. For example, the rules of the Yeung Wo Kongsi provided that

> [q]uarrels and troubles about claims in the mines should be referred to the company, where they shall be duly considered. If any should refuse to abide by the decision of the company, it will nevertheless assist the injured and defend them from violence. If, when foreigners do injury, a complaint is made, and the company exerts itself to have justice done, without avail, it ought to be

submitted to. Whatever is referred for settlement to the assembly of the five companies conjointly cannot again be brought before this company alone.

Where a man is killed, a reward shall be offered by the company for the capture and trial of the murderer, the money being paid only when he has been seized; the members of the company shall subscribe each according to what is just. If more than the anticipated amount is required, the friends of the deceased shall make up the deficiency. Complaint shall be made of offenders to the civil court, and proclamations for their arrest shall be placarded in the principal towns; but any one found guilty of concealing them shall pay all the expenses to which the company has been put. Difficulties with members of other companies shall be reported to the agents of this company, and, if justice demand, shall be referred for the judgment of the five companies conjointly. Offenses committed on shipboard, upon the sea, shall be referred to the five companies conjointly. Difficulties brought upon men by their own vices and follies will not receive attention. Thievery and receiving of stolen goods will not be protected; nor will troubles in bawdy-houses, nor those in gambling-houses, nor debts to such, nor extortions of secret associations, nor the quarrels of such associations, nor those who are injured in consequence of refusal to pay their licenses, nor smuggling, nor any violation of American laws. The company will not consider complaints from a distance of a doubtful character, or without sufficient proof. No reply will be made to anonymous letters, or those without date and a specification of the true origin and nature of difficulties. Names must be carefully given in all complaints from the interior. No payments of money will be made in the settlement of cases where the rules of the company are not complied with. Where the conduct of an individual is such as to bring disgrace on the company and upon his countrymen, he shall be expelled, and a notice to that effect be placarded in each of the five companies' houses; nor will the company be responsible for any of his subsequent villainies, or even make any investigation should he meet with any violent death. Costs connected with the settlement of disputes shall be borne by the party decided to be in the wrong. In difficulties of a pressing and important character in the mines a messenger shall be sent thence, and a judicious person shall at once accompany him to the place. In any quarrel where men are killed or wounded the person who originated it shall be held accountable. Any defensive weapons

> belonging to the company shall be given to individuals only after joint consultation, and the register of their names. Those requiring such weapons for defense shall give security for their return. If any shall take them on their own responsibility, they shall be held accountable for any consequences.
>
> Anyone using the seal of the company, or addressing a letter in its behalf unauthorized, shall be severely censured if the matter be unimportant; if a serious offense, he shall be handed over to a court of law. The parties and witnesses in cases shall be examined under oath. Representatives from the people of different counties and townships shall be notified by the agents of the company of the time of any meeting; and when assembled they shall not leave until the business be dispatched. Notices of meeting upon urgent business shall be marked with the words *urgent case;* the representatives so informed shall be fined ten dollars if not present within an hour of the time. In arbitration the agents of the company, the representatives and the witnesses shall all be put on oath.[49]

Through its judicial activities the kongsi extended itself over the Chinatown community. Its decisions were cause for much dissension within the Chinese settlement. The founders of the Kwong Duck, Hip Sing, and Suey Sing tongs alleged that their own decisions to disaffiliate from a clan or kongsi arose as a response to the unfair and arbitrary justice they witnessed in matters of disputes over business or property. So long as the Chinese had an inferior status in American courts, and so long as the Chung Wah Kongsi appeared as the only legitimate authority to both the Chinese and the whites in America, it was able to administer it form of justice with impunity.

The Chung Wah Kongsi also acted as the official representative of, and spokesman for, the Chinese to the American government and to the public. To this extent, American leaders and the general public permitted a form of indirect rule to grow up, not too different from the "Kapitan China" system established by British and Dutch colonial administrators in Southeast Asia. The Chung Wah Kongsi proclaimed itself to be the advocate for all Chinese in America whenever occasions arose for it to do so.[50] Composed of the respectable members of the Chinese community, it was recognized as such by nearly all those—white and Chinese alike—who sought to champion the cause of the Chinese immigrant. Only under certain adverse circumstances, or by accident, for instance, when the baptized Chinese Christians appealed to Reverend Otis Gibson to relieve them of the onerous burden of obtaining a debt voucher from the Six Companies in order to return to China, did the character and scope of kongsi power raise doubts among the non-Chinese supporters of the Oriental cause.[51]

Control of Work and Occupations

Kongsi control over jobs in and outside the Chinese colony was exercised in different ways. Common laborers were subjected to a system of contract labor managed by merchant-contractors. The latter not only obtained work for the immigrants but also supplied them with tools and necessities. Inside Chinatown the associations represented crafts, over which they exercised a monopoly. The Chung Wah Kongsi enforced a Chinese form of "property right" that it adapted to the merchandising scene in Chinatown. It also collected a transactions tax over merchant enterprises, and extended its authority over both mercantile and laboring classes.

Contract Labor

One of the many charges against the Chinese immigrants was they they were slaves to Chinese contractors. Most of these charges grew out of a poor understanding of the methods by which the Chinese in America had immigrated and were coupled with an inaccurate comparison of the credit-ticket system with the methods employed to bring Chinese laborers to Cuba and Latin America. In fact, a direct contract approach was utilized to bring agricultural labor from China to California in 1854, and to Arkansas and Louisiana in 1869.[52] But, aside from these two incidents, the Chinese seem to have come to America by means of the credit-ticket system.

American employers, however, did secure contract labor from China by subcontracting through the Six Companies or through individual merchants. Leland Stanford and his business colleagues built the western section of the first transcontinental railroad with Chinese labor secured through subcontracts with the Chung Wah Kongsi.[53] It is believed that several other railroads adopted similar practices. When the attempt was made to settle Chinese coolies on Southern plantations in 1869, the railroad involved offered a subsidy to the American contractors, while the Dutch shipping firm that was to bring in the Chinese engaged the services of a prominent Louisiana Chinese who had previously been the spiritual and political leader of the Chinese settlement in British Guiana.[54]

American employers seeking laborers went to Chinatown merchants who acted as employment agents.[55] The merchants somestimes acted as lone individuals, at other times as officers of a kongsi. In either case, however, they could doubtless have secured the authority and protection of their kongsi. The Chung Wah Kongsi acted as agents for the Central Pacific Railroad and perhaps for other railways. But in 1894, a spokesman for the Six Companies denied that they imported "contract or slave labor."

> This point is the American idea that the Six Companies import contract or slave labor. In fact, there have been and are some so-called contracts for laborers; but there have neither been contracts for slave labor, nor have the Six Companies had anything to do with them. These contracts are made between the American employer and some one of the Chinese merchants.[56]

Even those who vehemently denied that any of the Chinese were coolies recognized that they came here under the sponsorship of the Chinese merchants:

> They are no more "coolies" or "peons" because they come here under the auspices of men of their own nation than would be the immigrants to be brought here from Europe by the International Immigrant Union the officers of which are now soliciting funds in this city to bring over female servants from Germany, Ireland, and Scotland.[57]

Merchant control over Chinese labor was enhanced by the fact that he advanced passage-money and supplied provisions through his store for the arriving laborers. The cost of these was deducted, along with interest, from the laborer's earnings. Often, a merchant-contractor or his agent served as the "boss" of a labor gang, or appointed the boss from among the laborers selected. The boss received the total sum of the gang's wages and distributed the earnings after deducting what the laborer owed. A Chinese observer of the scene noted:

> A few years ago there was a contract made between a company that undertook to build a railroad in Mexico and a Chinese mercantile establishment, whose name is Quong Ying Kee. Since Quong Ying Kee could not find all the Chinese the company required, they sent back men to China to advertise for workmen. The laborers plainly understood they they were coming to work for a dollar a day, and to patronize Quong Ying Kee for their provisions. The foremen went to work for a dollar and a quarter a day. Whether Quong Ying Kee received any commission out of

> the wages or not, the writer has not been able to ascertain. If any wished to come to work and had no money to pay his passage, Quong Ying Kee would pay for him and get the money back by retaining about two thirds of his wages every month until the amount was fully paid. Some workers agreed to pay twice what Quong Ying Kee paid for their passage; others one and a half. This story was told to the writer by a person who was a foreman in this contract.[58]

The merchant-contractor-boss system pervaded nearly all forms of Chinese labor thus placing the control of labor and of labor's earnings in the hands of the Chinese merchant class.

> The American farmers and manufacturers often make contracts with the Chinese for laborers, ... When a farmer or a manufacturer wishes to hire a certain number of Chinamen to work for him, he generally goes into a Chinese store to ask the storekeeper to get them for him. When there is any contract made between the American employer and the Chinese merchant for laborers, the workmen always understand that they are to patronize this merchant for their provisions. There are benefits in these contracts both for the storekeepers and the laborers. The merchant gets his profit by selling more goods, and the laborers by getting work more easily.
>
> As most of the Chinese laborers do not understand the English language, it is necessary to have an interpreter where a large number of Chinese work together. All communications between the American employer and the Chinese laborer must be made through this interpreter. Therefore, when the employer wishes the Chinese to do a certain piece of work at a certain time, he only tells the interpreter all about it. Then the interpreter tell the Chinese to do what their employer wants them to. Of course the Chinese always obey the interpreter, for they know that it is the employer's command. Perhaps on some occasion an American may ask the Chinese laborers something about their work; they will tell him; "Go tell the boss (interpreter)." Thus we see how easily the American people may obtain...the idea that all Chinese laborers in the United States are slaves because they appear to be controlled or "bossed" by some one Chinaman.[59]

Craft and Labor Guilds

As organizers of closed craft or labor monopolies the territorial kongsis extended their economic hegemony from common labor to the higher professions in Chinatown. Among many examples that could be cited: the Hakka cooks are organized as the Tsung Tsin Association, a subdivision of their district association. Chinese tenant orchardists in the Sacramento Valley belonged to the Yeung Wo Association. The Sz Yup people, distributed over several kongsis, are small retailers whose associations protect their right to conduct business in most of the laundries, curio shops, and Cantonese restaurants of Chinatown.[60]

The Sam Yup Association early established its monopoly over the higher professions in Chinatown: tailoring, mending, clothing repair, and herbal medicine. In later years, acording to Rose Hum Lee, the higher professions in Chinatown were still largely in the hands of the Sam Yup and the Chung Shan peoples.

> An occupational census of the Chinatown in Butte, Montana, showed that the American Chinese whose mothers were American-born or from Sam Yup became the professionals. . . . By the same token, the professionals of San Francisco's Chinatown have their antecedents either in Chung Shan ancestry, American-born mothers, or Sam Yup territorial origin.[61]

Kongsi labor monopolies were also established. In terms of their activities these associations combined the functions of a craft union, a medieval guild, and a benevolent association and were, in fact, replicas of craft guilds found in China.

> Washermen, shoemakers and cigar-makers have formed such unions.
>
> The objects of these societies are to guard against a destructive competition between different establishments, to settle upon a schedule of prices for work, and to save the trade from being ruined by too many engaging in it. This is accomplished by requiring that a term of apprenticeship shall be served before an individual can be eligible to membership in the union; and then an initiation fee is demanded, so large that few will enter except as are disposed to devote themselves earnestly to their business, and when initiated at such a cost, they will be interested in efforts to sustain the respectability and profitableness of their calling.
>
> The money accumulated from fees and fines is expended in public dinners for the members of the union, in fitting up a place

> for the god which they may choose for their patron, and in the rites of his worship. Sick and unfortuante members are aided to some extent, and those who die are sure to receive an honorable burial, and this, to a Chinaman, is the most desirable of all things.
>
> If money remains in the treasury at the end of the year it is divided equally among the members, unless they choose to spend it in feasting, and in mirth and music.[62]

Labor guilds were not able to maintain their monopolies in occupations invaded by white laborers or taken over by merchants, and steadily lost influence over such occupations after 1882. Two examples are noteworthy. The cigar-makers guild declined rapidly after the American unions invented the "white label" to evict Chinese workers from the industry. After the formation of anti-Chinese laundry leagues the laundry guild was compelled to reduce its dues and confine its activities to Chinatown.

> Before the rise of steam laundries in California the fee for washmen was thirty dollars and the guild paid dividends so that every Chinaman wanted to join; but since 1882, the number of Chinese laborers has become so much less and the competition of white laundries so serious that the washmen's guilds are much less prosperous. Formerly the apprentice received thirty dollars a month and board but now the boss laundrymen complain that he [sic] wants two dollars a day and there is no profit left.[64]

Guild monopoly was carefully guarded and protected by strict rules. The Chinese who sought to invade a monopolized field were dealt with swiftly and severely: "If a nonguild employer starts a washhouse, the guilds will underbid him and run him out, but their constitution forbids them to underbid each other."[65]

Another method by which craft monopoly was maintained was the transplantaion to Chinatown of China's property-right system. Adapted to the economic conditions of the ghetto, this system regulated the number of businesses within the same occupational category that could be established on a city block. "The laundrymen divide the territory—as, for example, the laundries must be ten doors apart—and strictly enforce the rules."[66] Another feature of the "property-right" systems claims a permanent lien on all business property ever used by its members even after the property has been vacated or the shopkeeper gone bankrupt. The property right is officially recognized in such kongsi rules as those discovered to be still in force in New York's Chinatown in 1936, requiring that "business transactions of laundries, restaurants, and the like must be reported to the Association by the seller and buyer in person two weeks before the deal, so that the Association can make it known to the public and the deal be made as scheduled; otherwise the deal is not recognized by the Association as legal."[67] After the transaction has been made, kongsi protection continues in the form of severe fines and penalties meted out to those who establish competing businesses nearby.

The "basic property right" system limits the free movement, sale, or exchange of Chinese businesses and places considerable authority over the life and death of businesses in the hands of the kongsis. Once a piece of business property has been vacated, it cannot be bought, sold, rented, or leased until a sum of money has been paid to the previous tenant or his kongsi representative for the "property right."[68]

Over and above the business controls they acquired through the property right sytem, the kongsis collected a "transactions tax" and other sums from those businessmen needing an official witness to any commercial matter. Caucasians could not witness any Chinatown business transaction; any transaction authorized in accordance with American law remained invalid until it met the kongsis requirements. K.C. Wu, president of the Chung Wah Kongsi of New York, is reported to have said, "if we allow foreigners to act as witnesses at our business deals, there would be no Chung Wah Kung Saw." Failure to pay the tax placed the noncomplying business man in jeopardy of kongsi judicial exactions, of being boycotted, or of being accused of fraudulent practices and being ostracized from the community.[69] A host of other charges, taxes, and levies are evidence of kongsi influence on Chinatown businesses. "Each laundry or restaurant keeping its location must pay a fee of $2 per annum. . . . "[E]ach store or restaurant must pay the Association monthly dues according to its volume of business. . . . Laundries must pay $4 a year for a one-man laundry; $8 a year for a two-man laundry," and up. The Association charged $2.50 to call a meeting or settle a dispute.[70]

The Activities of the Secret Societies

Clans and kongsis maintained authority through the indispensability of their financial, social, legal, benevolent, and political services to the Chinese immigrants; secret societies gained adherents by providing equally indispensable services in the form of prostitution and gambling.

Gambling and prostitution provided otherwise unavailable opportunities for sojourning, homeless Chinese males. In few other activities could Chinese laborers achieve a reputation on the basis of individual performance alone. From his first day on board the ship from Canton or Hong Kong to the far-off day when he would return to China, the laborer was treated categorically, as a "Chinaman" by white Americans; as a member of a clan or kongsi in Chinatown. For his job, his credit, his protection from other Chinese, and his security from the depredations of hostile Americans, the immigrant was beholden to either a clan or a territorial association. His own merits and individual personality counted for nothing to white America and were matters of little concern to Chinatown associations. In the gambling den or the brothel, however, he could discover for himself or demonstrate to others his special luck[71] or his own sexual talent. In the brothel not only could he judge his own performances, but also he could win a sign of personal worth: A woman might become attracted to him. If he could purchase her freedom he would have his own concubine.[72] The Chinese laborer entered Chinatown's "dens of iniquity" more an individual than in almost any other place in his sojourn. Perhaps only in these places was it possible for him to obtain a sense of his personal worth, a chance to change his luck, a person to love and comfort him.

The secret societies made money from the importation and sale of women. By 1870, over six thousand women were said to have been imported to the United States as "slave girls."[73] The trade in women was so profitable that the tongs became very wealthy from it. Women from China were brought to America under contracts, and compelled to work as prostitutes. Brothel keepers paid tribute and protection money to one or more of the tongs, which also helped supply them with women. Several "slave girl" contracts have been captured by police or acquired by missionaries, and they leave no doubt about the unsavory character or extent of this business.[74] One such contract reads:

> An Agreement to assist the woman Ah Ho, because coming from China to San Francisco she became indebted to her mistress for passage. Ah Ho herself asks Mr. Yee Kwan to advance for her six hundred and thirty dollars, for which Ah Ho distinctly agrees to give her body to Mr. Yee for service a sa (sic) prostitute for a term of four years. There shall be no interest on the money. Ah Ho shall receive no wages. At the expiration of four years Ah Ho shall be her own master. Mr. Yee Kwan shall not hinder nor trouble her. If Ah Ho runs away before her time is out, her mistress shall find her and return her, and whatever expense is incurred in finding and returning her, Ah Ho shall pay. On this day of agreement Ah Ho with her own hands has received from Mr. Yee Kwan six hundred and thirty dollars. If Ah Ho shall be sick at any time for more than ten days, she shall make up an

> extra month of service for every ten days of sickness. Now this agreement has proof. This paper received by Ah Ho is witness.
>
> Tung Chee
>
> Twelfth Year, Ninth Month, and Fourteenth Day (October 1873).[75]

By 1885, there were approximately seventy brothels in San Francisco's Chinatown.[76] The business was quite lucrative. Women were sold as domestic servants for $100 to $500 each, and for prostitution purposes for from $1,500 to $3,000 depending on age and appearance. From the houses they were sold as concubines, and sometimes resold as credit-ticket prostitutes to several buyers consecutively. Late in the century, Donaldina Cameron, a missionary in Chinatown, made an attempt to end this female slave trade. Whenever possible Miss Cameron would kidnap girls from the brothels and bring them up at the mission home which today bears her name. However, the secret societies continued to derive a major part of their income from ownership or control of houses of prostitution.[77] Only when the immigrant population became aged and enfeebled and when the sex-ratio moved closer to balance did the traffic in women begin to die out in Chinatown.

The tongs exercised control over and sometimes owned the gambling houses in Chinatown. A gambling company might be started by a few partners who combined small sums of money for the purpose. Often the legitimate businessmen in Chinatown held an interest in the companies and rented out the cellars of their establishments for use as gambling dens. The secret societies collected tribute from the gambling companies in Chinatown. Occasionally, as in New York City in 1891, Chinatown gamblers formed their own guild for mutual protection, but the usual practice was for the secret society to provide protection for the gambling enterprise and to arrange for its legal defense if prosecuted in American courts.[78]

In addition to revenues obtained from gambling and prostitution, the tongs exercised authority through financial and judicial structures similar to those of the kongsis previously described. The judicial organ of the secret societies not only collected fines and levied taxes, but also tried its own members and its enemies—the latter *in absentia*—for criminal offenses and even meted out death sentences, dispatching its own "executioners" (bu hau doi) to carry out the sentence. If a member of one society was killed by a member of another, the judicial organ of the first would ordinarily order its members to seek out the murderer and kill him or bring him before its tribunal. In turn the killer would seek protection and defensive action from his own brotherhood.

If a secret society member was arested for crimes committed in service to the society, he would be defended by attorneys hired by his sworn brothers, and every attempt—including use of perjured testimony—would be made to prevent his conviction. Chinese who testified for the prosecution, regardless of their clan, kongsi, or tong affiliation, or Chinese interpreters who acted in good faith in the American courts in criminal cases involving secret society members, were subject to intimidation and on occasion were murdered. Loyalty to sworn brothers was the paramount secret society value, instilled in the members through an awesome initiation ritual, and enforced with unstinting vigor.[79]

The agents of the tong were "insured" in case of injury, death, or imprisonment while in tong service. Written contracts provided an indemnity if the agent were to be killed in the line of tong duty; medical care for injuries sustained; a small salary while temporarily incapacitated; a large compensation plus the costs of passage to China in case of permanent disability; and an annual sum in support of family or friends in case of lengthy imprisonment. In return, the "salaried soldier" of the secret society promised to act only in response to its orders, to serve the society's and not his own interests, and to obey all commands bravely and without question.[80]

With vice and criminal activities as an economic base from which it sought power in Chinatown, the secret societies came into conflict not only with the legitimate authority structure in Chinatown—the clans and kongsis—but also with American agencies of law enforcement. This dual structure of conflict—among the several Chinatown organizations on the one hand, and between Chinese organizations and American police agencies on the other—further isolated the Chinatown Chinese from the larger society and encouraged the common but erroneous observation that the Chinese were both clannish *and* homogeneous. As the foregoing has shown, the Chinatown Chinese were highly organized, but these organizations rested on different and conflicting bases and were often in conflict with one another. The homogeneity attributed to the Chinese is an illusion created by the isolation and insulation of Chinatown[81] from the rest of society—a condition caused by the internal conflict which bound the Chinese together in a kind of "antagonistic cooperation," and by the racist discrimination against the Chinese exerted by American institutions and law. The true paradox of Chinese society is that its "cohesion" is a consequence of its many and varied conflicts.

NOTES

1. Thomas and Znaniecki, *Polish Peasant in Europe and America*, pp. 1521-1647.
2. Charles P. Loomis, "The Old Order Amish As a Social System," in *Social Systems: Essays on Their Persistence and Change*, ed. Loomis (New York: Van Nostrand 1960), p. 230.
3. Thomas and Znaniecki, *Polish Peasant in Europe and America*, pp. 1535-37.
4. Wirth, *Ghetto*, pp. 18-39, 52-61.
5. A classic example is described by a legal historian: A murder having been committed in Chinatown, the San Francisco police were informed by the victim's family that one Tarm Poy was the criminal. He was arrested and indicted. The entire Fong Clan, of which the victim was a member, raised money for expense of the prosecution and retained an able attorney, Mr. Frank M. Stone (b. 1847)—one-time partner to the notorious anti-Chinese Senator A.A. Sargent—to assist in the case. In the course of the trial only one piece of evidence served to clinch the conviction, the name of Tarm Poy on the hat found at the scene of the crime. After the conviction, Tarm Poy's death sentence was commuted to deportation from California. Stone received, in addition to his fee, a solitaire diamond from the Fong Clan, raised by "contributions" ranging from 5 cents to twenty dollars from each clan member. A year later the chief prosecution witness revealed that the entire case against Tarm Poy had been fabricated by the rival Fong Clan out of revenge against his clan. The clinching testimony had been a manufactured perjury. Oscar T. Shuck, "Seniors of the Collective Bar—Frank M. Stone," *History of the Bench and Bar of California* (Los Angeles: Commercial Printing House, 1901), pp. 938-42.
6. The term *coolie* is used in its original designative meaning as presented by C.W. Brooks and certain Chinatown merchants: "Merely a laborer. In eighteen hundred and fifty-one I studied Sanskrit, so that I spoke it. The word 'coolie' is an old Sanskrit word, and means, in India, a laborer. The word *walla* refers to the next highest grade; then *baboo*, which menas the business man. The meaning of the word *coolie* is the same in China as in India." Testimony of Charles Wolcott Brooks, *Chinese Immigration, Its Social, Moral, and Political Effect*, p. 101.

> You speak of the Chinamen as *coolies*, and in one sense the word is applicable to a great many of them; but not in that in which you seem to use it. *Cooly* is not a Chinese word; it has been imported into China from foreign parts, as it has been into this country. What its original signification was we do not know; but with us it means a common laborer and nothing more. We have never known it used among us as a designation of class, such as you have in view—persons bound to labor under contracts which they can be forcibly compelled to comply with. The Irishmen who are engaged

> in digging down your hills, the men who unload ships, who clean your streets, or even drive your drays, would, if they were in China, be considered coolies; tradesmen, mechanics of every kind, and professional men would not. If you mean by coolies laborers, many of our countrymen in the mines are coolies, and many again are not. There are among them tradesmen, mechanics, gentry (being persons of respectability and who enjoy a certain rank and privilege), and schoolmasters, who are reckoned with the gentry, and with us considered a respectable class of people. None are coolies if by that word you mean bound men or contract slaves.

Letter of the Chinamen to His Excellency, Gov. Bigler (San Francisco, April 29, 1852, reprinted in Littel's *Living Age*, July 3, 1852, pp. 32-34. Emigration from China in the nineteenth century proceeded according to two systems, the one used for South America, the Caribbean area, and Cuba was involuntary contract servitude; the one for the United States, Malaysia, Canada was the credit-ticket system using a voluntary contract of debt indenture with the obligation to be paid from deductions from earnings. Involuntary contract labor to America was attempted in 1869, by Koopmanschap and Co. in order to provide cheap labor supply in the Arkansas and Mississippi valleys. Persia Crawford Campbell, *Chinese Coolie Emigration to Countries Within the British Empire* (London: King and Sons, 1923), pp. xvii-xix, 28-39, 150-51, and my discussion of the Kiipmanschap plan in Appendix I.

7. Campbell, *Chinese Coolie Emigration*, p. xvii.
8. Reprinted in Alexander McLeod, *Pigtails and Gold Dust* (Caldwell: Caxton, 1947), pp. 78-79. The contract is in the Wells Fargo Bank Historical Collection, San Francisco. Earlier translations have credited this as a contract with a British merchant. More recent translations, however, agree that it is with an American merchant. The Chinese referred to Caucasian foreigners as "red-headed devils," distinguishing only the country—England as the "Glorious Country," America as the "Flowery Country." Ibid., p. 79.
9. *Letter of the Chinamen*, pp. 32, 33. By "cooly" the Chinese signers specifically meant "persons bound to labor under contracts which they can be forcibly compelled to comply with." Ibid., p. 32. They rejected this definition as both incorrect and inapplicable to immigrant Chinese laborers. But they did not mention the credit-ticket indenture contract.
10. Ibid.
11. A.W. Loomis, "The Six Chinese Companies," *Overland Monthly*, vol. I, no. 3, September 1868, pp. 222-23.
    See also, Otis Gibson, *The Chinese in America* (Cincinnati: Hitchcock and Walden, 1877) pp. 49-51.
12. U.S. Congress, Senate, Joint Special Committee to Investigate Chinese Immigration, 44th Cong., 2d. sess., February 27, 1877, S. Rept. 689, pp. 22-24 (hereafter referred to as Sen. Doc. 689).
    Testimony of the Hon. Frank M. Pixley. Pixley, representing the city of

San Francisco, adopted a racist attitude in his testimony. To illustrate his prejudices it is best to insert here another part of his testimony.

> The Chinese are inferior to any race God ever made. . . . I think there are none so low. . . . Their people have got the perfection of crimes of 4,000 years. . . . The Divine Wisdom has said that He would divide this country and the world as a heritage of five great families; that to the Blacks he would give Africa; and Asia he would give to the Yellow races. He inspired us with the determination, not only to have prepared our own inheritance, but to have stolen from the Red Man, America; and it is now settled that the Saxon, American, or European groups of families, the White Race, is to have the inheritance of Europe and America and that the Yellow raes are to be confined to what the Almighty originally gave them; and as they are not a favored people, they are not to be permitted to steal from us what we have robbed the American savage of. . . . I believe that the Chinese have no souls to save, and if they have, they are not worth the saving.

For a criticism of this investigation see Mary Coolidge, *Chinese Immigration* (New York: Henry Holt, 1909), pp. 96-108;
Elmer Sandmeyer, *The Anti-Chinese Movement in California* (Urbana: University of Illinois Press, 1939), pp. 82-89.

13. "Address of the Chinese Six Companies to the American Public," April 4, 1876. Presented and read to the congressional committee by Colonel F.A. Bee, attorney for the Chinese Six Companies. Sen. Doc. 689, pp. 38-39.
14, Loomis, *Six Chinese Companies*, p. 223.
15. Gibson, *Chinese in America*, p. 339.
16. Coolidge, *Chinese Immigration*, p. 410. Emphasis added.
17. Leong, Gor Yun, *Chinatown Inside Out* (New York: Barrows, Mussey, 1936), pp. 49-50.
18. William Hoy, *The Chinese Six Companies* (San Francisco: Chinese Consolidated Benevolent Association, 1942), p. 23.
19. Loomis, *Six Chinese Companies*, p. 223.
20. Gibson, *Chinese in America*, pp. 341-43.
21. Ibid., pp. 343-44.
22. Sen. Doc. 689. Testimony of T.H King, p. 95. Professor Coolidge has attempted to discredit Captain King's testimony, since it was the most important in deciding whether or not there was a coolie trade to California. King was a San Francisco merchant, and had resided in China for ten years. While in China he had served as assistant to U.S. Consul Bailey and had been implicated in Bailey's embezzlement of consular fees. The point at issue for Professor Coolidge was whether or not the Chinese immigrants to California came under involuntary labor contracts or as "free" laborers; that is, laborers under no contract or under voluntary contracts. Testimony of Chinese at Hong Kong or

Canton to the effect that they were leaving voluntarily may be doubted. But the credit-ticket system just described includes the voluntary contract. Attacks on Captain King's honesty do not undermine his testimony, since he admits that consular irregularities permit the emigration of many coolies. Other witnesses also testified about the poor state of our consular system in China.
See Testimony of Brooks, *Chinese Immigration*, pp. 100-1.
In general see Coolidge, *Chinese Immigration*, pp. 48-52, 104-6;
Sandmeyer, *Anti-Chinese Movement*, pp. 25-29;
Campbell, *Chinese Coolie Emigration*, pp. 28-39.

23. See Appendix.
24. The Chung Wah Kongsi publicly acknowledged this state of affairs in an address prepared for the congressional investigation of 1876:

> The United States has been open to Chinese emigration for more than twenty years. Many Chinamen have come; few have returned. Why is this? Because among our Chinese people a few in California have acquired a fortune and returned home with joy. A desire to obtain a competency having arisen in the heart, our people have not shrunk from toil and trouble. They have expected to come here for one or two years and make a little fortune and return. Who among them ever thought of all these difficulties? Expensive rents, expensive living. A day without work means a day without food. For this reason, though wages are low, yet they are compelled to labor and live in poverty, quite unable to return to their native land.

Address of the Chinese Six Companies to the American Public. Presented and read to the congressional committee by Colonel F.A. Bee, attorney for the Chinese Six Companies, April 5, 1876, Sen. Doc. 689, p. 39.

25. Non-Chinese foreigners refused to pay the tax and drove off the collectors. See "Statement of L.A. Bensancon," *California Senate Journal, 2d sess., Appendix M,* No. 2 (1851). The attorney general of California believed the tax was unconstitutional and unsuccessfully brought suit to have it declared so. *People v. Naglee. California Senate Journal, 2d sess., Appendix* 1851, pp. 683-701.
26. Coolidge, *Chinese Immigration*, p. 57.
27. In 1852-54, the collector received 10% of his total collections; in 1854-61, he received 15%, the sheriff, 3%, Recorder, 3%; in 1861-69, the collector received 20%. Ibid., p. 37n.
28. Pun Chi, "A remonstrance from the Chinese in California to the Congress of the United States," trans. Reverend William Speer, *The Oldest and the Newest Empire: China and the United States* (Hartford: S.S. Scranton, 1870), pp. 575-81. The remonstrance was written in the late 1850s, or early 1860s, but not published until 1870.
29. Ibid.
30. McLeod, *Pigtails and Gold Dust*, pp. 54-55.

31. It should be remembered that after 1854, the Chinese lost the right of testimony in California court actions in which Caucasians were involved. *People v. Hall*, 4 California 399, (1854); *Speer v. See Yup*, 13 Cal. 73, (1855); *People v. Elyea*, 14 Cal. 144 (1855).
32. "New Rules of the Yeung Wo Ui-Kun," adopted 1854, trans. Speer, "Democracy of the Chinese," *Harper's Monthly*, November 1868, pp. 845-46.
33. Richard Hay Drayton, "The Chinese Six Companies," *Californian Illustrated Magazine*, August 1893, p. 472.
34. H.C. Bennett, "The Chinese in California, Their Numbers and Influence," *Sacramento Daily Union*, November 27, 1869, p. 8.
35. Cf. Robert Michels, *Political Parties* (New York: Free Press, 1915, 1958), pp. 86-96.
36. "New Rules of the Yeung Wo Ui-Kun," trans. Speer.
37. Fong Kum Ngon, *Chinese Six Companies*, p. 525.
38. Henry Burden McDowell, "A New Light on the Chinese," *Harper's Monthly Magazine*, December 1892, p. 14.
39. Loomis, "Holiday in the Chinese Quarter," *Overland Monthly*, February 1869, p. 147.
40. "New Rules of the Yeung Wo Ui-Kun," trans. Speer.
41. Loomis, "Six Chinese Companies," p. 223.
42. Leong Gor Yun, *Chinatown Inside Out*, pp. 51-52.
43. Ibid., p. 50.
44. Loomis, "Chinese 'Funeral Baked Meats,'" *Overland Monthly*, July 1869, p. 29.
45. For one recent critical description of the role and activities of the Chung Wah Kongsi see Rose Hum Lee, *The Chinese in the United States of America* (Hong Kong: Hong Kong University Press, 1960), pp. 144-61, 184.
46. Loomis, "Six Chinese Companies," p. 223.
47. Fong Kum Ngon, *Chinese Six Companies*, pp. 524-525.

> In the government of the four hundred clans, and the village and district life, the elders over sixty years of age, and the graduates (of whatever age) of the literary examinations, form one council or shan-sze, under a *fuyin* ("mayor"), or *tepao* ("dean") of their own. ...The government tax is paid and the land is divided up among the highest bidders by the council. ...Family disputes, debts, wayward youths, village works, wells, lawsuits (most of them on water rights), celebrations, processions, and the clan's policy toward other clans, and the government as represented in the mandarin, taotai, and viceroy—are all controlled by the council. Six clans send all the emigrants to America. Their names are Sam Yup; Yung Wo; Hop Wo; Yan Wo; Kong Chow; and Ning Yung, known to us as the famous "Six Companies of San Francisco."

J.S. Thompson, *The Chinese*, pp. 168-69.

48. Culin, "Customs of the Chinese in America," p. 193.
49. "New Rules of the Yeung Wo Ui-Kun," trans. Speer.
50. Some of its more important proclamations are:
"Letter of the Chinamen to His Excellency Governor Bigler." San Francisco, April 29, 1852;
Lai Chan Chuen, "Reply to the Message of His Excellency, Governor John Bigler" (1855) in Speer, *The Oldest and Newest Empire*, pp. 578-81;
Address of the Chinese Six Companies to the American Public, Report 689, p. 39;
The Chinese Question From a Chinese Stand-Point, June 1873, in Gibson, *Chinese in America*, pp. 285-92;
"Letter to A.J. Bryant, Mayor of the City and County of San Francisco," April 5, 1875, in Gibson, *Chinese in America*, pp. 306-8;
A Memorial From Representative Chinamen in America to His Excellency U.S. Grant, President of the United States, 1876, in Gibson, *Chinese in America*, pp. 315-23;
Chi, "A Remonstrance from the Chinese in California to the Congress of the United States," n.d., in Speer, *Newest Empire*, pp. 588-604.
51. Few "pro-Chinese" elements appear to have been acting without some special interest in mind. The agriculturalists wanted cheap labor. The Protestant missionaries sought conversions; when the Chinese proved recalcitrant, the missionaries lost interest. See Paul Taylor, "Foundations of California Rural Society," *California Historical Society Quarterly*, September 1945, pp. 193-228;
Robert Seagar II, "Some Denominational Reactions to Chinese Immigration to California, 1856-1892," *Pacific Historical Review*, February 1959, pp. 49-66.
A good example of unanalyzed commitment to the Six Companies is Coolidge, *Chinese Immigration*, esp. pp. 406-12.
52. See Appendix for information and citation on these two incidents.
53. Testimony of F.F. Low, *Chinese Immigration*, p. 70.
54. See Appendix.
55. As late as 1895, Chinese laborers were being secured by contract from Singapore:

> Vice-President Maxwell Somerville exhibited a series of photographs of Chinese laborers, obtained from a factor at Singapore. Various types were represented. Each man was photographed with his name written in Chinese characters on a slip of paper pinned on his blouse. Copies of the printed contracts between the employers and laborers were also shown, one in Chinese and another in English. The term of service is for three years. An advance of thirty dollars is made by the employer.

Proceedings of the Numismatic and Antiquarian Society of Philadelphia, November 7, 1895, pp. 99-100.
56. Fong Kum Ngon, *Chinese Six Companies*, pp. 523-24.

57. Bennett, "Chinese in California," p. 8.
58. Fong Kum Ngon, *Chinese Six Companies*, p. 524.
59. Ibid.
60. Chinese Chamber of Commerce, p. 5;
 Lee, *Chinese in the United States*, p. 146.
61. Lee, *Chinese in the United States*, pp. 385-386.
62. Loomis, "Six Chinese Companies," p. 226.
63. Sen. Doc. 633, pp. 411-13;
 Coolidge, *Chinese Immigration*, pp. 406-7.
64. Coolidge, *Chinese Immigration*, p. 407.
65. Ibid.
66. Ibid.
67. Leong Gor Yun, *Chinatown Inside Out*, p. 38.
68. For examples of the hardships of this system see ibid., pp. 40-49.
69. Ibid., pp. 36-39.
70. Ibid., pp. 37-38.
71. "Philosophically, gambling is not essentially bad; it is merely a test of luck. But this argument does not account for growth of the gambling business in Chinatown, though most gamblers use this as justification when they begin haunting gambling houses. The business has grown *because it is the only social outlet that holds out the possibility of economic freedom*, as much as because the Chinese are gamblers by nature." Leong Gor Yun, *Chinatown Inside Out*, p. 192. Emphasis added.
72. Not a few of the so-called tong wars to be discussed had as the immediate casus belli a dispute over purchase of the contract of a Chinatown courtesan.
73. H.H. Bancroft, "Mongolianism in America," p. 356, This figure is probably an exaggeration, but there is no doubt of the traffic in women; so also Gibson, *Chinese in America*, pp. 127-57; and sources cited in footnote 74.
74. For the sworn statements of imported prostitutes, see Reports of the U.S. Industrial Commission on Immigration... *Chinese and Japanese Labor in the Mountain and Pacific States*, XV, part IV (Washington: G.P.O., 1901), pp. 771-72, 783-91.
 For a description of the traffic see Charles Frederick Holder, "Chinese Slavery in America," *North American Review* CLXV July 1897, pp. 288-94.
 For the reproduction of a prostitution contract see Gibson, *Chinese in America*, p. 139.
 For general descriptions see Loomis, "Chinese Women in California," *Overland Monthly*, April 1869, pp. 344-50;
 Report of the Special Committee to...the *Board of Supervisors of the City and County of San Francisco*, September 1885, in William B. Farwell, *The Chinese at Home and Abroad* (San Francisco: A.L. Bancroft, 1885), vol. II, pp. 8-16.
 Apparently the women who came were déclassé; they are described as "big footed"; that is, as having never had bound feet. These women were

probably Hakkas who lived in boats around Hong Kong and Canton, or who were victims of the Hakka-Punti War.

75. Gibson, *Chinese in America*, p. 139. Another contract, nearly identical will be found on p. 140 of the same work.

76. "Official Map of Chinatown in San Francisco," prepared under the supervision of the Special Committee of the Board of Supervisors, July 1885, in Farwell, *Chinese at Home*, insert.

77. Voluntary statement of Lee Yow Chun, January 17, 1898;
Statement made by Lieutenant of Police William Price to Commissioner of Immigration Hart H. North, San Francisco, September 22, 1898;
Statement of Chun Ho, rescued slave girl...San Francisco, September 17, 1898;
Statement made by Donaldina Cameron...San Francisco, September 2, 1898;
Statement of Gon Sung...September 2, 1898;
Statement of Gui Ngun...September 2, 1898.
All in *Reports of the U.S. Industrial Commission on Immigration,*... pp. 773-92.
See also Gibson, *Chinese in America*, pp. 127-57;
Carol Green Wilson, *Chinatown Quest, The Life Adventures of Donaldina Cameron* (Stanford: Stanford U.P., 1950, 1931).

78. Stewart Culin, *The Gambling Games of the Chinese in America*, Publications of the University of Pennsylvania, Series in Philology, Literature, and Archaeology, vol I, no. 4, 1891;
Culin, "Customs of the Chinese in America," *Journal of American Folk-Lore*, July/September 1890, pp. 196-97.

79. Statement of J. Endicott Gardner, United States Chinese inspector, San Francisco, California, February 23, 1900;
Statement made by Lieutenant of Police William Price to commissioner of immigration...September 22, 1898. *Reports of the U.S. Industrial Commission*, pp. 768-71, 775-82.
Testimony of Mr. Ellis, chief of police of San Francisco; Testimony of An Chung; Testimony of Ah Gow; Testimony of Ah Dan; Testimony of Lem Schaum. *Report of Special Committee...Board of Supervisors of San Francisco*, 1885, pp. 50-56.
Stewart Culin, "The I Hing," pp. 54-55.
The Thirty-six articles which made up the oath sworn by members of the Hung League contained numerous prohibitions on revealing the secrets of the order and specific penalties for violation. Article 7 forbade members from informing on their brethern in criminal matters; Articles 15, 22, and 25 required that the brethern aid in the escape of a member from prison, prohibited informing authorities on disputes among members, and prohibited testifying against any member before a public tribunal. Gustave Schlegel, *Thian Ti Hwui. The Hung League or Heaven-Earth League. A Secret Society with the Chinese in China and India* (Batavia: Lange, 1866), pp. 135-43.
See also John Gilmer Speed, "Chinese Secret Societies of New York

City," *Harper's Weekly*, July 14, 1900, p. 658.
For a summary of the ritual of initiation into a tong see "Chinese Highbinders," *Current Literature* 27, March 1900, pp. 275-77.

80. A contract of the Chee Kung Tong demonstrates the mutual obligations that governed the relations between the agent of the tong and the organization.

> To Lum Hip, *salaried soldier:*
>
> It has been said that to plan schemes and devise methods and to held the seal is the work of the literary class, while to oppose foes, fight battles, and plant firm government is the work of the military.
>
> Now this tong appoints salaried soldiers, to be ready to protect ourselves and assist others. This is our object.
>
> All, therefore, who undertake the military service of this tong must obey orders and without orders you must not dare to act. If any of our brethern are suddenly molested it will be necessary for you to act with resolute will.
>
> You shall always work to the interest of the tong and never make your office a means of private revenge.
>
> When orders are given you shall advance valiantly to your assigned task. Never shrink or turn your back upon the battlefield.
>
> When a ship arrives in port with prostitutes on board and the grand master issues an order for your to go down and receive them you must be punctual and use all your ability for the good of the Commonwealth (or State).
>
> If in the discharge of your duty you are slain we will undertake to pay $500 sympathy money to your friends.
>
> If you are wounded a doctor will be engaged to heal your wounds, and if you are laid up for any length of time you will receive $10 per month.
>
> If you are maimed for life and incapacitated for work $250 shall be paid to you and a subscription taken to defray costs of your journey home to China.
>
> This paper is given as proof, as word of mouth may not be believed.
>
> Furthermore, whenever you exert your strength to kill or wound enemies of this tong, and in doing so you are arrested and imprisoned, $100 per year shall be paid to your friends during your imprisonment.
>
> Dated 13th day of 4th Month of 14th year Kwong Sui, Victoria, B.C. (Seal of Chee Kung Tong).

Letter of Instructions to a Highbinder or Salaried Solider. Exhibits attached to statement of J. Endicott Gardner. *Reports of the U.S Industrial Commission*, p. 771.

81. New York is a series of worlds within worlds, like the little ivory

spheres which the Chinese so deftly carve. Quite the inner one of these, by far the most conservative, estranged and difficult to penetrate understandingly, is that triangular blotch in the great city's very heart bounded by the rifts of Pell and Mott streets and Chatham square. If a stone barrier the breadth and height of the walls of Shanghai were built about this district, and the only entrance to this inner world were a "needle's eye," so far as concerns the welfare and the content of the average Chinaman within, such a cutting off from the world would be a kindness rather than a hardship. So complete is the Celestial's little world, and so all in all to one another are Chinamen in their own haunts, that they can do without the rest of the contiguous motley of foreign colonies, the government, its constitution, its laws, and its franchises. Insular as a caddis worm, the Chinaman has enclosed himself in a stone cell, out of which he moves rarely, and never very far. There are Chinamen who would be utterly lost two blocks away from their district, and who, although residents of the quarter for years, know nothing and care nothing for the white world save that which they gather from occasional glimpses through plate glass to and from Evergreen Cemetery, where the bodies of many departed Celestials lie until such time as their bones are gathered up to be transported back to the Flowery Kingdom and to be mingled with the dust of the fathers.

Speed, "Chinese Secret Societies of New York City," p. 658.

Conflict in Chinatown ||8

|| INTRODUCTION

The so-called tong wars, said to be characteristic of nineteenth-century Chinatowns, have usually been treated in three ways: (1) as romantic mysteries of an exotic and strange people; (2) as incidents which erupted from time to time to upset the harmoniousness of an otherwise peaceful and hardworking people; and (3) as a "social problem" indicative of social disorganization. None of these descriptions is accurate. The first—to be found in literary and cinematic stereotypes and human interest articles in metropolitan newspapers[1]—is too fanciful to be relevant for a sociological analysis of Chinatown's structure of conflict. The second—a frequent concomitant of Sinophilic journalism[2]—misunderstands the relation of conflict to Chinatown social organization. The third—a common feature of sociological writing on the Chinese community[3]—does not comprehend the socio-cultural aspects of Chinatown's pattern of antagonism.

A noted American sociologist has observed that "Conflict is an ever present process in human relations."[4] In Chinatown conflict and order are parts of the same process that Charles H. Cooley noted when he observed, "The more one thinks of it, the more he will see that conflict and cooperation are not separate things, but phases of one process which always involves something of both."[5] Conflict has been an endemic feature of overseas Chinese life. Its presence does not indicate social disorganization. Indeed, conflict contributes to the persistence of Chinatown as a community.[6]

CAUSES OF CONFLICT

Social conflicts within and between groups in Chinatown were struggles for scarce "resources": wealth, status, power, and—an especially scarce "item" in Chinatown—women. Although our knowledge of the *casus belli* for the many conflicts that broke out in Chinatown is inadequate, four major causes for intergroup strife may be discerned: (1) rival aspirations for control over business operations in Chinatown or for control of its entire political economy; (2) transplantation of mainland civil wars or revolutions to Chinatown; (3) revolts of the poor against the ghetto community's governing plutocracy; and (4) rival claims to a woman.[7]

Power Struggles

As the secret societies grew in number and membership they challenged the right of the clan-kongsi elite to rule in Chinatown. In the late 1880s, a war was declared between the Suey Sing Tong and the Wong Clan in San Francisco. "...This was more than a war between two factions. It was a war to determine the status of the tongs, whether they were to remain or be ruled by the larger families."[8] A few years later, after a costly but unsuccessful attempt by the Chung Wah Kongsi to test the constitutionality of the Geary Act, several secret societies united in a violent and vituperative campaign designed to persuade Chinatown's denizens to renounce their allegiance to the "Six Companies."[9]

At the turn of the century, several powerful secret societies in New York City and San Francisco fought one another for control over the lucrative gambling, smuggling, and prostitution rackets operating in Chinatown.[10] In these fights the stakes were high, and the battles fierce. In the course of these struggles, smaller secret societies were destroyed by annihilation or they were absorbed into larges ones. In the end, a precarious secret society oligopoly over illegal business emerged in Chinatown, just as a conflict-ridden criminal oligopoly emerged in American society outside of Chinatown.

Mainland Wars Transplanted Overseas

The rivalries between various language groupings, which were in part responsible for the lawlessness of southeastern China, were transplanted overseas by the immigrants. The Hakka-Punti War was fought in Kwangtung between 1855 and 1868, and overseas wherever Hakkas and Cantonese ("Punti") came into contact.[11] In Malaya, "the

Hakkas in Penang and afterward in Perak formed the bulk of the Hai San secret society, whose struggle with the Ghee Hins (Cantonese) for the possession of the Larut tin fields gave rise to the Larut wars of 1862-73."[12] In 1854, the Sam Yup Kongsi fell out with the Yan Wo (Hakka) Kongsi at China Camp and at Weaverville, California. In one battle 900 Yan Wo "soldiers" met 1,200 of the Sam Yup "army" and fought until the Sam Yup declared themselves victorious and retired. Both groups of antagonists secured military assistance from local Californians who trained them in the use of firearms.[13]

After 1900, many of the so-called tong wars were between supporters of rival parties[14] seeking to overthrow the Manchu Dynasty. It is well known that Sun Yat sen's revolution was mounted from various overseas Chinese bases, especially those in the Dutch East Indies, but the role played by the American Chinese has not been fully clarified. Although the several secret societies and the various kongsis were able to unite in support of antidynastic action in China and better treatment of Chinese settlers in the Dutch colony,[15] no such unity was achieved in the United States. The Chee Kung Tong apparently lent its support to Dr. Sun's anti-Manchu movement, but after the Republic was proclaimed the various tongs supported rival rebel groups and fought one another accordingly. These fights coincided with struggles for power in Chinatown among the various tongs.[16]

Revolts of the Poor

Some of Chinatown's hostilities were primitive "class conflicts." They represented the nonideological revolts of inarticulate poor people against a system which they resented but could not replace.[17] The violent altercation between the Yee Clan and the On Yick Tong, ostensibly began because of an argument over a prostitute, also reflected the impoverished cooks' and waiters' resentment of the Yee Clan's wealth and status. One of the most powerful clans in the United States,[18] many of the Yees were Chinatown merchants; its clan treasury allegedly had hundreds of thousands of dollars. In contrast, the On Yick Tong consisted of poor and lowly laborers:

> ...[T]he On Yick Tong seems hardly worthy of mention. It had a little over one hundred members in San Francisco, less in Stockton, California, and a few in Portland.
>
> ...[T]he On Yicks were poor and lowly. Most...were cooks and restaurant workers. There were few gamblers in their ranks. It was considered the smallest on the tong roster. During weekdays there was hardly an On Yick to be seen on the streets of

> Chinatown, as everyone worked. Only on Saturday nights and on Sundays did they assemble.[19]

Rival Claims Over Women

With the extreme imbalance in Chinatown's sex ratio, it is not surprising that fights broke out over rival claims to a woman. These quarrels between rival suitors often became pretexts for intertong or clan-tong warfare.[20] This was especially the case if the woman in question was under contract to work in a brothel owned or controlled by a secret society. Should one of these women marry a Chinese before her term of service was up, the employer charged her with breach of contract. Sometimes the would-be groom was unwilling to buy up the woman's contract and sought to kidnap her. Rivalries over women were one of the most frequent causes for conflict in nineteenth-century Malayan and American Chinatowns.[21] Nearly every tong war described by Gong and Grant, John Gilmer, Speed, and Robert Wells Ritchie has as its background a quarrel—between rival suitors or between a suitor and a brothel keeper—that erupted into an interassociation fight.

MODES OF CONFLICT

Violence

In an illuminating discussion of certain features of African social structure, Max Gluckman has argued

> that in these societies custom establishes certain conflicts between men, and may thus produce quarrels among them. Custom at least controls the places where quarrels may take place. But custom also brings into work mechanisms which inhibit the development of the quarrels and which exert pressure for settlement.[22]

A parallel is to be found in overseas Chinese society. In Chinatown, local conditions as well as custom, established conflicts between men: wars for wealth, status, power, and women broke out frequently, but custom dictated whether and how these deadly quarrels would be initiated, fought, and resolved. The traditional ways of initiating, fighting, and settling disputes in Chinatown were affected very little by the customs or the constraints imposed by the larger society.

From accounts of inter-association struggles presented in popular books and essays and in recent newspapers,[23] it is possible to construct the stages through which conflicts are initiated, fought, and settled.

Stage 1

For any of a variety of reasons, an altercation occurs between two persons or two groups.[24] In the Sam Yup-Hakka dispute, for example, some of the latter rolled a huge boulder down on the mining claim of the Sam Yups. The wars between the On Yick Tong and the Yee Clan and between the On Leong Tong and the Four Brothers' Association erupted after a dispute over "ownership" of a prostitute. Many fights arose out of attempts to eliminate business rivals. After 1913, a number of intertong wars broke out over political support for "left," "centrist," or "right" factions in the civil war in China.

After an immediate exchange of uncivilities, the offended parties repair to their respective association headquarters to seek aid from their compatriots.

Stage 2

The councils of the respective societies take under advisement the complaint of the offended members. If it is felt that the men have been improperly aggrieved and that the insult reflects on the entire society, the council decides that vengeance or reparations must be exacted from the offending society. If reparations are demanded, and if the other society agrees to pay, negotiations are undertaken in order to determine the nature and amount of the payment. A recent dispute between the Bing Kung and Hop Sing tongs was settled peacefully after five months of difficult negotiations. In some cases, however, the members' anger impedes any negotiated conclusion to hostilities. The On Yick-Yee dispute became violent after individual reprisals on both sides made the continuation of negotiations between the council heads impossible.[25]

If vengeance is deemed necessary, the offended society posts a declaration of war (*chun hung*) in the streets of Chinatown. The declaration names the enemy and states, in abusive language, the impending fate of the wrongdoer. The chun hung of the Sam Yup Kongsi posted against the Yan Wo (Hakka)) Society illustrates the form of these declarations:

> **Challenge From the Sam Yup Company at Rock River Ranch to the Yun Wo Company at Chinese Camp**

> There are a great many now existing in the world who ought to be exterminated. We, by this, give you a challenge, and inform you beforehand, that we are the strongest, and you are too weak to oppose us. We can, therefore, wrest your claim, or anything else from you and give you notice to drive you away before us, and make you ashamed of yourselves. You are nothing as compared to us. We are durable as stone, but you are pliant as a sponge.
>
> Your force would have no more effect against us than an egg would against a stone. You want to coax us to come to terms. That we refused to do. We mean to fight you, and expel you all from your localities. If you don't stand and fight us, we will consider you no better than so many brutes; and, as such, we will harness you to our own desires. There are plenty of us, well-equipped, and ready, at any time, to meet you and fight you, wherever you choose; and [we] will make you run into your holes and hide yourselves. But we need not go to that trouble. We have only to speak and you will become frightened. You won't stand like men; you die perfect worms, or like the dog who sits in the door and barks, but will go no further. If you won't accept this challenge, we tell you, by the way, to go and buy lots of flour, and hide yourselves, and we'll kill every man of you that we come across. Shame! Shame![26]

If a society declares a particular person to be the target for its vengeance, a notice of proscription is sometimes posted, couched in vulgar and abusive language. The chun hung posted for Chun Ti Chu, president of the Sam Yup Kongsi, after his abortive and costly attempt at having the Geary Act declared unconstitutional read:

> The President of the Sam Yup Company contains twelve stinkpots which are inexplicable. He has no literary talent. He bought his position with money. His father was a reformed thief. ...He shields guilty criminals, and tries to free them. He provoked people to anger at a meeting and tried to escape. Therefore all people had better close their noses before passing his door.[27]

Stage 3

Once vengeance has been decided upon, open "warfare" breaks out. Stores in Chinatown close down, tourists avoid the area, and the streets are haunted by the paid mercenaries of the belligerents. The object in these fights is to extract sufficient "blood" to repay the insult. Usually only the "salaried soldiers" of the societies participate in the actual hostilities, though occasionally innocent bystanders or noncombatants are casualties. In 1871, in Los Angeles, a policeman was killed in the course of a tong war; a mob of Los Angeles's white citizens descended upon Chinatown and killed over a score of Chinese, few of whom had been actually involved in the fighting.

Sometimes a "war" consists only of plot and counterplot to assassinate rival association leaders. Such were the "wars" in which twelve San Francisco tongs united against the oppressive exploitation of the Sam Yup Kongsi leader, Fong Chong (alias "Little Pete");[28] against his predecessor, Loke Tung; and against the aforementioned Chun Ti Chu.

In some wars the strain imposed by conflicting loyalties to clan on the one hand and tong on the other can become very serious. In one struggle between the On Yick Tong and the Yee Clan, members of the latter were put into a very difficult position since all the tongs rallied to the cause of the beleaguered On Yick group and there were Yees in every tong, including the On Yick.[29] Gaut Sing Dock, a mercenary affiliated with the Hip Sing and eight other tongs, allegedly murdered Yees so wantonly that Yee Toy, a leader of the Hip Sing Tong, killed him in an act of revenge for his clan brothers.

Stage 4

After the fighting has gone on for some time, peace overtures are broached. Sometimes these arise from among the belligerents themselves, at other times from neutral interested parties. In the latter instance, peace is sometimes imposed by threat or by force.

The war that broke out when the Hip Sing Tong challenged the On Leong Tong for control of Chinatown's vice operations was marked by a complicated strategy. At this time an anti-corrpution campaign was being carried forward in New York City by Rev. Charles Parkhurst and his Society for the Prevention of Crime, a group of private citizens who raided criminal haunts in order to embarrass the police. Huey Gow and Mock Duck, leaders of the Hip Sing Tong, told Rev. Parkhurst where On Leong gambling activities went on, utilizing these non-Chinese authorities to eliminate their competitors. Meanwhile, the On Leong Tong had bribed the New York sheriff; the city's police were on their side. The warring secret societies played off a dispute between the district attorney's office and the New York police to their own advantage. During the course of the scandal that erupted over the corruption of the public authorities, On Leong and Hip Sing gunmen carried on a shooting war in New York City, Boston, and Philadelphia. At length a truce was negotiated when state supreme court Judge Warren W. Foster, who had familiarized himself with

Chinese feuds, arranged for a peace conference to be held in his office. After due deliberation, and

> with due pomp and solemnity the judge produced elaborate articles of peace, duly engrossed and sealed, and ordered the plenipotentiaries to sign them. Very gravely the names were affixed: those of Tom Lee and Jim Gum, his lieutenant; Mock Duck, Wong Git, and Wong Sam, the wicked secessionists. A very formal joint banquet of the tongs in honor of Judge Foster and members of the District Attorney's staff followed and clinched the peace proceedings.[30]

Although the role played by the Chung Wah Kongsi is not clear, that body seems to have held out the threat of economic reprisals or betrayal of the tongs to the police:

> The Ching Wah Gung Shah decreed that the war between the On Leongs and Hip Sings must stop. It stopped.[31]

Intertong disputes and wars between tongs and kongsis sometimes did not end until the Chinese government had intervened. In the final years of Manchu rule in China, the imperial government suspected that an anti-Manchu revolution would be mounted with the economic and military aid of overseas Chinese, and that revolutionary support would come mainly from the secret societies. Overseas Chinese consular officials often intervened in kongsi-tong disputes in behalf of pro-Manchu kongsis. To prevent the further organization of secret societies Ho Yow, the Chinese consul in San Francisco, once suggested that the United States grant an unusual extraterritorial right over "corporations" to the Chinese Consulate.

> Q. What would you think of a law of Congress that would provide that mere membership upon the part of any alien in this country in any organization that has for its purpose the commission of crime or violation of law would be a felony and any alien found belonging to such organization should be deported?
> A. If such a law could be enforced I think it would be an excellent thing, but it is very hard to prove that they are other than what they represent them[selves] to be, seemingly innocent organizations, as they are [in]corporated under the State Laws.
> Q. How would it be to specify the different things which are considered violation of the law, such as blackmail, etc.?
> A. I would make this suggestion: Before any organization can be

perfected the by-laws must be submitted to the representative of their own country and secure the official indorsement before the organization can be perfected.
Q. I had in mind, Mr. Consul, the organization of a special court or tribunal before which might be tried all the questions which may arise, such as to deportation, etc., and rather than vest such great power in any one man, I thought it would be wise to have a court of three or four members and the consul or highest official at each port representing each country to act as *ex officio* member of such court?
A. I think it is a very good thing and quite agree with you.[32]

The Chinese consul general, working with the Chung Wah Kongsi and the San Francisco police, helped to end the war between the Hop Sing and Suey Sing tongs in 1900. When the hostilities first broke out, Ho Yow posted a notice in the name of the emperor of China:

> Implore my people to keep the peace. In a country so far from our native land, a colony such as exists in San Francisco should be in continuous peace. We should be as one brother to another. There should be no more quarreling; it is shameful in the eyes of other nations. Only two companies are engaged in the present war, and this is not their first quarrel. These men must change their ways, and not be like wild beasts in the jungle. If this trouble is not settled without further blood, I will invoke the aid of the Six Companies and the Merchants' Association, and bring the offenders to American justice.[33]

After six men had been killed, Ho Yow and the Chinatown merchants were able to effect a temporary truce during the shopping days preceding the celebration of Chinese New Year. But, with the murder of a Suey Sing member, the truce was broken, and the fighting resumed. Thereupon, true to this promise, Ho Yow, joined by the leading merchants, his own private detective force, and the San Francisco police, arrested all those Chinese without the immigration certificates required by the Geary Act and had them deported. The war ended. The deportations had cut deeply into the ranks of the tongs, many of whose gunmen were illegal immigrants.[34]

The business boycott and shooting war between the Sam Yup Kongsi and the peoples of the Sz Yup, organized as twelve united tongs, was also ended through the mediation of Ho Yow. The Sam Yup leader having been killed, the consul initiated negotiations between the warring factions and settled all issues except one: a resentment over the refusal of the Sam Yup to recognize that a Sz Yup man, Wong Chu, wrongfully accused of murder, was innocent, as an American court had decided. Ho Yow proceeded from that point.

> His first effort was to get both sides to dismiss their lawyers.... Wong-Chu was treated as an innocent man, the decree of the American court in his favor being recognized. The Sam Yups agreed to pay the full expense of his trial and to recognize him as an injured man; the See Yups were to permanently renounce a certain legal firm which had been inordinately active in keeping the disturbances alive, and this they agreed to do. Upon these terms with the payment of the money stipulated, peace was declared, the boycott was called off, the fighting men were forbidden to do any more shooting, and it was formally promulgated by the warring factions that all persons might proceed in the open without apprehension of bodily molestation. Business at once revived, and so grateful were the Chinese for the mediation of Mr. Ho, that in accordance with their request he was raised to the position of Consul general....

The peace treaty concluding a "war" is sealed by a banquet to which the belligerents are invited. If the war has been settled such that one group has been declared at fault, that group is required to host and pay for the feast. However, the honor of the loser is not wholly demeaned by this custom: tradition and proper etiquette require that the host be duly honored at the banquet which he sponsors. By custom, no reference is made to the feud just concluded.

In 1913, a Chinese Peace Society was formed in San Francisco; soon after, another was established in New York City. Composed of kongsi and tong leaders, the society has as its principal purpose the prevention of violent outbreaks in Chinatown: by 1917, the "Chinese Peace Society,...with a neutral as chairman, had caused many a war to be averted, through careful arbitration of the problems,...which might have caused conflicts."[36]

After 1924, the Chung Wah Kongsi in New York City and elsewhere, was reorganized with representation accorded not only to the kongsis, but also to the secret societies, a recognition that many Chinese held dual affiliations. In the reorganization:

> The board of the society consists of one representative from each tong and one from each of the business houses. The most active members of the board are representatives of the On Leong and Hip Sing tongs, the Ning Yang and Lun Sin guilds, the Gee

> Kung Tong, or Freemasons, the Chinese Chamber of Commerce, and the Kim Lun which was founded by Sing Dock...These seven representatives are empowered to make final decisions.[37]

Nonviolent Modes of Conflict

Not all disputes in Chinatown were characterized by violence. Chinatown's political and commercial rivals sometimes exploited the same weaknesses and corruptibility that American captains of industry utilized between 1865 and 1910: public law was made into an instrument of private vengeance.[38] In Chinatown, however, such aggrandizements remained community-bound. Although both kongsis and secret societies sought the aid of American agencies of enforcement to remove their competitors or cripple their operations, the kongsis, headed by respectable businessmen, were usually more successful at this than the unsavory tongs. During the first thirty years of tong-kongsi conflict (1855-85), the Chung Wah Kongsi attempted to persuade city police to shut down Chinatown gambling dens and deport Chinese prostitutes, hoping to strike down the economic base from which secret society power sprang. In 1855, Lai Chun Chuen, representing the then unfederated kongsis, wrote in response to California Governor Bigler's accusation that Chinese "vagabonds gather in various places and live by gambling."

> But collections of gamblers as well as dens of infamous women are forbidden in China by law. These are offenses that admit of a clear definition. Our mercantile class have a universal contempt for such. But obnoxious as they are, we have no power to drive them away. We have often wished these things were prevented, but we have no influence that can reach them. We hope and pray that your honorable country will enact vigorous laws by which brothels and gambling places may be broken up, and thus worthless fellows be compelled to follow some honest employment, gamblers to change their calling, and, moreover, your own policemen and petty officials be deprived of many opportunities of trickery and extortion. Harmony and prosperity may then prevail, and the days await us when each man can in peace engage in his own sphere of duty. Such is the earnest desire of the merchants who present this.[39]

A few years later the kongsis petitioned the United States Congress to banish vice from Chinatown. Their petition approached each of the evils differently. Prostitution could be prevented by deporting all abandoned Chinese women to China:

> At first all the abandoned women who came to California were boat women from the seacoast.... At that time, we Chinese proper, fearing that other people would mistake these for our own females, and thus disgraceful conceptions of us be spread abroad, specially requested your authorities to banish them. But the local authorities, not comprehending the evil, would not consent to their removal.... It is now our request that you will enact laws for the correction of this grievance. We beseech you to stringently require commanders of vessels, while they carry these women away, to bring no more of them back. And a time should be fixed within which all here shall be compelled to leave, themselves providing the means, and returning to their own people. Thus will we be rid of this spreading poison and be relieved of this disgrace.[40]

Gambling could be prevented by publicizing and enforcing the recent statute prohibiting it:

> In our Middle Kingdom gambling is forbidden by law. Formerly, on account of its not being forbidden in your honorable country, many men learned this vice, and the results have been deeply injurious. Now we are fortunate in having a law against it passed by you and put into operation. If only men knew that they must rigidly obey it, and if from this time forth there shall be no secret granting of licenses, then we might hope that those who had learned this vice might return to honest occupations.[41]

Last and most important, the merchants sought to eliminate the leaders of the secret societies. The *Remonstrance* requested that the Chinese merchants be empowered to name the criminals in Chinatown that American authorities ought to prosecute:

> Among our Chinese there are some bad people; and only the Chinese can know who they are. If you will permit the Chinese merchants, they will prepare private statements as to such persons, vouching for them by the signature of their names. Thus rogues may be justly punished, and will understand that the laws are to be respected, and will be deterred from the commission of crimes; and they will return to the ways of virtue.[42]

That this last proposal was aimed at enlisting police aid in the competitive struggles of the kongsis against the secret societies and those Chinese who refused to accept kongsi authority was recognized by Reverend William Speer, a missionary who championed civil rights for Chinese in America. While he regarded the greater part of the *Remonstrance* as reasonable and just, Speer opposed any move that would permit the kongsi leaders to denounce Chinatown's few independent Christians:

> There is a reasonableness and justice in the requests and suggestions which should cause them to be weighed and adopted, if only we except that of the reference of questions relating to the characters of persons accused of crimes to the opinion of "The Chinese Merchants," meaning probably their Association, or Exchange, in San Francisco. Personal prejudices, jealousies among the people of different clans, and displeasure with some who leave the religion and customs of their fathers and adopt those of our country, might make such an opinion one which it would be unsafe for our courts to follow.[43]

The secret societies sometimes eliminated their enemies by informing the police of their illegal activities. Loke Tung and Fong Chong, both of whom were kongsi as well as tong officials, commonly acted as stool pigeons to the police and then took over the gambling operations of the jailed criminals.[44] Loke Tung is said to have organized a real estate syndicate, leased a large number of dwelling units in Chinatown, and charged such exhorbitant rents to the Sz Yup people that they were forced to crowd together and thus violate San Francisco's "cubic air ordinance" or leave the area.[45] Loke Tung's depredations so aroused the Sz Yup people that they united in their efforts to resist him. Eventually he was murdered by a professional assassin hired by the vengeance-seeking Chin Clan, a member of which he had killed.[46]

|| CONCLUSION

Conflict and Social Organization

A noted sociologist has pointed out that while at one time a high rate of socially pathological behavior—crime, suicide, alcoholism, and so forth—was believed to indicate social disorganization, or a state of anomie, further "study showed that many places—for example, many slums marked by high rates of crime—which looked, because something was obviously wrong, as if they must be disorganized were not in fact disorganized, if that word means a lack of social control and of intimate contact between men. Indeed these areas were overorganized rather than underorganized."[47] Our investigations suggest that Chinatown should be included in the list of such "overorganized" communities.

Order in Chinatown is manifested in its institutions of law and arbitration and in its regulation of conflict. Not all disagreements resulted in violence. Within the clan and the kongsi, disputes were settled by arbitration. The Chung Wah Kongsi acted as supreme arbiter in cases appealed to its executive board. However, not all of its decisions were accepted. Many resulted in withdrawal of the aggrieved party from the association and some were followed by a declaration of war. But the existence of law and order also implies the existence of its opposite: resistance and rebellion, and methods to cope with these.[48]

Rebellion, feuds, and violence in Chinatown—while lamentable from the point of human suffering—do not demonstrate disorganization, but rather the reverse. In Chinatown disagreement, dispute, hostilities, and settlement are patterned. Traditional folkways govern the manner in which individual resentments shall be channeled. Institutions have been established in which the aggrieved may complain and through which their feelings may be assuaged (or hurt further). Hostilities, including violence, are not chaotic and without organization. Indeed, the mode of hostility, the form and targets of violence, and the way to cessation of a struggle are each institutionalized.

That conflict and social organization in Chinatown are related is not surprising. Similar conclusions have been reached by investigations of so-called primitive societies. In the latter, conflict is as much a part of the institutionalized order as other social activities. Among the Kagoro, for example, when fights within a community broke out, only clubs, stones, and blunt weapons were permitted; in fights against neighboring villages, spears, slings and unpoisoned arrows were used; but in wars against aliens, spears and arrows were poisoned and stratagems were employed.[49] The Tiwi of northern Australia settled arguments about wife seduction by having accuser and accused face each other in a ring; after an abusive harangue, the accuser was permitted to hurl spears at his opponent who might dodge them for a while but who eventually had to let himself be hit. Wars with neighboring villages were carried on by armed groups who performed much the same rite of accusation and spear hurling as just described, only on a wider scale.[50]

Among the overseas Chinese, there is no "primitive society";

nevertheless the clan, kongsi, and secret society attempt to order the relations of their members and, in the case of the first two groups, to settle disputes by submission to higher authority. Although feuds do break out and violence is not unknown, there is among the Chinese a body of norms and practices throught which even murderous feuds are regulated.

Conflict and Group Cohesion

Georg Simmel and Lewis Coser have emphasized the several group-binding functions of social conflict.[51] The study of conflict in Chinatown indicates that there, as elsewhere, it has been a paradoxical basis for order and the enhancement of social solidarity.

Conflict bound Chinese together, first, with the group in which they were members; second, in that special effect of antagonistic cooperation, the binding of opponents in deadly embrace; third, within the overseas Chinese community toward which their struggles were directed.

The clan, kongsi, and secret society were each strengthened by conflicts with opponents. The conflict promoted the in-group feeling of each combatant and heightened the morale of group membership. This conforms to the generally accepted sociological proposition "that the distinctions between 'ourselves, the we-group, or in-group, and everybody else, or the others-groups, out-groups' is established in and through conflict."[52] However, this kind of association, alone, would not have made for a Chinese community, but rather only for the solidarity of the units arrayed against one another within Chinatown.

The conflict between the various associations in Chinatown bound them together and directed the attention and energies of one upon the other. Had family unification been possible or business organized in a less competitive spirit the secret societies might have become otiose. But, as conditions actually were, clans, kongsis, and tongs regarded each other with enmity. Moreover, their battles with one another had an inertia: each served to harden opposition and further bind the groups into patterned antagonism. Eventually conflict became ritualized and took on its own formality—the public declaration of war, the diplomatic negotiations, the treaty of peace, and the peace-securing banquet. Formalization also encouraged each antagonist to take a latent interest in the organization of its opponent, since only a rationally organized group could carry out "wars" and accede to peace overtures according to defined norms. Conflicts served to stabilize the rules of war; in this sense, they helped sustain order in a disharmonious community. The antagonistic elements could function without fear of a Hobbesian chaos.[53]

Conflict in Chinatown was "inner-directed"; it made no sense unless carried out within and in relation to the ghetto community. Clan feuds were directed against each other and not against American families or Irish clans. Clan-tong "wars" were fought over scarce resources: women, status, wealth, and power inside Chinatown. Insofar as elements not native to Chinatown—police, clergy, diplomats, and the representatives of the Chinese government—played a part in these struggles, they served as *ad hoc* catalysts, invoked to balance the power of one or another combatant. They were not utilized and indeed were avoided or repelled if they showed interest in upsetting the organization and folkways of Chinatown.

It was not in the interest of the elites of the various fighting groups to promote assimilation of the Chinese into American society. Assimilation would draw off the loyalties of association members; provide immigrants and their offspring with alternative modes of mobility outside Chinatown; and help to eliminate illegal community enterprises. The clans and kongsis established their right to "represent" the Chinese to American authorities, while the secret societies co-opted or corrputed the lesser elements in the outer society.

Their intramural conflicts served to isolate the Chinese communities from the larger society in the United States, and probably elsewhere. External antipathy set the boundaries beyond which neither individual Chinese nor Chinese social organizations could function. Internal conflict created rival groups who contended *with one another and not with outside elements.* The struggles reinforced the hostile organizations, institutionalized and channeled the conflict, and directed the energies of the contenders toward one another.

|| NOTES

1. For analyses of stereotyped imagery of the Chinese see
   Dorothy B. Jones, *The Portrayal of China and India on the American Scene, 1896-1955* (Cambridge, Mass.: Massachusetts Institute of Technology Press, 1955), pp. 13-36;
   William P. Fenn, *Ah Sin and His Brethern in American Literature* (Peking: College of Chinese Studies, 1933).
   For shorter analyses see
   Jacobus ten Broek, Edward Barnhart, and Floyd Matson, *Prejudice War, and the Constitution* (Berkeley: University of California Press, 1954), pp. 29-32;
   Rose Hum Lee, *The Chinese in the United States of America* (Hong Kong: Hong Kong University Press, 1960), pp. 261, 357-72.

2. Nineteenth-century writers were occasionally wont to dismiss tong wars by contrasting the secret society struggles with more ideological movements, and by showing that the "personal" grievances for which tong members fought resulted only in harm to Chinese antagonists:

> But you say, There is the terrible 'Hip Shing Tong,' the highbinders' society. Yes, even in New York this branch of the evil society exists; but against that let me place the imported Mafia of Italy, the nihilism of Russia, the anarchism of Germany and Italy; and while we weight one against the other, let us remember that while the Hip Shing Tong may sometimes become the instrument of private vengeance for personal wrongs, the anarchist club and the nihilist society hurl their death-dealing blows at great social and political institutions, and attack and destroy the pure and innocent without reason or cause.

Helen F. Clark, "The Chinese of New York Contrasted with their Foreign Neighbors," *The Century Magazine*, vol. LIII, no. 1, November 1896, p. 110.

3. Lee, *Chinese in the United States of America*, pp. 161-73, 334-41.
4. Kingsley Davis, *Human Society* (New York: Macmillan, 1948, 1949), p. 157.
5. *Social Process* (New York: Scribner's Sons, 1918), p. 39, quoted in Lewis Coser, *The Functions of Social Conflict* (New York: Free Press, 1956), p. 18.
6. For a general discussion of the positive functions of social conflict see Coser, *Social Conflict.*
7. The conflicts in Malaya were similar to those in the United States:

> The reasons for these clashes were many. One was the right to control lucrative "rackets" in a given area. Another was the traditional rivalry between the different tribes of Hakkas, Hokkiens, Cantonese, Hylam, Teochews, etc., which, unlike in China proper, were brought to live together for the first time in Malaya. Yet a third reason was jealousy over women.

Leon Comber, *Chinese Secret Societies in Malaya: A Survey of the Triad Society from 1800 to 1900* (Locust Valley: J.J. Augustin, 1959), p. 95.

8. Eng Ying Gong and Bruce Grant, *Tong War!* (New York: Nicholas L. Brown, 1930), p. 50.
9. Richard Hay Drayton, "The Chinese Six Companies," *California Illustrated Magazine*, August 1893, pp. 472-77.
10. Gong and Grant, *Tong War!*;
Lee, *Chinese in the United States*, pp. 161-73, 300-6, 334-40, 425-28.
11. A history of the Hakkas by Reverend E.J. Eitel will be found in the *China Review* II, 1873-74. It is quoted at length in Mervyn L. Wynne, *Triad and Tabut: A Survey of the Origins and Diffusion of Chinese and*

Mohammedan Secret Societies in the Malay Peninsula, A.D. 1800-1935 (Singapore: GPO, 1941), pp. 59-61.
A semifictional account of Hakka migrations and conflicts in China will be found in James Michener, *Hawaii* (New York: Random, 1959).

12. Wynne, *Triad and Tabut*, p. 60.
See also Comber, *Chinese Secret Societies*, pp. 94-173.
13. Alexander McLeod, *Pigtails and Gold Dust* (Caldwell: Caxton, 1947), pp. 53-56.
14. A similar kind of conflict occurred in Greek immigrant society. See Theodore Saloutos, *They Remember America: The Story of the Repatriated Greek-Americans* (Berkeley: University of California Press, 1956), pp. 24-48. When Greece was at war many immigrants returned to fight for their country, pp. 35-40.
15. Lea Williams, *Overseas Chinese Nationalism: The Genesis of the Pan-Chinese Movement in Indonesia, 1900-1916* (New York: Free Press, 1960), esp. pp. 184-202.
16. Lee, *Chinese in the United States*, pp. 174-75;
Gong and Grant, *Tong War!*, pp. 153, 210;
Leong Gor Yun, *Chinatown Inside Out* (New York: Barrow, Mussey, 1936), pp. 72-75, 136-38, 142;
Culin, "The 'I Hing,'" pp. 54, 58.
17. Hobsbawm's description of the various European social bandits and primitive rebels applies also to the Chinese immigrant:

> The men and women with whom this book is concerned differ from Englishmen in that they have not been born into the world of capitalism as a Tyneside engineer, with four generations of trade unionism at his back, has been born into it. They come into it as first-generation immigrants, or what is even worse, it comes to them from outside, insidiously by the operation of economic forces which they do not understand and over which they have no controls, or brazenly by conquest, revolutions and fundamental changes of law whose consequences they may not understand, even when they have helped to bring them about. They do not as yet grow with or into modern society: they are broken into it, or more rarely—as in the case of the gangster middle class of Sicily—they break into it. Their problem is how to adapt themselves to its life and struggles. . . .

E.B. Hobsbawm, *Social Bandits and Primitive Rebels* (New York: Free Press, 1959).
18. The Yee Clan achieved notoriety with its dramatic withdrawal from the Sz Yup Kongsi. It was most numerous in Pittsburgh; in San Francisco its members operated some of the finer Chinese restaurants.
Lee, *Chinese in the United States*, pp. 64, 145, 173-75.
19. Gong and Grant, *Tong War!*, p. 195.
20. See ibid.;

John E. Bennett, "The Chinese Tong Wars in San Francisco," *Harper's Weekly*, August 11, 1900, pp. 746-46;
John Gilmer Speed, "Chinese Secret Societies of New York City," *Harper's Weekly*, July 14, 1900, p. 658;
Robert Wells Ritchie, "The Wars of the Tongs," *Harper's Weekly*, August 27, 1910, pp. 8-10.

21. Comber, *Chinese Secret Societies in Malaya*, pp. 95, 101-2, 132, 183-84, 193-95.
22. Max Gluckman, *Custom and Conflict in Africa* (Oxford: Basil Blackwell, 1960), p. 137.
23. See San Francisco *Examiner*, Janaury 3, 1958, p. 7; May 3, 1958, p. 1; May 5, 1958, p. 1; May 7, 1958, p. 8; May 9, 1958, p. 3;
San Francisco *Chronicle*, January 3, 1958, p. 9; January 4, 1958, p. 1.
24. The "Chinese Funeral Procession Riots" in Singapore (1846) broke out on the occasion of death rites for a secret society leader who had incurred many enemies in his lifetime;
the riots of 1851, over the denunciation of a Chinese convert to Christianity;
the 1854 *emeute* over a quarrel between a Hokkien and a Cantonese over 5 catties (7 pounds) of rice;
the fights against Singapore police in 1854-66 over abusive anti-Chinese legislation;
The Penang riots over the murder of a diamond merchant and an outbreak of gang street-fighting.
Comber, *Chinese Secret Societies in Malaya*, pp. 63-76, 78-93, 94-108, 109-36.
25. In Malaya the Ghee Hin-Toh Peh Kong "war" broke out after the latter society trumped up a casus belli and refused the proffered negotiations of the former society. Ibid., p. 111.
26. McLeod, *Pigtails and Gold Dust*, pp. 53-54.
27. Drayton, *Chinese Six Companies*, p. 475.
Chun Ti Chu is described by his supporters as "one of the ablest and smartest Chinese here. He can fight as well as talk. He is a fine shot and the highbinders [Tong mercenaries] fear him as much as they hate him. He is brave enough to stand off three or four highbinders." Ibid.
28. The career of Fong Chong is fascinating. A well-educated Chinese, he operated criminal syndicates in and outside of Chinatown. He maintained good relations with the police, who believed his death was the result of resentment against his informing on criminal activities in Chinatown. Apparently he used the police to close down the operations of his "business" rivals. Several brief biographical sketches are available:
John P. Young, *San Francisco, A History of the Pacific Coast Metropolis* (San Francisco: J.S. Clarke, 1912), vol. II, pp. 816-817;
Gong and Grant, *Tong War!*, pp. 66-93;
Statement made by Lieutenant of Police William Price to Commissioner of Immigration Hart H. North, at San Francisco, California, September 22, 1898, in Reports of the U.S. Industrial Commission, pp. 775-82.

29. In Nuerland a similar situation occurs when a clan or lineage goes to war against a village in which one of its members is a resident. Gluckman argues that the cross-pressures put upon the village resident by this situation impel him to seek to compromise the issue to avoid making a choice between his obligation to his kin and his loyalty to his village. This may be the case in Chinatown, though I have found no evidence on the matter. Gluckman, *Custom and Conflict*, pp. 1-12.
30. Ritchie, *Wars of the Tongs*, p. 9.
A substantially similar account will be found in Gong and Grant, *Tong War!*, pp. 170-75. These events took place in 1905.
31. Ritchie, *Wars of the Tongs*, p. 9.
32. *Statement of the Hon. Ho Yow, His Imperial Chinese Consul General at San Francisco, to Thomas F. Turner*, April 4, 1900. *Report of the U.S. Industrial Commission*, pp. 791-92.
33. Bennett, "Chinese Tong Wars in San Francisco," p. 746.
34. Ibid., pp. 746-47.
35. Ibid., p. 747.
36. Gong and Grant, *Tong War!*, p. 211.
37. Ibid., p. 287. See also
Leong Gor Yun, *Chinatown Inside Out*, pp. 77-78;
William Hoy, *The Chinese Six Companies* (San Francisco: Chinese Consolidated Benevolent Association, 1942), p. 22.

> Several changes have taken place within the Benevolent Association's structure...[T]he key leader in most cities is selected because he is not a member of a tong; it is believed that this will preserve the altruistic nature of the Association and procure more public support from the dominant society, as well as the Chinese living outside the Ghetto. However, the tongs are represented on the board of control. The strength of tong control over the Benevolent Association depends on the number of tongs there are in a given city (six or more in San Francisco) and whether the other organizations are controlled by them. Thus separation is apparent but not real....Though the Benevolent Association's affiliated leaders outnumber the tong or tongs, the inclusion of the latter causes the leaders to turn to the tong for help rather than devise fair methods of control.

Lee, *Chinese in the United States*, pp. 156-57, 160.
38. For the unsavory activities of America's early industrial leaders see
Gustavus Myers, *History of the Great American Fortunes*, 3 vols. (New York: Chas. H. Kerr, 1909-1911);
Ferdinand Lundberg, *America's Sixty Families* (New York: Citadel Press, 1938, 1960), pp. 50-243.
For some characteristic vignettes of this period see
Robert L. Heilbroner, *The Worldly Philosophers* (New York: Simon & Schuster, 1961), pp. 182-85, 203-6.

39. Lai Chun Chuen, "Reply to the Message of Governor Bigler," in Speer, *The Oldest and Newest Empire: China and the United States* (Hartford: S.S. Scranton, 1870), pp. 579-80.
40. Pun Chi, "A Remonstrance from the Chinese in California to the Congress of the United States," in Speer, ibid., pp. 600-1.
41. Ibid.
42. Ibid.
43. Ibid., pp. 603-4.
    For the life of Speer see
    Robert Seagar II, "Some Denominational Reactions to Chinese Immigration to California, 1856-1892," *Pacific Historical Review*, February 1959, pp. 49-50.
    The Chung Wah Kongsi made one last attempt to petition for American aid in the destruction of the tongs in *A Memorial from Representative Chinamen in America to His Excellency U.S. Grant, President of the U.S.A.*, reprinted in Otis Gibson, *The Chinese in America* (Cincinnati: Hitchcock and Walden, 1879), pp. 315-23. In this petition the Six Companies, joined by the president of the Chinese Young Men's Christian Association, complained of the Supreme Court decision which permitted the landing of prostitutes (*Chy Lung v. Freeman*, 92 U.S. 275), asserted that gambling and prostitution benefitted an unscrupulous class of white Americans, and urged "an honest and impartial administration of municipal government in all its details, even including the police department."
44. "Q. Why was it that Little Pete was killed? Was it at the instigation of the Sam Yups or the See Yups?
    "A. The See Yups.
    "Q. What had he done to the See Yups?
    "A. Of course, as I say, there are two factions that are all the time fighting. Little Pete was a very intelligent Chinaman, and they accused him of informing the police, on account of raids made by them—which he did, as a matter of fact."
    Statement made by Lieutenant of Police William Price, p. 777.
45. The only report of this use by Chinese of the hated "cubic air ordinance," a law passed to discriminate against Chinese patterns of domestic arrangement (see Appendix), is in
    Gong and Grant, *Tong War!*, p. 58.
46. Ibid., pp. 59-65.
47. George C. Homans, *The Human Group* (New York: Harcourt, 1950), p. 337.
48. See the discussion in
    E. Adamson Hoebel, The Law of Primitive Man (Cambridge: Harvard U.P., 1954), pp. 24-28, 328-30, and *passim*.
49. M.G. Smith, "Kagoro Political Development," *Human Organization*, Fall 1960, p. 141.
50. C.W.M. Hart and Arnold R. Pilling, *The Tiwi of North Australia* (New York: Henry Holt, 1960), pp. 79-86.

51. Coser, *Social Conflict.*
52. Ibid., p. 35;
    E.A. Ross, *The Principles of Sociology* (New York: Century, 1930), p. 162.
53. Coser, *Social Conflict,* pp. 121-33.

Summary and Conclusion || *IV*

No state of society or laws can render men so much alike, but that education, fortune, and tastes will interpose some differences between them; and, though different men may sometimes find it to their interest to combine for the same purposes, they will never make it their pleasure. . . . [F]ar from supposing that the members of modern society will ultimately live in common, I am afraid that they may end by forming nothing but small coteries. . . .

[W]hatever may be the progress of equality, in democratic nations a great number of small private communities will always be formed within the genral pale of political society. . . .

Alexis de Tocqueville

Some Factors Affecting the Integration of Immigrants into the Larger Society ‖9

The modes of life of the Chinese and Japanese in America represent two different patterns of immigrant adjustment. The former established and maintained communal autonomy and transplanted institutions of nineteenth-century southeastern China to Chinatown. The latter have become one of the most acculturated of immigrant groups in America. An examination of the overseas experiences of the two groups indicates the role that certain key factors have played in shaping these two patterns of immigrant adjustment.

SOCIAL PREPAREDNESS OF THE IMMIGRANT GROUP

Talcott Parsons has suggested that the separation of kinship from other social roles is a characteristic of modern society.[1] As a corollary, the present study suggests that the integration of an immigrant group into a modern society is facilitated to the extent its kinship organization has "modernized" in the preemigration period. A kinship system in which the conjugal unit is subordinated to the extended family is less "modern" than one in which the immediate family is largely disobliged from the bonds of extended kinship.[2] In Japan, modernization of the kinship structure began two centuries prior to emigration. Japan's industrial revolution, which began with the Meiji Restoration in 1868, continued the structural changes begun two hundred fifty years earlier. When Japanese immigrants came to the United States at the close of the nineteenth century, they had already built their kinship system around the primacy of the nuclear family. To that extent they were in a position to form families and rear children in a manner close to that of white Americans and far from that under the rules, roles, and relationships of extended kinship.

In China, however, extended kinship social organization had not diminished to any significant extent prior to the time of emigration to America. The large-scale lineage communities of the emigrant prefectures remained intact through most of the nineteenth century. Structural changes in southeastern China's kinship system did not become noticeable until the twentieth century. Chinese immigrants to the United States were obliged to a clan system. To that extent they have built their social lives around the clan associations that ministered to their needs in Chinatown.

Variations in the familistic regulation of filial obligation, residence requirements, and inheritance have consequences for the integration of an immigrant group into American society. The traditional Chinese family system placed equal filial obligations upon all sons. These obligations were reinforced by the requirement of patrilocal residence and by the custom that wives remain in the homes of their parents-in-law even in the absence of their husbands. A Chinese immigrant looked homeward and did not consider himself to be a permanent settler in America.

Chinese family customs had serious consequences for the immigrants' life in Chinatown. Except for women forced into indenture as prostitutes or domestic servants, and the wives of Chinese merchants, permitted to emigrate under American law, few Chinese women journeyed overseas in the nineteenth century. Only rarely did Chinese wives violate the traditional expectation that they await their husbands' return in the homes of their parents-in-law. Denied access to Caucasian women because of miscegenation statutes and racial and cultural differences, the Chinese immigrant was compelled either to accept a womanless sojourn or to seek sexual gratification from prostitutes. The long-lasting shortage of women in the overseas Chinese community delayed the birth of a second generation among the Chinese in America. That generation might have discarded many of the traditional beliefs and practices of its parents and dissociated itself from Chinatown associations. More often than not, the children of the Chinese immigrants were born in China—conceived just before the husband left or during a temporary return visit—and came to the United States as adolescents or young adults. While this China-born generation often reflected the social changes that had gone on in China during their fathers' sojourn, they were still culturally distant from their age-peers in Caucasian-American society and dependent upon Chinatown institutions for jobs and social life.

The Japanese Issei grew up within a system of primogeniture that freed younger sons from the obligation of patrilocal residence and permitted them to establish branch families at places of their own choosing. Wives could join their immigrant husbands without violating tradition. Japanese immigrants were not consigned to living out their sojourn in all male communities, nor were they compelled to live celibate or resort to prostitutes. As soon as they were financially able, Japanese immigrants sent for wives from Japan, settled down to domestic life, and produced a second generation destined to become even more "modern" than themselves.

INSTITUTIONS OF KINSHIP

The Chinese transplanted their system of clanship overseas. The surname associations of the overseas Chinese are unique: similar associations cannot be found, to my knowledge, among any other immigrant groups in the United States. Bound together by assumed ties of blood, these clans united their members with one another, against other clan groups, and in a kinship organization unfamiliar to most white Americans. Ties of blood, language, and community united those who hailed from the same locality into powerful kongsis, organizations apparently similar to European immigrants' landsmannschaften or Japanese kenjinkai, but having a much greater claim on the lives of their members. The authority of the kongsis was traditional, stemming from that of similar associations in China's premodern cities. Rebels, pariahs, outcasts, and criminals organized themselves into overseas equivalents of China's secret societies. Occasionally associated with revolution in China, these societies functioned for the most part as criminal associations.

Japan's urbanization and the centralized government established by the Tokugawa shoguns did much to erode local allegiance and repudiate traditional organizations. By the time of emigration, Japanese clans were virtually nonexistent, kenjinkai impotent, and secret societies scattered and for the most part irrelevant to those departing for the United States. The Japanese immigrants established no overseas clans. Kenjinkai had a brief importance among the early immigrants but failed to become dominant institutions in community life. Except for a few patriotic and military societies with ultranationalistic beliefs and few members, secret societies did not flourish among the Issei. Criminal associations like the Chinese Triad have not been found among overseas Japanese.

|| IMMIGRANT ENVIRONMENT

Whether an immigrant group will become or produce a people culturally undifferentiated from the larger society appears to be a function of the accumulation of favoring or discouraging factors. The culture and social organization of an immigrant group certainly determine its place with respect to the "takeoff" into integration and how "far"—socially speaking—it must travel to reach its destination. But the conditions of life which the immigrants encounter further determine whether and at what pace the road to integration will be traveled.

The occupational and settlement patterns were not the same for the two immigrant peoples. These differences added to those cultural "givens" with which each had arrived and modified each group's adjustment to life in America. Their ghettoization in cities and their unusual situation with respect to women placed the Chinese in a poor position to establish a domestic life or to relinquish dependency upon Chinatown associations. The Japanese were not troubled by similar obstacles.

The wage-labor contracted through Chinese "bossess"—who were, often enough, officials of clans or kongsis or who had influence with these officials—added another element to the dependency of the Chinese. Their later eviction from white man's work and exile into the shops and stores of Chinatown only served to increase the subservient position of the immigrant. The Japanese, on the other hand, shortly after their arrival, entered into small-scale agriculture. Kenjinkai lost their short-lived prominence as employment agencies and could not become the "kongsis" of Little Tokyo, where no more than one-half of the immigrant Japanese lived in a ghetto more a product of white racism than ethnic congregative sentiment.

The congregation of Chinese in urban ghettos, the violent hostility with which their presence was greeted, and their dependence on traditional leaders for protection increased their isolation in and insulation from the rest of American society. The dispersal of the Japanese in the rural hinterlands, at the fringes of large cities, and in Little Tokyos separated them from one another and did not facilitate communal domination. Resistance to legislative and extralegal racism occurred, but the groups organized to protect Japanese interests and to defend the rights of Japanese immigrants and their children sprang from the immediate needs of the immigrants, not from those of the traditional associations.

POWER AND CONFLICT IN THE IMMIGRANT COMMUNITY

The focus of power and the pattern of conflict within an immigrant community are important factors affecting the community's integration. In Japanese American communities protest and agitation has been directed outward toward obtaining an equal place for Japanese in American society. Neither Issei nor Nisei leaders sought an autonomous Japanese community within the United States. There have not been violent struggles for community power among overseas Japanese. What struggles occurred were over tactics, strategy, and policy in the movement toward integration.[3]

The power elites of Chinatown have, on the other hand, worked to maintain a separate communal existence within American society. The inner workings of Chinatown's community administration are a mystern today to most Americans. Inside the Chinese ghetto a traditional oligarchy of merchants legislates for and administers the community and acts as the spokesmen for the Chinese people before the larger society. Disputes are settled according to a juridical tradition unrelated to and often inconsistent with American law.

Conflict in Chinatown, unlike that in Japanese communities, is inner-directed. The several associations—clans, kongsis, and secret societies—struggle against one another for control of the community and for the undivided allegiance of its denizens. The focus of this conflict tends to reinforce the ghettoization of the Chinese. Quarrels among the Chinese are intramural and concern matters understood by denizens of Chinatown. Its isolation, in turn, reacts on Chinatown society, slowing down or disouraging changes that might arise if its people had extensive contacts with peoples of the larger society. "Other things being equal, the more isolated a society the slower it is to change. It remains dependent upon tradition, upon ascribed rather than achieved status, upon sacred values and transcendental ends. It misses the stimulating effect of cultural cross fertilization."[4]

The social distance between Chinatown and American society acts as an auxiliary to the social solidarity of the Chinese people. Depsite a certain amount of dissatisfaction with life in Chinatown, the majority of Chinatowners are understandably unwilling to exchange their way of life for that of the "foreigner."[5] The Chinese matter-of-factly look to those fellow Chinese possessed of "face and favor" for leadership and guidance. Chinatowners expect justice at the hands of clan and kongsi officials but distrust the white man's courts. They regard the fights between associations in Chinatown as a private matter, subject to the traditional rules of negotiation and settlement employed in pre-revolutionary China and in the early days of overseas Chinese settlement. Urban police often share the latter attitude, preferring to allow the Chinese to settle their own disputes so long as serious violence or a public outcry does not occur. Habitual ways of life are not easily discarded. Certainly they will not be given up because outsiders assert the moral superiority of another way of life.

NOTES

1. "Some Principal Characteristics of Industrial Societies," in *Structure and Process in Modern Societies*, ed. Talcott Parsons (New York: Free Press, 1960), pp. 132-68, esp. pp. 147-49.
2. See the discussion in Kingsley Davis, *Human Society* (New York: Macmillan, 1948, 1949), pp. 414-29.
3. It is my impression that Japanese today are in a position similar to that of the successful blacks described in E. Franklin Frazier, *Black Bourgeoisie* (New York: Free Press, 1959). The barrenness of assimilation has impressed itself on several thoughtful Nisei, one of whom asked me after some discussion of differences between second-generation Chinese and Japanese, "Don't you find Nisei boring? I do."
4. Davis, *Human Society*, p. 156.
5. The following does not apply to the growing number of American-born, American-educated Chinese who have elected to come under the regular jurisdiction of American laws or institutions but to maintain habits of food and language. This generation has not suffered so seriously because of the sex ratio or because of occupational restrictions. But new immigrants to America come under the aegis of Chinatown institutions and adopt many of the older attitudes. See Rose Hum Lee, *The Chinese in the United States of America* (Hong Kong: Hong Kong University Press, 1960), pp. 76-81, 113-31, 200-51, 313-31, 373-404.

Appendix ||

|| CALIFORNIA AND THE CHINESE[1]

California immigration legislation was first designed to prevent Asian labor from competing for jobs with white men. In 1852, the California state senate turned down George B. Tingley's infamous Senate Bill, No. 63, "An Act to Enforce Contracts and Obligations to Perform Work and Labor," commonly known as the Coolie Bill.[2] While California thus refused to authorize the importation of contract labor, it did not prevent the arrival of those persons who had voluntarily bound themselves to work off debt indentures held by clans, kongsis, or the "Six Companies." A "Capitation tax" of fifty dollars per person was required of the master, owner, or consignee of any vessel having on board persons ineligible to become citizens in 1855, but this statute was declared an unconstitutional attempt by the state to regulate commerce.[3] Despite this decision, on April 26, 1858, the state legislature passed a new law, holding that no Chinese or Mongolian might land at any port or be permitted to enter the state unless driven ashore by stress of weather or by an unavoidable accident, adding a penalty of fine or imprisonment for those in charge of any ship violating this law. However, this law—together with the 1862 "Police tax" that required a monthly tax of $2.50 from all Mongolians 18 years of age or over and not engaged in licensed mining or the production of rice, sugar, tea, or coffee[4]—was declared unconstitutional in 1863.[5] Although Governor Leland Stanford believed the "police tax" to be "stringent and oppressive," he hoped that the state legislature might find a Constitutional means to reach "the object desired, the discouragement of Chinese immigration, and not its total prohibition."[6]

Beginning in 1870, California put into law another of its attempts to restrict Chinese immigration. A law that year forbade the landing of any Chinese or Japanese female unless satisfactory evidence of her voluntary coming, correct habits, and good character was presented. Fines ranging from $1 to $10,000, and prison sentences from 2 to 12 months were imposed for each person illegally landed. The law was extended to apply to males. Although this act was not enforced because of the recently passed Civil Rights Act, a similar act of 1874, led to an appeal to the United States Supreme Court. This second law required that the state commissioner of immigration investigate all passengers on incoming ships who were not citizens of the United States to ascertain whether any were lunatic, idiotic, or likely to become a public charge, or a criminal, or "a lewd or debauched woman." For each such person the owner, master, or consignee of the ship was required to post a bond of $500 against that passenger's becoming a charge to any city for two years, or convey said passenger from the state. In the Supreme Court proceeding *Chy Lung v. Freeman*, the justices found the law to be unconstitutional, exceeding the police power of the state, violating the Burlingame Treaty between the United States and China, denying the passengers the equal protections of the law, and prohibited by the Civil Rights Act. After this decision, the anti-Chinese element determined to rely on the federal Congress, rather than the state legislature, for relief. But for over thirty years California had also enacted discriminatory and punitive legislation to discourage the Chinese.[7]

Between 1851 and 1882, the city of San Francisco and the state of California enacted a host of repressive and discriminatory pieces of legislation intended to restrict the rights and occupations of the immigrants. The effect which this legislation had on immigration cannot be definitely ascertained, but it served notice on the Chinese that they were to have little or no standing in the public courts and legislature.

During this period, California's legislation was of three kinds.[8] The first, consisted of attempts to restrict or limit immigration of Chinese to California. This legislation ran afoul of the constitutional provision assigning control over immigration to the Congress. The second category was legislation designed to discourage Chinese from staying in California by making occupational and social life burdensome, expensive, and dangerous. Much of this legislation fell before the protections established by the Fourteenth Amendment to the Constitution. The third was state and local legislation that enacted the hostile and prejudiced attitudes of an enraged proletariat subjected to demagogues and unscrupulous politicians. This legislation also violated the rights guaranteed to all persons under the equal protections and due process clauses of the Fourteenth Amendment, and was, usually, declared unconstitutional.

THE ANTI-CHINESE MOVEMENT, 1852-1900

The Chinese were not only subjected to legal discrimination and public vilification, but also to the unconstrained hostilities of the non-Chinese laborers with whom they came in contact. Believed to be unfair competition in labor, unassimilable as a people, of low moral character, and dangerous to peaceful society,[9] the Chinese immigrants were the victims of one of the most outrageous attacks on a whole people that has ever been perpetrated by an enraged citizenry.

In 1851, the Chinese merchants of San Francisco had made a favorable impression on the populace. Regarded as industrious, quiet, and "able to live under our laws as if born and bred under them," the Chinese storekeepers were looked upon as a welcome addition to the heterogeneous population of the frontier state: "We shall undoubtedly have a very large addition to our population; and it may not be many years before the halls of Congress are graced by the presence of a long-queued Mandarin sitting, voting, and speaking beside a don from Santa Fe and a Kanaker from Hawaii. . . . The 'China boys' will yet vote at the same polls, study at the same schools, and bow at the same altar, as our own countrymen."[10]

But within a year the appearance of Chinese laborers in the mines aroused quite a different response. In Marysville, the non-Chinese miners drew up a resolution asserting that "no Chinaman was to be thenceforth allowed to hold any mining claim in the neighborhood."[11] There followed a general uprising against the Chinese resulting in their expulsion from the mining claims.

> [T]he excitement in regard to the Chinese is rapidly extending along the banks of the North Fork of the American river and daily expulsions are taking place. This morning some sixty Americans ranged down the river some four miles, driving off two hundred—quietly removing their tents, strictly respecting their persons and property—except in one instance, when a Celestial seemed inclined to be obstreporous, his "cradle" was thrown into the river. The same company intended to proceed en

> masse to Horseshoe Bar this afternoon, to concert measures with the miners there to "start" some four hundred located in that place. A band of music is engaged to accompany the expedition! Nearly all of the eighty thousand or ninety thousand American miners are fully determined to submit no longer to have the public lands robbed of their only treasure.[12]

In 1858 and 1859, there was again a movement to expel the Chinese from the placers, and Chinese miners were routed out from Vollecito, Douglas Flat, Sacramento Bar, Coyote Flat, Sand Flat, Rock Creek, Spring Creek, and Buckeye.[13]

However, by far the greatest outrages against the Chinese took place as part of the uncontrolled labor agitation of the late 1860s and during the decades of the '70s and '80s. Consequent upon a period of sudden unemployment, the white urban, unemployed proletariat, led by avaricious politicans and self-seeking demagogues, came to believe that the source of their difficulty was unfair Chinese labor competition. Especially after 1867, did the attacks on the Chinese increse in number and destruction in the cities where the new Workingmen's party flourished. In that year a mob of several hundred attacked and beat 30 Chinese workers and their white foreman. In port cities newly arrived Chinese became victims of youths and hoodlums who robbed and stoned them as they walked from the docks to their ui-kuns.

In 1871, in the midst of a tong war in Los Angeles, a gang descended upon Chinatown, hanged 15 Chinese, including several women and children, from lampposts and awnings and killed 6 more. In the spring of 1876, Chinese were driven out of such small mining camps as Truckee, Chico, and the Lemm Ranch, as their quarters burned, and many killed. For two months, in 1877, anti-Chinese riots raged unchecked in San Francisco. In the first month alone 25 laundries estimated to be worth $20,000 were burned to the ground. A few years later the Chinatown of Tacoma, Washington, was set afire and anti-Chinese violence flared up in Portland, Seattle, and Olympia. The residents of Pasadena, Santa Barbara, Santa Anna, Oakland, and twelve other cities expelled their Chinese populations.[14]

An anti-Chinese riot in Denver resulting in one death, many casualties, and $20,000 damage, in 1880, and the infamous massacre of 28 Chinese who refused to join a strike in Rock Springs, Wyoming, in 1885, aroused protest from the Chinese government. In the first case, the secretary of state replied that, the local authorities having done all they could, the Chinese had had the same protection as American citizens. The Rock Springs *émeute* occasioned negotiations with China and included agreement by the United States to pay an indemnity amounting to over $200,000.[15]

After the passage of the restrictive legislation of 1882, the violent attacks on the Chinese gradually began to subside. An attempt to expel the Chinese from Los Angeles in the 1880s did not obtain popular support.[16] Prejudice and local discrimination remained high, however, and those Chinese who desired to escape from the Chinatown ghetto were prevented from doing so by housing restrictions in other parts of the city.[17] As late as 1909, outrages against the Chinese were still not unkown:

> After the exclusion law was passed, the persecution of the Chinese might have been expected to die out; and certainly the traditional forms of physical persecution should have become less and less frequent. Yet within five years [the] Chinese of San Francisco have been stoned in the streets, have been arrested and held to pay all the fines of themselves and their white companions; fined for gambling and prostitution while white establishments close by flourished without molestation under police protection; fined for sanitary nuisances while the Italian quarter, no less bad, received no attention; and have been denied the right to buy or lease property outside the Chinese quarter. In the country districts of California they have had their ears and their queues cut off, their cabins burned, their property stolen and destroyed without being able to secure protection or redress. The tradition that a Chinaman has no rights is dying, but it is certainly by no means dead.[18]

THE FEDERAL GOVERNMENT AND CHINESE IMMIGRATION

Between 1841 and 1861, American diplomatic and consular relations with China were limited to the treaty ports, by the emperor's edict requiring that all such matters be handled there,[19] and by his permissive policy allowing the coolie trade to be policed by local officials.[20] As the *Robert Browne* incident illustrates, American officials did not protest the trade, but demanded protection and indemnity for American merchants who engaged in it. In 1852, an American ship, *Robert Browne,* cleared Amoy, bound for California with over four hundred Chinese aboard. However, the Chinese passengers received such harsh treatment from the Captain, that they mutinied, killed him, and forced the sailors to bring the ship into a port at the Ryukyu Islands. After Dr. Peter Parker, an interim American chargé d'affaires and medical missionary, had complained to the Chinese government that "a merchant vessel of his country had had its captain, mate, and crew killed by Chinese passengers who stole the ship's cargo and escaped on shore,"[21] the mutineers were captured by a combined force of American and British sailors, and returned to their various villages or to Canton for trial.

In 1858, the United States minister to China formally offered to negotiate the cessation of the coolie trade:

> Recently residents of South China have often been enticed and carried to foreign countries in great numbers to do hard labor in strange lands. If Chinese coastal officials are willing to cooperate, means can certainly be found in accord with the wishes of China to negotiate the cessation of this kind of evil practice.[22]

An imperial edict of the same date rejected his proposal pointing out that "The...items...are...matters which local officials must handle, nor do they have to wait for these barbarians to ask them."[23] Three weeks later, the nominal prime minister of China and the Grand Council addressed the same proposal, commenting: "The American barbarians' request for the prohibition of opium and of enticing people from the ports...are both prohibited by Chinese law and must be administered by local officials..."[24] Local officials, however, were not always ready to enforce the law, and sometimes conspired to violate it. It seems fair to suggest that the coolie trade from China was not treated effectively in diplomatic negotiations. Reforms were made in particular cases. After agitation against the Chinese arose in California, attention was turned to Washington for legislative relief.

In 1862, the evils of the coolie trade received wide public attention when the House of Representatives released its report on Chinese contract laborers brought to Cuba and South America. In light of these exposures, the anti-Chinese agitation in California, and, perhaps, because by 1860, "the constant traffic was practically monopolized by the American clipper ships,"[25] Congress passed a law prohibiting "the Coolie trade by American citizens in American vessels."[26] However, the statute contained enough loopholes and ambiguities to to limit its effectiveness. It served to put the coolie traffic under a modicum of consular regulation.[27]

The regulations which governed the emigration of Chinese to America, both before and after the passage of the act of 1862, did not in fact prohibit contract emigration, but required that the emigrant coming under contract certify that he was departing China of his own free will. The burden of determining whether contract labor emigration was "free" or involuntary fell upon the American consuls who sometimes utilized their control over departures to line their own pockets.

> The cooly act enables the consul to exact large fees from every cooly, which the ships pay, and requires them to charge more charter money. The consul also having the option, can make obstacles and compel the Chinese to pay large fees to remove. The consuls also require many conditions from ships in the shape of large unofficial fees or indirect revenue. That makes the cooly trade to California a very remunerative one for consuls; consequently it is in their interests to continue it. . .[28]

The Chinese immigrant was to be apprised of the nature of his contractual obligations by what appeared to be an elaborate set of safeguards:

> By emigration regulations in force at Hong Kong, all laborers under contract to labor abroad must, before leaving, have their contracts read or translated to them personally and alone, and their distinct assent obtained, fourteen days before they can legally embark. After a fortnight it is again read to them by an emigration officer, and inquiry made if they have changed their minds. If still anxious to go they are sent on shipboard, where they are offered by the Consul a last opportunity of withdrawing, who certifies that they executed their contracts voluntarily; and thus having, after reflection, thrice publicly reaffirmed the fact, they clear legally from Hong Kong.[29]

However, Chinese agents, known as crimps, working for foreign labor contractors, kidnapped or inveigled unsuspecting Chinese into dockside sheds and tortured them. The tortures were unbelievably cruel and included tying up by the thumbs, repeated immersion in water, and beatings. Torture continued until the immigrant consented to falsely swear that he was voluntarily leaving the country. Then these hapless victims were sold for from $13 to $20 and shipped to Macao or overseas.[30]

It was especially difficult to establish whether a credit-ticket contract was entered into freely by the immigrant, or whether he was working off a debt incurred involuntarily. A governor of California testified:

> [P]ractically all Chinese come here through means advanced by

> these companies [that is, the Six Chinese Companies] or individuals, or by people here through these companies. I think it is by no means sure that the Southern Pacific Railroad Company is not importing Chinese today through these companies. I know the Central Pacific Railroad did it.... Their contract is simply to repay the amount advanced for their passage, with a sufficient bonus to compensate them for the risk, interest, etc. In other words, if they advanced forty dollars for passage, they exacted that they should pay one hundred dollars, perhaps, in return to be deducted from wages—five dollars a month or ten dollars a month, after they arrive; after they work that out they are free.[31]

But even supposing that the consuls sought scrupulously to enforce the law, and that the activities of the crimps were curbed, the non-Chinese consul still had the nearly insurmountable task of seeking to enforce foreign laws on a people whose language he could neither speak nor understand, and whose customs and mores were alien to his own. The American consul relied on his Chinese secretary or interpreter, who thus gained control over departures.

> Mr. Haymond: Suppose the consul desired, in good faith, to make inquiries, and these people were brought there under duress, would not some influence there prevent them from disclosing the truth?
>
> A: ... [W]hat is needed in American foreign diplomatic service is educated interpreters or officers, with some kind of an understanding of their language, who can go among the people and explain to them their rights. Our consuls are appointed from Iowa, Wisconsin, etc., and the first thing they do is to read about China. Then they go there and hire a Chinese clerk on whom they are entirely dependent.[32]

That the act of 1862 did not prevent involuntary contract labor from being shipped to America was illustrated by a sheme to import thousands of Chinese laborers to the South to replace the recently emancipated blacks on plantations and in railroad construction.[33] The principals in this plan were the Dutch merchants, Koopmanschap and Co., of San Francisco, the St. Louis and Pacific Railroad, the Union Pacific Railroad, and the Chinese coolie broker, Tye Kim Orr, a resident of Louisiana who had been the evangelical leader of the free Chinese settlement in British Guiana until a scandal caused him to leave.[34]

After the Civil War, planters in the Arkansas Valley complained of a serious labor shortage. A suggestion that Chinese laborers be imported was supported by some of the more powerful interests in the country. Not only did many planters come forth to champion the cause of coolie immigration, but many newspapers also supported the venture.[35]

In 1869, a labor convention at Memphis, Tennessee, considered the practicability of obtaining immigrants from China, whose habits of life, the climate and productions of their own country, fitted them in an eminent degree for field labor in the production of cotton, sugar, rice, and tobacco.[36] At the convention Tye Kim Orr convinced the delegates that they need not fear that Chinese immigrants would "demoralize our own citizens," The New Orleans Chamber of Commerce reported:

> Some arguments were made, particularly against immigrants from China, as tending to demoralize our own citizens. These were entertained by a very small number only, and were evidently abandoned after the statements made by Mr. Tye Kim Orr, an intelligent, native Chinaman, now a resident of the Lafourche. His statement of facts as to his country, his people, their habits of industry, endurance, and frugality, as also the productions of that country, were listened to with marked attention.[37]

Cornelius Koopmanschap, representing his shipping firm, told assembled planters that his steamers had already carried 30,000 Chinese to California, and that with the opening of the Pacific Railroad Chinese coolies could reach the Missisippi Valley in 40 or 50 days at a per capita expense of about $100. The general passenger agent of the St. Louis and Pacific Railroad not only agreed to publish the proceedings of the convention gratis, but also offered "a free ticket over that road to San Francisco and return, to any agent who may go to assist immigrants in reaching the Union Pacific Railroad."[38]

The plan having been accepted, Tye Kim Orr was dispatched to China and began his recruitment of Chinese laborers despite American laws which forbade the practice.[39] Recruitment practices were generally unsavory, yet they were not seriously interfered with by the local American authorities. The assistant to the American consul testified to having permitted Chinese to board ships bound for New Orleans "seldom knowing the purport more than that they were going for three or five years, for as many dollars per month, to labor as directed, often knowing that they were to be cared for if sick, and sent back at the expiration of the contract, or their bodies, if dead, and so otherwise ignorant that they were very easily scared if anyone intimated to them that they were being deceived."[40] In one instance a sea captain purchased the son from a family being sold by a Chinese broker who held the family as security for a loan to the father.[41] Those Chinese who discovered they had been deceived into becoming contract laborers tried desperately to escape their plight. "Sometimes they refused to go on board at Hong Kong, as was the case with a few cargoes once, a few years ago, going to New Orleans, when they nearly all jumped overboard, some drowning in Hong Kong Harbor."[42]

The first cargo of two hundred Chinese bound for New Orleans cleared Hong Kong in 1870, in the *Ville de St. Lo* under charter to Koopmanschap and Co. of San Francisco.[43] There can be little doubt that a coolie trade to the South would have continued and profoundly affected the racial composition of that region, had not British authorities intervened to stop it. Under pressure from the Anti-Slavery Society, the Aborigines Protection Society, and the Social Science Association, in 1870, the British government closed the port of Hong Kong to all passenger carriers except those departing for ports within the British Empire. Subsequently, British-Portuguese cooperation virtually closed the port of Macao to American coolie traders.[44] The Chinese who had been brought to the South were used less as agricultural laborers than as replacements for blacks on railway projects.

By 1880, the anti-Chinese movement had spread to cities east of the Mississippi River. In 1870, Chinese laborers had been recruited to North Adams, Massachusetts, to break a strike of shoemakers. Anti-Coolie meetings in Boston protested reducing American labor to the standards of "rice and rats." In 1877, Chinese were brought to break a cutlery workers' strike in Beaver Falls, Pennsylvania. A few years earlier the Cincinnati *Enquirer* denounced the employment of Chinese labor in cigar-making.[45] The labor movement was virtually united in its desire to rid America of what it considered to be its greatest enemy: an alien and unassimilated laboring class willing to work at less than a living wage.[46]

Washington's response to the pressure to halt the coming of Chinese to America included renegotiation of the Burlingame Treaty in 1880, and the first Chinese restriction law in 1882. According to Article I of the former:

> Whenever in the opinion of the Government of the United States the coming of Chinese Laborers to the United States, or their residence therein, affects or threatens to affect the interests of that country, or to endanger the good order of the said country or any locality within the territory thereof, the Government of

> China agrees that the Government of the United States may regulate, limit, or suspend such coming and residence, but may not absolutely prohibit it. The limitation shall apply only to Chinese who may go to the United States as laborers, other classes not being included in the limitations. Legislation taken in regard to Chinese laborers will be of such a character only as is necessary to enforce the regulation, limitation, or suspension of immigration, and immigrants shall not be subject to personal maltreatment or abuse.[47]

The Restriction Act of 1882[48] provided for a ten year exclusion of skilled and unskilled laborers and those engaged in mining, while it permitted the landing of merchants, students, and itinerants upon their presentation of an official certificate attesting to their status. However, the law contained so many confusing, ambiguous, and complicated clauses and requirements that its effect was to promote both evasions by the Chinese and unusually harsh treatment of legitimate arrivals by immigration inspectors.[49] Subsequent amendments obviated some confusions and inequities but created new ones. In 1887, at the request of the Chinese government, negotiations were opened to draft a new treaty. In 1888, this treaty was signed by the two governments and submitted for ratification. Before amendment by the Senate the treaty provided:

> Art. I—For a period of twenty years the coming of Chinese laborers shall be absolutely prohibited.
>
> Art. II—The preceding articles shall not apply to any Chinese laborer having wife, child, parent, or property or debts to the amount of one thousand dollars; and such right of return shall be exercised within one year of departure.
>
> Art. III—Chinese subjects, not laborers, to have admission to produce a certificate vised by the diplomatic representatives at the port of departure. Chinese in transit to have the same privileges as before.
>
> Art. IV—Guaranteed to the Chinese residents all the rights of the most favored nation except naturalization, and the United States reaffirmed its intention "to exert all its powers to secure protection to the persons and property of all Chinese subjects in the United States."
>
> Art. V—While expressly denying the legal obligation to grant indemnity, agreed to the payment of $276,619.75 as full indemnity for all losses and injuries suffered by the Chinese in the United States.[50]

The Senate added a clause to Article I reading: "and this prohibition shall extend to the return of Chinese laborers who are not now in the United States whether holding return certificates under existing laws or not," and another to Article II requiring that "no such Chinese laborer shall be permitted to enter the United States by land or sea without producing to the proper officer of Customs the return certificate hereinafter required." Even before the treaty was ratified a bill embodying its main points was passed and signed by President Cleveland. Upon the release of a London press dispatch announcing that the Chinese government had rejected the treaty, the Scott Act was introduced into the House of Representatives providing that any Chinese who had not returned to the United States before the passage of the act was to be refused admittance, that no more certificates permitted under sections 4 and 5 of the act of 1882 would be issued, and that all certificates issued earlier were void. The Scott Act was passed by both houses and subsequently signed by President Cleveland, who, on receipt of China's proposed revisions of the unratified treaty of 1888, felt justified in substituting the Congressional legislation for the treaty. He argued the Chinese government had acted in bad faith in refusing to accept the original treaty.[51] The Scott Act shocked both the Chinese government and the Chinese Six Companies. The former protested in vain to the American secretary of state for the next four years. The Chung Wah Kongsi raised a hundred thousand dollars to test the constitutionality of the act, but the Supreme Court, although it noted that the act violated the treaty, held that Congressional modification of a treaty is always a right of Congress.[52]

Anti-Chinese sentiment continued to affect Congress for the next few years, kept alive by the outcries of organized labor and by the anti-Oriental movement in the Pacific Coast states. The Fifty-second Congress (1892) disposed of twelve different bills for the regulation of Chinese immigration before passing the Geary Act.

This act—

1. continued all existent laws regulating the coming of the Chinese for ten years;
2. placed the burden of proof of their right to be in America on the Chinese;
3. fixed a one-year prison sentence for unlawful residence, to be followed by deportation to the country to which the illegal resident was subject;
4. denied bail to the Chinese in habeas corpus proceedings;
5. required that all Chinese laborers now resident in the United States apply within one year for a certificate of residence or be

subject to deportation;
6. required that the certificate contain complete identification of the individual, a duplicate to be kept on file in the office of the collector of Internal Revenue;
7. established penalties for the falsification of a certificate.[53]

The passage of the Geary Act was the occasion of the greatest outcry of protest from the Chung Wah Kongsi and the imperial Chinese government. The former advised its members not to register since the law would be declared unconstitutional. Agents of the Six Companies traveled throughout the United States to raise a fund for legal defense. Many Chinese complied with the directives issued by the Six Companies, only to find themselves subject to deportation when the Supreme Court sustained the law in a 5-3 decision. The faith of the Chinese in the protective abilities of the Six Companies was profoundly shaken, and the secret societies utilized the occasion to put a price on the head of Chun Ti Chu, president of the Sam Yup Association, who had issued the directive against registration. Chagrined by its defeat, the Six Companies threatened to send all the Chinese to Canada and Mexico.[54] When, as a result of the Court's decision, nearly the entire Chinese population in the United States became subject to deportation, Congress enacted the McCreary Amendment, extending the time for registration six months, but reclassifying all Chinese engaged in mining, fishing, huckstering, and laundering as laborers.[55] In order to restore order to San Francisco's Chinatown, still in revolt against both the Geary Law and the Six Companies for deluding the Chinese about their rights, the Chinese government dispatched a Mandarin, to the city's Chinese consulate.[56] Subsequently a new Sino-American Treaty was ratified (1894) which while nearly identical with the abortive treaty of 1888—

1. included the acknowledgment by the government of China of the propriety of recent American immigration legislation;
2. granted China the right to require registration of American laborers in China;
3. provided that the United States would annually furnish the Chinese government with a list of all Americans in China, except government officials and their servants;
4. permitted the right of Chinese in transit to cross the United States;
5. permitted Chinese with families, property, or debts to return to the United States.

In 1901, the last great debate over the exclusion of the Chinese began. Although largely sprung from the continuing anti-Chinese movement in California, the exclusionist forces had by this time captured all but the syndicalist elements of the American labor movement. A Chinese Exclusion Convention was held that year at the Metropolitan Temple in San Francisco with prominent exclusionists reiterating the by now familiar changes that the Chinese were "nonassimilable," "undesirable," "destructive competition," "servile," and "immoral," and that exclusion was the only way to preserve Western civilization.[57]

The view of the American Federation of Labor appeared in a widely circulated pamphlet by Samuel Gompers and Herman Gustadt, entitled *Meat vs. Rice,* which restated all the standard accusations against the Chinese in extremely inflammatory language.[58]

Congress, in 1902, approved a bill to continue all existing exclusion laws, insofar as they were not inconsistent with treaty obligations, and extended the laws to cover insular possessions acquired by the United States with the annexation of Hawaii and the take-over of the Philippines. Two years later the Chinese government notified the United States that the treaty of 1894 would be terminated in 1904, thus making all laws on exclusion dependent upon the treaty of 1880. To remedy this, Congress reenacted parts of the act of 1888, the Geary Act, and the McCreary Amendment, and the act of 1902 indefinitely and unconditionally. The net effect of this was to prohibit all Chinese from coming to the United States except officials, merchants, teachers, students, and travelers, but to permit the return to the United States of those Chinese having families, property, or debts. Furthermore, the renewed exclusion was extended to all of the United States territories and possessions, and Congress was given authority to propose further legislation needed to enforce these acts.[59]

|| CONCLUSION

Chinese immigration to California had not become a matter of national attention until 1875. Up until that time federal attempts to halt or regulate the coolie trade were confined to occasional negotiations with the Chinese government and a law prohibiting involuntary contract labor immigration, passed in 1862. In 1882, following a revision of the Burlingame Treaty in 1880, the first Chinese restriction law was passed. Ten years later it was renewed. In 1904, after the negotiation of three treaties and the enactment of eight federal laws to regulate Chinese immigration, an amendment was added to existing laws that virtually excluded all Chinese except government officials, merchants, teachers, students, and travelers.[60] This law remained substantially unchanged until Chinese were placed under quota restriction in 1943. Despite these legal restrictions and a sometimes ruthless enforcement of the exclusion law, Chinese entered the United States illegally, or by exploiting loopholes in the law.

NOTES

1. A portion of this research was done while I was assistant to Professor Jacobus ten Broek in 1957.
2. *California State Journal,* 3rd sess., 1852, pp. 168, 192, 205, 217, 305-7. The bill was passed by the assembly in 1852, but kiled in the Senate after the reading and wide circulation of the opinion of Senator Philip A. Roach, who was to be a leader in the fight for Chinese exclusion for the next thirty years. "Minority Report of the Select Committee on Senate Bill. No. 63. Appendix, March 20, 1852, pp. 669-75.
3. *People* v. *Downer.* 7 Cal. 169, 1857, citing the "Passenger Cases," 7 Howard 122. But an earlier law of 1852, requiring the masters of vessels to give a per capita bond of $500 as indemnity against the costs of medical and other relief of alien passengers, or to commute the bond by a payment of not less than five nor more than ten dollars per passenger, remained in force until 1870 when it was declared unconstitutional. Mary Coolidge, *Chinese Immigration* (New York: Henry Holt, 1909), p. 70.
4. This exemption reveals that Californian opposition to Chinese contract labor was selective. Labor for agriculture was needed, and Chinese as late as 1854, were shipped to California as contract laborers for agricultural work. See House of Representatives, 34th Cong., 1st sess., Ex. Doc. 185. No. 12 for the translation of a contract for Chinese agricultural labor in California. Persia Crawford Campbell, *Chinese Coolie Emigration to Countries Within the British Empire* (London: King and Sons, 1923), Campbell, p. 94, 94n. Even in his famous minority report on the "Coolie Bill" in 1852, Philip Roach favored contract coolies for agriculture:

   > "There is ample room for its employment in draining the swamplands, in cultivating rice, raising silk, or planting tea. Our State is supposed to have great natural advantages for those objects; but if these present not field enough for their labor, then sugar, cotton, and tobacco invite their attention. For these special objects, I have no objection to the introduction of contract laborers, provided they are excluded from citizenship; for those staples cannot be cultivated without "cheap labor"; but from all other branches I would recommend its exclusion. I do not want to see Chinese or Kanaka

carpenters, masons, or blacksmiths, brought here in swarms under contracts, to compete with our own mechanics, whose labor is as honorable and as well entitled to social and political rights as the pursuits designated "learned professions" *Minority Report of the Select Committee on Senate Bill. No. 63, op. cit.*, p. 671.

5. *Lin Sing* v. *Washburn*, 20 Cal. 534 (1863).
6. Coolidge, *Chinese Immigration*, pg. 72.
7. *Chy Lung* v. *Freeman*, 92 U.S. 275; Elmer Sandmeyer, *The Anti-Chinese Movement in California* (Urbana: University of Illinois Press, 1939), pp. 52-53; Otis Gibson, *The Chinese in America* (Cincinnati: Hitchcock and Walden, 1877), pp. 140-57; Coolidge, *Chinese Immigration*, pp. 418-19.
8. The legislation has been admirably summarized and criticized in the several studies of the anti-Chinese movement. Lucille Eaves, *A History of Labor Legislation in California*, Berkeley: University of California Press, 1909), pp. 105-95; Ira B. Cross, *A History of the Labor Movement in California*, (Berkeley: University of California, 1935), pp. 73-130; Coolidge, *Chinese Immigration*, pp. 55-82; Sandmeyer, *Anti-Chinese Movement*, pp. 40-77. Briefer accounts include B.J.O. Schrieke, *Alien Americans*, (New York: Viking, 1936), pp. 3-22; Grace H. Stimson, *The Rise of the Labor Movement in Los Angeles*, (Berkeley: University of California Press, 1959), pp. 60-68.
9. "The burden of our accusations against them is that they come in conflict with our labor interests; that they can never assimilate with us; that they are a perpetual unchanging and unchangeable alien element that can never become homogeneous; that their civilization is demoralizing and degrading to our people; that they degrade and dishonor labor; that they never become citizens, and that an alien, degraded labor class, without desire of citizenship, without education and without interest in the country it inhabits, is an element both demoralizing and dangerous to the community within which it exists."
U.S., Congress, Senate, Joint Special Committee to Investigate Chinese Immigration, 44th Cong., 2d sess., February 27, 1877, S. Rept. 689, p. 22 (hereafter referred to Sen. Doc. 689. Testimony of the Hon. Frank pixley. The remarks about citizenship are particularly onerous in view of the legal prohibitions upon naturalization for Chinese. Actually several Chinese had applied for citizenship. See Coolidge, *Chinese Immigration*, p. 77n.; *Daily Alta Californian*, May 12, 1851.
10. *Daily Alta Californian*, May 12, 1851.
11. *Marysville Herald*, May 4, 1852.
12. *Sacramento Union*, May 2, 1852.
13. *Sacramento Union*, December 29, 30, 1858; March 5-10, July 16, 25, 1859; Coolidge, *Chinese Immigration*, 255, 255n.
14. Coolidge, *Chinese Immigration*, pp. 254-73. For an admirable brief summary see Jacobus ten Broek, Edward Barnhart, and Floyd Matson, *Prejudice, War, and the Constitution* (Berkeley: University of California Press, 1954), pp. 11-22. See also Alexander McLeod, *Pigtails and Gold Dust* (Caldwell: Carton, 1947), pp. 57-70, 187-98.

15. Coolidge, *Chinese Immigration*, pp. 194-200, 271-73. For the anti-Chinese view of the Rock Springs riot see A.A. Sargent, "The Wyoming Anti-Chinese Riot," *Overland Monthly*, November 1885, pp. 507-12. For a reply see J., "The Wyoming Anti-Chinese Riot—Another View," December 1885, pp. 573-76. The treaty was not ratified but the indemnity was voted in subsequent legislation.
16. Stimson, *Labor Movement*, pp. 60-67.
17. In 1901, the editor of a Chinese language newspaper found it impossible to move his family from Los Angeles to any part of San Francisco other than Chinatown. Coolidge, *Chinese Immigration*, pp. 438-39.
18. Ibid., p. 275. Professor Coolidge adds; "All these and many other petty instances are within the personal knowledge of the writer and are by no means unusual."
19. One result was that Chinese bound for Cuba or Peru had supposed they were emigrating to California. See Watt Stewart, *Chinese Bondage in Peru: A History of the Chinese Coolie in Peru, 1849-1874* (Durham: Duke University Press, 1951), p. 16.
20. On this point and general Sino-American relations see Earl Swisher, *China's Management of the American Barbarians. A Study of Sino-American Relations, 1841-1861, With Documents* (New Haven: Far Eastern, 1951), pp. 1-16, 179-205 and passim.
21. Swisher, *American Barbarians*, p. 200.
22. *American Memorandum: United States Minister Reed Lists his Proposals for the Revision of the Treaty of Wang-hsia*, May 9, 1858, in Swisher, *American Barbarians*, p. 449.
23. Imperial Edict, May 9, 1958; ibid, p. 453.
24. Ibid., p. 472.
25. Campbell, *Coolie Emigration*, p. 116.
26. Ibid., p. 127n. It should be noted that American ships discussed here were used to take contract laborers to Cuba and South America; credit-ticket immigrants to America.
27. American-British diplomatic rivalry in the Far East, and the corruption of American and Chinese officials made enforcement of coolie prohibition nearly impossible. The coolie trade at Whampoa in 1859, was supported by Consul Perry when other nations had sought to regulate it or prohibit it. Abuses there having been publicized, the coolies were ordered to be returned to the city for examination. But the American ship *Messenger* transshipped the coolies to Macao. Chinese Minister Lou held the American responsible for evasion and Ward, American minister plenipotentiary, forced the return of the coolies. Ministers Reed and Ward repeatedly asked the secretary of state to request congressional regulation. When the Chinese government proposed to invesitgate the coolie trade at Whampoa, and retained Mayers of the British consulate to act as interpreter, the American vice-consul refused him admission to American coolie ships. See ibid., pp. 125, 126-29.
28. Testimony of Thomas H. King, former assistant consul in China. Sen. Doc. 689, p. 93. King served with Consul Bailey at Hong Kong from 1871

to 1879. Bailey embezzled $35,000 to $40,000 in consular fees during his term of office. Coolidge, *Chinese Immigration*, p. 50n. Professor Coolidge is most adamant in denying that there was an involuntary contract coolie trade to California.

> President Lincoln's message in 1861, the voluminous report on the Coolie trade in the House in 1862, and the correspondence between Minister Burlingame and Secretary of State Seward in 1866, all show clearly that the State Department, as well as the commissioners, ministers, and consults in China were engaged in preventing the shipment of Chinese laborers under contract to Cuba, the West Indies, and South America. Nowhere in these papers is there even a suggestion that contract coolies had been shipped to this country. Moreover, almost every intelligent American who has studied Chinese life or written upon it, all the missionaries among them, the better-educated immigration officials in this country and many employers of Chinese, unite in declaring that they came just as freely as the immigrants at Atlantic ports. Ibid., p. 48.

In partial refutation see Campbell, *Coolie Emmigration*, pp. 26-39, 86-160.

29. Testimony of C.W. Brooks. Sen. Doc. 689, p. 101-102. See also C.W. Brooks, "The Chinese Labor Problem," *Overland Monthly*, November 1869, pp. 407-19, esp. p. 416. Brooks was consul for Japan in San Francisco for 16 years.
30. Campbell, *Coolie Emigration*, p. 118. Again this method was chiefly used to obtain immigrants to Central and South America and for contract labor to the American South in 1869-70. So dangerous did life become at Shanghai that the Chinese population threatened the European community with riots. Ibid., pp. 119-20; Swisher, *American Barbarians*, pp. 627, 629.
31. Testimony of F.F. Low, former governor of California. Sen. Doc. 689, p. 70.
32. Testimony of C.W. Brooks. Sen. Doc. 689, p. 102.
33. To my knowledge no extensive research has been done on this important episode in Reconstruction history. I have searched diligently for documents and correspondeed with leading historians of the South on this matter, including T. Harry Williams and Kenneth M. Stampp, and with the naval historian, John H. Kemble. However, the documentation and analysis are my own.
    [Author's note to 1984 edition: See Lucy M. Cohen, *Chinese in the Post-Civil War South: A People Without a History* (Baton Rouge: LSU Press, 1984), pp. 67-95, 120-23, 180-82.]
34. In the American reports to be cited below, no mention of Tye Kim Orr's previous career is made, and perhaps it was unknown. But in a British report on the coolie trade, written in 1871, there is this comment on the Chinese settlement in British Guiana:

> One tide—some forty miles or so up the Demerara river is a settlement of free Chinese. During the reign of Governor Hincks, and, I was told, chiefly on the suggestion of Mr. Des Voeux, a tract of land on the Camoudi Creek was assigned for the habitation of Chinese Coolies whose indentures had expired.... The matter was taken up by the Governor and the Court of Policy and a large number, most of them Christians, were removed to the creek, under the leadership of an evangelist, O Tye Kim.... So long as O Tye Kim remained with the people, he exercised over them a very beneficial influence. But in a weak moment he made a serious moral slip, and, finding exposure inevitable, absconded. I heard of him again the other day from a well-known Chinese missionary, who told me he had since seen him in China, whither he had gone, after a residence in the United States, and had engaged in some illegal scheme of immigration to that country. Edward Jenkins, *The Coolie—His Rights and Wrongs* (New York: Routledge and Sons, 1871), pp. 114-16.

35. Quotations from all of these papers in support of the plan may be found in William M. Burwell, "Science and the Mechanic Arts Against Coolies," *De Bow's Review*, July 1869, pp. 557-71, esp. pp. 566-71.
36. *Report of the New Orleans Chamber of Commerce*, July 26, 1869, quoted in "Our Chamber of Commerce," *De Bow's Review*, August 1869, p. 699.
37. Ibid., p. 700. Tye Kim Orr also tried to convince William M. Burwell, editor of *De Bow's Review*, that Chinese were good factory laborers. "We received a call from Mr. Tye Kim Orr, a native of China, who has been for two years a resident of Donaldsville, Louisiana. He is an intelligent young man, speaking the English language, and converted to the Christian belief. He was invited by one of our prominent citizens to accompany him to the Memphis Labor Conventin. He contributed greatly to the information of that body, and may be designated as one of the agents to visit China for the purpose of encouraging immigration. He informs us that large classes of his countrymen are skilful (sic) in the manipulation of thread and would make good operatives in our cotton factories." *De Bow's Review*, July 1869, p. 630.
38. Ibid., p. 700-01.
39. This recruitment not only evaded the act of 1862, but also appears to have defied a resolution of Congress passed on January 16, 1867.

> Whereas the traffic in laborers transported from China and other eastern countries, known as the coolie trade is odious to the people of the U.S., is inhuman and immoral, and whereas it is abhorrent to the spirit of modern international law and policy which have substantially extirpated the African slave trade to permit the establishment in its place of a mode of enslaving men differing from the former in little else than the employment of fraud instead of force to make its victims captive, be it therefore resolved that it is the duty of this Government to give effect to the moral sentiment

> of the nation through all its agencies for the purpose of preventing the further introduction of coolies into this hemisphere or adjacent islands.

Cited in Campbell, *Coolie Emigration*, p. 151n.

40. Testimony of Thomas H. King, Sen. Doc. 689, p. 93.
41. Russel H. Conwell, *Why and How. Why the Chinese Emigrate and the Means They Adopt for the Purpose of Reaching America* (Boston: Lee and Shephard, 1871).
42. Testimony of King, Sen. Doc. 689, p. 93.
43. Campbell, *Coolie Emigration*, p. 151.
44. Ibid., pp. 152-60.
45. Boston *Transcript*, June 13, 1870; Cincinnati *Enquirer*, January 8, April 11, June 24, 1870; Cleveland *Leader*, January 19, June 17, 20, 23, July 27, 1867, June 6, 1870; Ohio State *Journal*, November 3, 1873; quoted in Carl Wittke, *We Who Built America* (New York: Prentice-Hall, 1948), pp. 460-61.
46. "The political issue after 1877, was racial, not financial, and the weapon was not merely the ballot, but also 'direct action'—violence. The anti-Chinese agitation in California, culminating as it did in the Exclusion Law passed by Congress in 1882, was doubtless the most important single factor in the history of American labor, for without it the entire country might have been overrun by Mongolian labor and the labor movement might have become a conflict of races instead of one of classes." Selig Perlman, *The History of Trade Unionism in the United States* (New York: Augustus Kelley, 1922, 1950), p. 62.
47. The Sino-American Treaty of 1880, reprinted in J.S. Tow, *The Real Chinese in America* (New York: Academy Pres, 1923), p. 153.
48. For a discussion of the arguments for and against this bill and the one that preceded it, vetoed by President Hayes, see Coolidge, *Chinese Immigration*, pp. 168-82.
49. Ibid., pp. 183-90.
50. Ibid., p. 194.
51. Ibid., pp. 183-202.
52. *Chae Chan Ping* v. *United States*, 130 U.S. 581 (1889); Coolidge, *Chinese Immigration*, pp. 202, 202n. But in March 1890, "Tsui Kwo Yin, successor to Chang Yen Hoon, reminded Mr. Blaine that the Chinese Government had waited eight months for a reply to its protests against the Scott Act, which the Supreme Court had declared was a violation of the treaty." Ibid., p. 203.
53. Sandmeyer, *Anti-Chinese Movement*, pp. 103-04; Coolidge, *Chinese Immigration*, pp. 209-33. For Geary's defense of the act see Thomas J. Geary, "The Law and the Chinaman," *The Californian Illustrated Magazine*, July 1893, pp. 304-13; "A Revival of the Chinese Question," probably written by Charles F. Holder, Ibid., pp. 321-23.
54. *Fong Yue Ting* v. *United States*, 149 U.S. 698 (1893); Richard Hay Drayton, "The Chinese Six Companies," *The Californian Illustrated*

Magazine, August 1893, pp. 472-73; Fong Kum Ngon, "The Chinese Six Companies," pp. 525-26; Coolidge, *Chinese Immigration*, pp. 220-21; Sandmeyer, *Anti-Chinese Movement*, pp.104-5; MacLeod, *Pigtails and Gold Dust*, pp. 222-25.

55. Coolidge, *Chinese Immigration*, pp. 221-33; Sandmeyer, *Anti-Chinese Movement*, p. 105.

56. Richard Hay Drayton, "The Chinese Six Companies," *California Illustrated Magazine*, August 1893, p. 477.

57. How Yow, "Chinese Exclusion; A Benefit or a Harm," *North American Review* CLXXIII (1901): 314-30; James D. Phelan, "Why the Chinese Should be Excluded," pp. 663-676. *Chinese Exclusion: Memorial to the President and the Congress of the United States*, November 21, 1901; *Proceedings*, California Chinese Exclusion Convention, San Francisco: November 21, 22, 1901; *For the Re-Enactment of the Chinese Exclusion Law;* California's Memorial to the President and the Congress of the United States. Adopted by the Chinese Exclusion Convention, San Francisco: November 21, 22, 1901. All contained in *Pamphlets on Chinese Exclusion*. Phelan Collection. University of California.

58. *Meat* v. *Rice. American Manhood Against Asiatic Coolieism. Which Shall Survive?* Published by the American Federation of Labor. Printed as Sen. Doc. 137, 1902. In Pamphlets, Phelan Collection.

59. Sandmeyer, *Anti-Chinese Movement*, pp. 106-8.

60. Sandmeyer, *Anti-Chinese Movement*, pp. 96-108; Coolidge, *Chinese Immigration*, pp. 145-233.

Bibliography*

DOCUMENTS

United States

Reports of the United States Industrial Commission on Immigration. *Chinese and Japanese Labor in the Mountain and Pacific States,* vol. 15, part IV, 1901. Prepared under the direction of the Industrial Commission by Thomas F. Turner, pp. 745-802.

Sixteenth Census of the United States, U.S. Summary, Race by Nativity and Sex for the United States, 1850-1940.

U.S. Congress, Senate, Joint Special Committee to Investigate Chinese Immigration, 44th Cong., 2d session, February 27, 1877, S. Rept. 689.

———, Immigration Commission. Immigrants in Industry. *Japanese and Other Immigrant Races in the Pacific Coast and Rocky Mountain States, 61st Cong., 2d session, Sen. Doc. 633, vol. III (Washington, D.C.: Government Printing Office, 1911).*

**Covers materials from pp. 35-253 only.*

California

"People v. Naglee." *California State Journal*, 2d. session, 1851, Appendix, pp. 683-701.

Report to the California State Senate of Its Special Committee on Chinese Immigration. *Chinese Immigration: Its Social, Moral, and Political Effects, Sacramento, 1878.*

Roach, Philip. "Minority Report of the Select Committee on Senate Bill No. 63." California State Journal, 3rd session, March 20, 1852, pp. 669-75.

"Special Message from the Governor of California to the Senate and Assembly of California in Relation to Asiatic Emigration." *California Senate Journal*, 3rd session, April 23, 1852.

"Statement of L.A. Bensancon." *California Senate Journal*, 2d session, 1851, Appendix M.N. 2.

II HISTORY

Carey, Charles H. *A General History of Oregon, Prior to 1861.* 2 vols. Portland: Metropolitan Press, 1935.

Cash, W.J. *The Mind of the South.* New York: Vintage, 1960.

Chapman, Charles E. *A History of California: The Spanish Period.* New York: Macmillan Publishing Co., Inc., 1921.

Coulton, G.G. *Medieval Village Manor, and Monastery.* New York: Harper "Torchbooks," 1960.

Crofts, Alfred, and Percy Buchanan. *A History of the Far East.* New York: Longmans, Green and Co., 1958.

Cross, Ira B. *A History of the Labor Movement in California.* Berkeley: University of California Press, 1935.

Eaves, Lucille. *A History of Labor Legislation in California.* Berkeley: University of California Press, 1909.

Fuller, George W. *A History of the Pacific Northwest.* New York: Alfred A. Knopf, Inc., 1931.

Ormsby, Margaret A. *British Columbia: A History.* Vancouver: The Macmillans in Canada, 1958.

Perlman, Selig. *The History of Trade Unionism in the United States.* New York: Augustus M. Kelley, 1950.

Pirenne, Henri. *A History of Europe.* 2 vols. New York: Doubleday & Company, 1956.

Stimson, Grace Heilman. *Rise of the Labor Movement in Los Angeles.* Berkeley: University of California Press, 1955.

Teggart, Frederick J. *The Theory and Processes of History.* Berkeley: University of California Press, 1941.

Warren, Sidney. *Farthest Frontier: the Pacific Northwest.* New York: Macmillan Publishing Co., Inc., 1949.

Young, John P. *San Francisco—A History of the Pacific Coast Metropolis.* 2 vols. San Francisco: J.S. Clarke, n.d.

ANTHROPOLOGY, SOCIOLOGY, AND POLITICAL SCIENCE: THEORY AND CASE STUDIES

Albert, Ethel M. "Socio-Political Organization and Receptivity to Change: Some Differences Between Ruanda and Urundi." *Southwestern Journal of Anthropology,* Spring 1960, pp. 46-74.

Arendt, Hannah. *The Origins of Totalitarianism.* 2d ed. New York: Meridian, 1958.

Barnes, Harry Elmer, and Teeters, Negley K. *New Horizons in Criminology.* 2d ed. New York: Prentice-Hall, Inc., 1943, 1951.

Barth, Ernest A.T., and Abu-Laban, Baha. "Power Structure and the Negro Sub-Community." *American Sociological Review,* February 1959, pp. 69-76.

Bendix, Richard. *Max Weber: An Intellectual Portrait.* New York: Doubleday & Company, Inc., 1960.

———, and Lipset, Seymour Martin. "Karl Marx' Theory of Social Classes." *Class, Status and Power,* edited by Bendix and Lipset, pp. 26-35 (New York: The Free Press, 1953.

Blumer, Herbert. "Collective Behavior." In *New Outline of the Principles of Sociology.* 2d rev. ed., edited by Alfred McClung Lee, pp. 167-224.

Brogan, D.W. *Politics in America.* New York: Doubleday, Anchor, 1960.

Coser, Lewis. *The Functions of Social Conflict.* New York: The Free Press, 1956.

Davie, Maurice R. *World Immigration.* New York: Macmillan Publishing Co., Inc., 1949.

Davis, Kingsley. *Human Society.* New York: Macmillan Publishing Co., Inc., 1948.

———. *The Population of India and Pakistan.* Princeton: Princeton University Press, 1951.

———, and Casis, Ana. "Urbanization in Latin America." In *Cities and Society*, edited by Paul K. Hatt and Albert J. Reiss, Jr., pp. 141-156. New York: The Free Press, 1951, 1957. (Reprinted from *The Milbank Memorial Fund Quarterly* 24 (April 1946: 186-207).

Evans-Pritchard, E.E. *Witchcraft, Oracles, and Magic Among the Azande.* London: Oxford University Press, 1937.

———. *The Nuer: A Description of the Modes of Livelihood and Political of a Nilotic People.* London: Oxford University Press, 1940.

Frazier, E. Franklin. *Black Bourgeoisie: The Rise of a New Middle Class in the United States.* New York: The Free Press, 1957.

Glazer, Nathan. *American Judaism.* Chicago: University of Chicago Press, 1957.

Gluckman, Max. *Custom and Conflict in Africa.* Oxford, England: Basil Blackwell, 1960.

Hart, C.W.M., and Pilling, Arnold R. *The Tiwi of North Australia.* New York: Holy-Dryden, 1960.

Hawthorn, Harry B., ed. *The Doukhobors of British Columbia.* Vancouver, B.C.: University of British Columbia, J.M. Dent and Sons (Canada) Ltd., 1955.

Hobsbawm, E.J. *Social Bandits and Primitive Rebels.* New York: The Free Press, 1959.

Hodgen, Margaret T. *Change and History.* New York: Wenner-Gren Foundation—Viking Fund Publications in Anthroplogy, no. 18, 1952.

Hoebel, E. Adamson. *The Law of Primitive Man.* Cambridge, Mass.: Harvard University Press, 1954.

Hollingshead, A.B. "Human Ecology." In *New Outline of the Principes of Sociology*, 2d rev. ed., edited by Alfred McClung Lee, pp. 67-120. New York: Barnes & Noble Books, 1951.

Homans, Goerge C. *The Human Group.* New York: Harcourt, Brace Jovanovich, Inc., 1950.

Johnson, Harry M. *Sociology: A Systematic Introduction.* New York: Harcourt, Brace Jovanovich, Inc., 1960.

Klapp, Orrin E., and Padgett, L. Vincent. "Power structure and Decision-Making in a Mexican Border City." *American Journal of Sociology*, January 1960, pp. 400-6.

Laponce, J.A. *The Protection of Minorities.* Berkeley: University of California Press, 1960.

Loomis, Charles P. *Social Systems: Essays on their Persistence and Change.* New York: D. Van Nostrand Company, 1960.

McDonagh, Edward C., and Richards, Eugene S. *Ethnic Relations in the United States.* New York: Appleton-Century-Crofts, 1953.

Martindale, Don. *American Social Structure.* New York: Appleton-Century-Crofts, 1960.

Mayer, Adrian C. *A Report on the East Indian Community in Vancouver.* Vancouver, B.C.: Institute of Social and Economic Research, 1959.

Merton, Robert K. *Social Theory and Social Structure.* rev. ed. New York: The Free Press, 1957.

Michels, Robert. *Political Parties: A Sociological Study of the Oligarchical Tendencies of Modern Democracy.* (translated by Eden and Cedar Paul. New York: The Free Press, 1915; 1958).

Park, Robert Ezra. *Race and Culture.* New York: The Free Press, 1950.

Parsons, Talcott. *The Social System.* New York: The Free Press, 1951.

———. *Structure and Process in Modern Societies.* New York: The Free Press, 1960.

Petersen, William. *Planned Migration: The Social Determinants of the Dutch Canadian Movement.* Berkeley: University of California Press, 1955.

Polsby, Nelson W. "Three Problems in the Analysis of Community Power." *American Sociological Review* December 1959, pp. 796-804.

Quinn, James A. *Urban Sociology.* New York: American Book Company, 1955.

Radcliffe-Brown, A.R., and Forde, Daryll, eds. *African Systems of Kinship and Marriage.* London: Oxford University Press, 1950.

Richmond, Anthony H. *The Colour Problem.* Harmondsworth, Middlesex: Penguin Books, 1955.

Riis, Jacob A. *How the Other Half Lives: Studies Among the Tenements of New York.* New York: Sagamore Press, 1890, 1957.

Rose, Arnold. *The Negro in America.* Boston: Beacon Press, 1944-48.

Roucek, J.S., ed. *Social Control.* 2d ed. New York: D. Van Nostrand Company, 1956.

Saloutos, Theodore. *They Remember America: The Story of the Repatriated Greek-Americans.* Berkeley: University of California Press, 1956.

Selznick, Philip. *The Organizational Weapon.* New York: McGraw-Hill Book Company, 1952.

Simmel, Georg. *The Sociology of Georg Simmel.* translated and edited by Kurt H. Wolff. New York: The Free Press, 1950.

Sjoberg, Gideon. *The Preindustrial City: Past and Present.* New York: The Free Press, 1960.

Smith, M.G. "Kagoro Political Development." *Human Organization,* Fall 1960, pp. 137-149.

Stycos, J. Mayone. "Community Cohesion Among the Greeks of Bridgetown." In Race Prejudice and Discrimination, edited by Arnold M. Rose, pp. 300-9. New York: Alfred A. Knopf, Inc., 1953. Reprinted from an article entitled "The Spartan Greeks of Bridgetown: Community Cohesion." *Common Ground* 8 (Spring 1948), pp. 24-34.

Taft, Donald R., and Robbins, Richard. *International Migrations.* New York: Ronald Press, 1955.

Thomas, W.I., and Znaniecki, Florian. *The Polish Peasant in Europe and America.* 2 vols. New York: Dover Publications, Inc., 1958.

Weber, Max. *The City.* translated and edited by Don Martindale and Gertrud Neuwirth. New York: The Free Press, 1958.

Wirth, Louis. *The Ghetto.* Chicago: University of Chicago Press, Phoenix Books, 1956.

Wittke, Carl. *We Who Built America.* Englewood Cliffs, N.J.: Prentice-Hall, Inc., 1948.

Wolfinger, Raymond E. "Reputation and Reality in the Study of Community Power." *American Sociological Review* October 1960, pp. 636-44.

|| SOUTHEAST ASIA AND THE PACIFIC

Boeke, J.D. "The Village Community in Collision with Capitalism." In *Class, Status, and Power.* edited by S.M. Lipset, pp. 541-46. New York: The Free Press, 1953.

Furnivall, J.S. *Colonial Policy and Practice.* New York: New York University Press, 1948, 1956.

Gullick, J.M. *Indigenous Political Systems of Western Malaya.* London: University of London, Athlone Press, London School of Economics Monographs on Social Anthropology, no 17, 1958.

Kuykendall, Ralph S. *The Hawaiian Kingdom, 1778-1874.* 2 vols. Honolulu: University of Hawaii Press, 1953, 1957.

Lasker, Bruno. *Human Bondage in Southeast Asia.* Chapel Hill: University of North Carolina Press, 1950.

Schurz, William Lytle. *The Manila Galleon.* New York: E.P. Dutton & Co., Inc., 1959.

Spencer, J.E. *Land and People in the Philippines.* Berkeley: University of California Press, 1954.

CHINA AND THE CHINESE

Anderson, [Lady] Flavia. *The Rebel Emperor.* London: Gollancz, 1958.

Bancroft, H.H. "Mongolianism in America." In *Essays and Miscellany,* edited by Bancroft, pp. 309-418. San Francisco: History Co., 1890.

Barnett, A. Doak. *Communist China and Asia.* New York: Harper & Row, Publishers, 1960.

Barnett, Milton L. "Kinship as a Factor Affecting Cantonese Economic Adaptation in the United States." *Human Organization* Spring 1960, pp. 40-46.

Bennett, H.C. "The Chinese in California, Their Numbers and Significance." *Sacramento Daily Union* November 27, 1869, p. 8.

Bennett, John E. "The Chinese Tong Wars in San Francisco." *Harper's Weekly,* August 11, 1900, pp. 746-47.

Bodde, Derk. *China's Cultural Tradition: What and Whither?* New York: Rinehart, 1957.

Brooks, C.W. "The Chinese Labor Problem." Overland Monthly, November 1869, pp. 407-19.

Broom, Leonard. "Jamaica." In *Race: Individual and Collective Behavior,* edited by Edgar T. Thompson and Everett C. Hughes, pp. 131-141. Adapted from Leonard Broom, "The Social Differentiation of Jamaica." *American Sociological Review,* April 1954, pp. 115-24.

Bryce, James. "Kearneyism in California." In *The American Commonwealth.* vol. II, pp. 425-48. New York: Macmillan Publishing Co., Inc., 1901.

Burwell, William. "Science and the Mechanic Arts Against Coolies." *De Bow's Review,* July 1869, pp. 557-71.

———. "The Cooley-ite Controversy." *De Bow's Review,* August 1869, pp. 709-24.

Campbell, Persia Crawford. *Chinese Coolie Emigration to Countries Within the British Empire.* London: King and Sons, 1923.

"The Celestials at Home and Abroad." *Littel's Living Age,* no. 434, August 14, 1852.

Chang, Chung Li. *The Chinese Gentry: Studies on Their Role in Nineteenth-Century Chinese Society.* Seattle: University of Washington Press, 1955.

Chapman, Mary. "Notes on the Chinese in Boston." *Journal of American Folk-Lore,* October/December 1892, pp. 321-24.

Chen Po-ta. *A Study of Land Rent in Pre-Liberation China.* Peking: Foreign Languages Press, 1958.

Chinese Chamber of Commerce. *San Francisco's Chinatown: History, Function and Importance of Social Organizations.* Mimeographed. San Francisco, 1953.

"Chinese Highbinders." *Current Literature,* March 27, 1900, pp. 275-77.

Clark, Helen F. "The Chinese of New York Contrasted With Their Foreign Neighbors." *The Century Magazine,* vol. LIII, no. 1, November 1896, pp. 104-13.

Comber, Leon. *Chinese Secret Societies in Malaya: A Survey of the Triad Society from 1800 to 1900.* Locust Valley, New York: J.J. Augustin, 1959.

"Comments of Rev. Ernest Faber on the Paper of D.J. Macgowan at the Meeting of December 16, 1886 of the North China Branch, Royal Asiatic Society." *Journal of the Royal Asiatic Society North China Branch—Proceedings,* vol. XXI, no. 2, August/December 1886, pp. 252-54.

Conant, Melvin. "Southeast Asia." In *Race: Individual and Collective Behavior,* edited by Edgar T. Thompson and Everett C. Hughes, pp. 44-49. New York: The Free Press, 1958.

Conwell, Russel. *Why and How. Why the Chinese Emigrate and the Means They Adopt for the Purpose of Reaching America.* Boston: Lee and Shephard, 1871.

Coolidge, Mary. *Chinese Immigration.* New York: Henry Holt, 1909.

Coughlin, Richard J. *Double Identity: The Chinese in Modern Thailand.* Hong Kong: Hong Kong University Press, 1960.

Coulter, Annie D. "The Economic Aspect of the Chinese Labor Problem." M.A. thesis, University of California, 1902.

Culin, Stewart. "The I Hing, or 'Patriotic Rising,' A Secret Society Among the Chinese in America." *Proceedings of the Numismatic and Antiquarian Society of Philadelphia for the years 1887-1889,* November 3, 1887, pp. 51-58.

———. "China in America: The Social Life of the Chinese in The Eastern Cities of the United States." Paper read before the American Association for the Advancement of Science, Section of Anthropology, New York, 1887, Philadelphia, 1887.

———. "Customs of the Chinese in America." *Journal of American Folk-Lore.* July/September 1890, pp. 191-200.

———. "Chinese Secret Societies in the United States." *Journal of American Folk-Lore.* January/March 1890, pp. 39-45.

———. "The Gambling Games of the Chinese in America." *Publications of the University of Pennsylvania, Series in Philology, Literature, and Archaeology,* vol. I, no. 4, 1891.

———. "Chinese Games with Dice and Dominoes." Report of the

United States National Museum, Smithsonian Institute, 1893, pp. 489-537.

———. "The Religious Ceremonies of the Chinese in the Eastern Cities of the United States." An Essay read before the Numismatic and Antiquarian Society of Philadelphia, April 1, 1886. Philadelphia: privately printed, 1887.

Doyen, F.T. "In Nankin." *Overland Monthly*, August 1868, pp. 170-76.

Drayton, Richard Hay. "The Chinese Six Companies." *Californian Illustrated Magazine*, August 1893, pp. 472-79.

Eberhard, Wolfram. *A History of China from Earliest Times to the Present*. London: Routledge and Kegan Pual, 1948.

———. *Conquerors and Rulers: Social Forces in Medieval China*. Leiden: E.J. Brill, 1952.

Elegant, Robert S. *The Dragon's Seed: Peking and the Overseas Chinese*. New York: St. Martin's Press, Inc., 1959.

Elliott, Alan J.A. *Chinese Spirit Medium Cults in Singapore*. London: London School of Economics and Political Science, Department of Anthropology. Monographs on Social Anthropoligy, no. 14, 1955.

Fairbank, John King. *The United States and China*. 2d rev. ed. Cambridge, Mass.: Harvard University Press, 1958.

Fang, John T.C. *Chinatown Handy Guide*. San Francisco: The Chinese Publishing House, n.d.

Farwell, Willard B. *The Chinese at Home and Abroad, Together with the Rpeort of the Special Committee of the Board of Supervisors of San Francisco, on the Condition of the Chinese Quarter of that City*. San Francisco: A.L. Bancroft and Co., 1885.

Fei Hsiao-Tung. *China's Gentry: Essays in Rural-Urban Relations*. rev., edited by Margaret Park Redfield. Chicago: University of Chicago Press, 1953.

———. "Peasantry and Gentry: An Interpretation of Chinese Social Structure and Its Changes." In *Class, Status, and Power*, edited by R. Bendix and S.M. Lipset, pp. 631-50. New York: The Free Press, 1953.

———, and Chang Chih-I. *Earthbound China: A Study of Rural Economy in Yunnan*. London: Routledge and Kegan Paul, 1949.

Fenn, William Purviance. *Ah Sin and His Brethren in American Literature*. Peiping: College of Chinese Studies, 1933.

Feuerwerker, Albert. *China's Early Industrialization: Sheng Hsuan-huai (1844-1916) and Mandarin Enterprise*. Cambridge, Mass.: Harvard University Press, 1958.

Fitzgerald, C.P. *China: A Short Cultural History*. London: The Cresset Press, 1935.

Fong Kum Ngon (Walter N. Fong). "The Chinese Six Companies." *Overland Monthly*, May 1894, pp. 519-26.

Fong, Ng Bickleen. *The Chinese in New Zealand.* Hong Kong: Hong Kong University Press, 1959.

Forman, Alan. "Celestial Gotham." *The Arena* VII (1893): 620-21.

Freedman, Maurice. *Chinese Family and Marriage in Singapore.* London: Her Majesty's Stationery Office, Colonial Research Studies, no. 20, 1957.

———. *Lineage Organization in Southeastern China.* London: University of London-Athlone Press, London School of Economics Monographs on Social Anthropology, no. 18, 1958.

———. "Jews, Chinese and Some Others." *British Journal of Sociology*, March 1959, pp. 61-70.

———. "Immigrants and Associations: Chinese in Nineteenth-Century Singapore." *Comparative Studies in Society and History*, October 1960, pp. 25-48.

Fried, Morton H., ed. *Colloquium on Overseas Chinese.* New York: International Secretariat, Institute of Pacific Relations, 1958.

Geary, Thomas J. "The Law and the Chinaman." *The Californian Illustrated Magazine*, July 1893, pp. 304-313.

Gibson, Otis. *The Chinese in America.* Cincinnati: Hitchcock and Walden, 1877.

Giles, Herbert A. "The Family Names." *Journal of the Royal Asiatic Society, North China Branch*, vol. XXI, no. 2, August/December 1886, pp. 255-88.

Gong, Eng Ying, and Grant, Bruce. *Tong War!* New York: Nicholas L. Brown, 1930.

Goodrich, L. Carrington. *A Short History of the Chinese People.* 3rd ed. New York: Harper & Row, Publishers, 1959.

Granet, Marcel. *Chinese Civilization*, translated by Kathleen Innes and Mabel R. Brailsford. New York: Meridian Books, 1958.

deGroot, J.J.M. *The Religion of the Chinese.* New York: Macmillan Publishing Co., Inc., 1910.

———. *Religion in China.* New York: G.P. Putnam's Sons, 1912.

Hayner, Norman S., and Reynolds, Charles N. "Chinese Family Life in America." *American Sociological Review*, October 1937, pp. 630-37.

Hittell, John S. *The Resources of California.* San Francisco: A. Roman, 1874.

Ho, Ping-ti. *Studies on the Population of China, 1368-1953.* Cambridge, Mass.: Harvard University Press, 1959.

———. "Aspects of Social Mobility in China, 1368-1911." *Comparative Studies in Society and History*, June 1959, pp. 330-359.

Ho, Yow. "Chinese Exclusion—A Benefit or a Harm." *North American Review* CLXXIII (1901): 314-30.

Holder, Charles Frederick. "Chinese Slavery in America." *North American Review*, July 1897, pp. 288-94.

Hoy, William. *The Chinese Six Companies*. San Francisco: Chinese Consolidated Benevolent Association, 1942.

Hsu, Francis L.K. *Under the Ancestors' Shadow: Chinese Culture and Personality*. London: Routledge and Kegan Paul, 1949.

———. *Religion, Science, and Human Crises: A Study of China in Transition and Its Implications for the West*. London: Routledge and Kegan Paul, 1952.

Hudson, G.F. *Europe and China: A Survey of Their Relations from the Earliest Times to 1800*. Boston: Beacon Press, 1931, 1961.

J. "The Wyoming Anti-Chinese Riot—Another View." *Overland Monthly*, December 1885, pp. 573-76.

Jenkins, Edward. *The Coolie—His Rights and Wrongs*. New York: Routledge and Sons, 1871.

Kaye, Barrington. *Upper Nankin Street, Singapore*. Singapore: University of Malaya Press, 1960.

Lee, Rose Hum. *The Chinese Communities in the Rocky Mountain Region*. Ph. D. dissertation, University of Chicago Library, 1947.

———. "Social Institutions of a Rocky Mountain Chinatown." *Social Forces*, October 1945, pp. 1-11.

———. "The Decline of Chinatowns in the United States." *American Journal of Sociology*, March 1949, pp. 422-32.

———. "Chinese Dilemma." *Phylon Quarterly*, 2nd quarter, 1949, pp. 137-40.

———. "Research on the Chinese Family." *American Journal of Sociology*, May 1949, pp. 497-504.

———. "Occupational Invasion, Succession, and Accommodation of the Chinese of Butte, Montana." *American Journal of Sociology*, July 1949, pp. 50-58.

———. "Chinese Americans." In *One America: The History, Contributions, and Present Problems of Our Racial and National Minorities*, edited by Frances J. Brown and Joseph S. Roucek, pp. 309-18. Englewood Cliffs, N.J.: Prentice-Hall, Inc., 1952.

———. "Delinquent, Neglected, and Dependent Chinese Boys and Girls of the San Francisco Bay Region." *Journal of Social Psychology* 36 (1952): 15-34.

———. "The Recent Immigrant Chinese Families of the San Francisco-Oakland Area." *Marriage and Family Living*, February 1956, pp. 14-24.

——. "The Established Chinese Families of the San Francisco Bay

Area." *The Midwest Sociologist,* December 1957, pp. 19-25.

———. "The Stranded Chinese in the United States." *Phylon Quarterly,* 2nd quarter, 1958, pp. 180-94.

———. *The Chinese in the United States of America.* Hong Kong: Hong Kong University Press, 1960.

Leong Gor Yun. *Chinatown Inside Out.* New York: Barrows Mussey, 1936.

"Letter of the Chinamen to his Excellency, Governor Bigler." San Francisco, April 29, 1852 in *Littel's Living Age,* July 3, 1852, pp. 32-34.

Loomis, A.W. "Chinese in California: Their Signboard Literature." *Overland Monthly,* August 1868, pp. 152-56.

———. "The Six Chinese Companies." *Overland Monthly,* September 1868, pp. 221-27.

———. "The Old East in the New West." *Overland Monthly* I (October 1868), pp. 360-67.

———. "Our Heathen Temples." *Overland Monthly,* November 1868, p. 453-61.

———. "What Our Chinamen Read." *Overland Monthly,* December 1868, pp. 525-30.

———. "Holiday in the Chinese Quarter." Overland Monthly, February 1869, pp. 144-53.

———. "Chinese Women in California." *Overland Monthly,* April 1869, pp. 344-50.

———. "How Our Chinamen Are Employed." *Overland Monthly,* March 1869, pp. 231-40.

———. "Medical Art in the Chinese Quarter." *Overland Monthly,* June 1869, pp. 496-506.

———. "Chinese Funeral Baked Meats." *Overland Monthly,* July 1869, pp. 21-28.

———. "Occult Science in the Chinese Quarter." *Overland Monthly,* August 1869, pp. 160-69.

Li Chien Nung. *The Political History of China, 1840-1928,* edited and translated by Ssu-yu Teng and Jeremy Ingalls.

Lin Yueh-hwa. *The Golden Wing: A Sociological Study of Chinese Familism.* London: Kegan Paul, Trench, Trubner, 1948.

Liu Hui-Chen Wang. *The Traditional Chinese Clan Rules.* Locust Valley, N.Y.: J.J. Augustin, 1959.

Lyman, Stanford M. "Factors Affecting the Location of Chinese and Japanese in the United States: A Socio-Demographic Study."

Macgowan, D.J. "Chinese Guilds or Chambers of Commerce and Trades Unions." *Journal of the Royal Asiatic Society North China Branch,* vol. XXI, no. 2, August/December 1886, pp. 133-92.

Maddux, Percy. *City on the Willamette, The Story of Portland Oregon.* Portland: Benfords and Mort, 1952, pp. 77-95.

McDowell, Henry Burden. "A New Light on the Chinese." *Harper's Monthly,* December 1892, pp. 3-17.

McLeod, Alexander. *Pigtails and Gold Dust.* Caldwell, Idaho: The Caxton Press, 1947.

Meadows, Thomas Taylor. *The Chinese and Their Rebellions.* Stanford: Academic Reprints, [1856].

Merrill, A.P. "Southern Labor." *De Bow's Review,* July 1869, pp. 586-92.

"Our Chamber of Commerce—The Chinese Labor Question." *De Bow's Review,* August 1869, pp. 669-701.

Pamphlets on Chinese Exclusion, Phelan Collection. University of California Library.

Phelan, James D. "Why the Chinese Should be Excluded." *North American Review* CLXXIII (1901): 663-76.

Purcell, Victor. *The Chinese in Southeast Asia.* London: Oxford University Press, 1951.

"A Revival of the Chinese Question." *Californian Illustrated Magazine,* July 1893, pp. 321-23.

Reynolds, C.N. "The Chinese Tongs." *American Journal of Sociology,* March 1935, pp. 612-23.

Ritchie, Robert Wells. "The Wars of the Tongs." *Harper's Weekly,* August 27, 1910, pp. 8-10.

Sandmeyer, Elmer. *The Anti-Chinese Movement in California.* Urbana: University of Illinois Press, 1939.

Sargent, A.A. "The Wyoming Anti-Chinese Riot." *Overland Monthly,* November 1885, pp. 507-12.

Seagar II, Robert. "Some Denominational Reactions to Chinese Immigration to California, 1856-1892." *Pacific Historical Review,* February 1959, pp. 49-66.

Schlegel, Gustave. *Thian Ti Hwui. The Hung-League or Heaven-Earth-League. A Secret Society With the Chinese in China and India.* Batavia: Lange and Co., 1866.

Scholz, Hartmut. "The Rural Settlements in the Eighteen Provinces of China." *Sinologica* 3 (1953): 37-49.

Schrieke, B.J.O. *Alien Americans.* New York: The Viking Press, Inc., 1936.

Shih, Vincent Y.C. "The Ideology of the Taiping T'ien-Kuo." *Sinologica* 3 (1953): 1-15.

Shuck, Oscar T. "Seniors of the Collective Bar—Frank M. Stone." *History of the Bench and Bar of California.* Los Angeles: Commercial Printing House, 1901, pp. 938-42.

Siu, Paul C.P. "The Sojourner." *American Journal of Sociology*, July 1952, pp. 32-44.

Skinner, G. William. *Chinese Society in Thailand: An Analytical History*. Ithaca: Cornell University Press, 1957.

———. *Leadership and Power in the Chinese Comunity of Thailand.* Ithaca: Cornell University Press, 1958.

Speed, John Gilmer. "Chinese Secret Societies of New York City." *Harper's Weekly*, July 14, 1900, p. 658.

Speer, William. "Democracy of the Chinese." *Harper's Monthly*, November 1868, pp. 836-48.

———. *The Oldest and Newest Empire: China and the United States.* Hartford: S.S. Scranton, 1870.

Sterry, Nora. "Social Attitudes of Chinese Immigrants." *Journal of Applied Sociology*, July/August 1923, pp. 325-33.

Stewart, Watt, *Chinese Bondage in Peru: A History of the Chinese Coolie in Peru, 1849-1874*. Durham: Duke University Press, 1951.

Swisher, Earl. *China's Management of the American Barbarians: A Study of Sino-American Relations, 1841-1861, with Documents.* New Haven: Far Eastern Publications, 1953.

Ta Chen. "Chinese Migrations with Special Reference to Labor Conditions." *Bulletin of the United States Bureau of Labor Statistics*, no. 340. Washington: G.P.O., 1923.

Taylor, Paul S. "Foundations of California Rural Society." *California Historical Society Quarterly*, September 1945, pp. 193-228.

Teggart, Frederick J. *Rome and China: A Study of Correlations in Historical Events*. Berkeley: University of California Press, 1939.

Teng Ssu-yu. *New Light on the History of the Tai Ping Rebellion.* Cambridge, Mass.: Harvard University Press, 1950. Mimeographed.

Thompson, John Stuart. *The Chinese.* Indianapolis: The Bobbs-Merrill Co., Inc., 1909.

T'ien Ju-K'ang. *The Chinese of Sarawak.* London: London School of Economics and Political Science. Monographs on Social Anthropology, no. 12, 1953.

Tow, Julius S. *The Real Chinese in America.* New York: Academy Press, 1923.

Tsien Tche-Hao. "La Vie Sociale des Chinois a Madagascar." *Comparative Studies in Society and History*, January 1961, pp. 170-81.

Vaughan, J.D. *The Manners and Customs of the Chinese of the Straits Settlements.* Singapore: Mission Press, 1879.

Walsh, R.F. "Chinese and the Fisheries." *The Californian Illustrated Magazine*, November 1893, pp. 883-40.

Warrington, Allen. "The Formation and Organization of the Chinese Companies: 1849-1854."

Weber, Max. *The Religion of China: Confucianism and Taoism.* New York: The Free Press, 1951. Translated and edited by Hans H. Gerth.

"The Why and Wherefore of Chinese Tongs." *Current Opinion,* November 1922, pp. 621-22.

Williams, Lea E. *Overseas Chinese Nationalism: The Genesis of the Pan Chinese Movement in Indonesia, 1900-1916.* New York: The Free Press, 1960.

Williams, S. Wells. *The Middle Kingdom.* New York: Charles Scribner's Sons, 1882, 1913.

Willmott, Donald Earl. *The Chinese of Semarang: A Changing Minority Community in Indonesia.* Ithaca: Cornell University Press, 1960.

Wilson, Carol Green. *Chinatown Quest: the Life Adventures of Donaldina Cameron.* rev. ed. Stanford: Stanford University Press, 1950.

Wolfe, Burton. "The Chinese Immigration Puzzle." *Chicago Jewish Forum,* Fall 1959, pp. 33-39.

———. "Chinatown USA: The Unassimilated People." *The California Liberal,* February 1960, pp. 1, 3-5.

Wong, Everett. "The Exclusion Movement and the Chinese Community in San Francisco." Master's thesis, University of California, 1954.

Wright, Arthur F. *Buddhism in Chinese History.* Stanford: Stanford University Press, 1959.

Wynne, Mervyn Llewelyn. *Triad and Tabut.* Singapore: Government Printing Office, 1941.

Yang, C.K. *The Chinese Family in the Communist Revolution.* Cambridge, Mass.: Harvard University Press, 1959.

———. *A Chinese Village in Early Communist Transition.* Cambridge, Mass.: Harvard University Press, 1959.

Yang, Martin. *A Chinese Village: Taitou, Shantung Province.* London: Kegan Paul, Trench, Trubner, 1948.

|| JAPAN AND THE JAPANESE

Adams, Romanzo. "Japanese Migration Statistics." *Sociology and Social Research,* May/June 1929, pp. 436-45.

Bellah, Robert H. *Tokugawa Religion: The Values of Pre-Industrial Japan.* New York: The Free Press, 1957.

Boxer, C.R. *The Christian Century in Japan, 1549-1650.* Berkeley: University of California Press, 1951.

Broom, Leonard, and Kitsuse, John I. "The Validation of Acculturation: A Condition of Ethnic Assimilation." *American Anthropologist* 57 (1955): 44-48. Abridged in *Principles of Sociology: A Reader in Theory and Research,* edited by Kimball Young and Raymond Mack, pp. 117-20. New York: American Book Company, 1960.

———. *The Managed Casualty: The Japanese-American Family in World War II.* Berkeley: University of California Press, 1956.

———, and Riemer, Ruth. *Removal and Return: The Socio-Economic Effects of the War on Japanese Americans.* Berkeley: University of California Press, 1949.

Dore, R.P. *City Life in Japan: A Study of a Tokyo Ward.* Berkeley: University of California Press, 1958.

Embree, John F. *A Japanese Village: Suye Mura.* London: Kegan Paul, Trench, Trubner, 1946.

Fujita, Michinari. "Japanese Associations in America." *Sociology and Social Research,* January/February 1929, pp. 211-28.

Grodzins, Morton. *Americans Betrayed: Politics and the Japanese Evacuation.* Chicago: University of Chicago Press, 1949.

Hearn, Lafcadio. *Japan: An Interpretation.* Tokyo and Rutland, Vt.: Charles E. Tuttle, 1904, 1955.

Ichihashi, Yamato. *Japanese in the United States.* Stanford: Stanford University Press, 1932.

Irie, Toraji. "History of Japanese Migration to Peru," translated by William Himel. *Hispanic-American Historical Review,* August/October 1951, pp. 436-52, 648-64.

Ishii, Ryoichi. *Population Pressure and Economic Life in Japan.* London: P.S. King and Son, 1937.

Iyenaga, T., and Sato, Kenoski. *Japan and the California Problem.* New York: G.P. Putnam's Sons, 1921.

Kataoka, W.T. "Occupations of Japanese in Los Angeles." *Sociology and Social Research,* September/October 1929, pp. 53-58.

Kawakami, K.K. *The Real Japanese Question.* New York: Macmillan Publishing Co., Inc., 1921.

LaViolette, Forrest E. "Canada and Its Japanese." In *Race: Individual and Collective Behavior,* edited by Edgar T. Thompson and Everett C. Hughes, pp. 149-55. New York: The Free Press, 1952.

Leighton, Alexander H. *The Governing of Men: General Principles and Recommendations Based on Experience at a Japanese Relocation Camp.* Princeton: Princeton University Press, 1945.

Lind, Andrew W. *Hawaii's Japanese: An Experiment in Democracy.* Princeton: Princeton University Press, 1946.

Nodera, Isamu. "Second Generation Japanese and Vocations." *Sociology and Social Research,* May/June 1937, pp. 464-66.

Norbeck, Edward. *Pineapple Town, Hawaii.* Berkeley: University of California Press, 1959.

Obana, T. "The American-Born Japanese." *Sociology and Social Research,* November/December 1934, pp. 161-65.

Roucek, Joseph S. "Japanese Americans." In *One America: The History, Contributions and Present Problems of Our Racial and National Minorities,* edited by Francis J. Brown and Joseph S. Roucek, pp. 319-34. Englewood Cliffs, N.J.: Prentice-Hall, Inc., 1952.

Sansom, George B. *Japan: A Short Cultural History.* rev. ed. New York: Appleton-Century-Crofts, 1943.

Smith, Thomas C. *The Agrarian Origins of Modern Japan.* Stanford: Stanford University Press, 1959.

Strong, E.K. *Japanese in California.* Stanford: Stanford University Press, 1933.

Taeuber, Irene. "Family, Migration, and Industrialization in Japan." *American Sociological Review,* April 1951, pp. 149-57.

———. *The Population of Japan.* Princeton: Princeton University Press, 1958.

Ten Broek, Jacobus; Barnhart, Edward A.N., and Matson, Floyd. *Prejudice, War, and the Constitution.* Berkeley: University of California Press, 1954. (Japanese American Evacuation and Resettlement, vol. III)

Thomas, Dorothy Swaine with the assistance of Charles Kikuchi and James Sakoda. *The Salvage.* Berkeley: University of California Press, 1952. (Japanese American Evacuation and Resettlement, vol. II

———, and Nishimoto, Richard. *The Spoilage.* Berkeley: University of California Press, 1946. (Japanese American Evacuation and Resettlement, vol. I

Weber, Max. *The Religion of India: The Sociology of Hinduism and Buddhism.* Translated and edited by Hans. H. Gerth and Don Martindale, pp. 270-82. New York: The Free Press, 1958.

Young, Charles; Reid, Helen R.Y., and Carrothers, W.A. *The Japanese Canadians,* edited byy H.A. Innis. Toronto: University of Toronto Press, 1938.

Yoshida, Yosaburo. "Sources and Causes of Japanese Emigration." *Annals of the American Academy of Political and Social Science,* September 1909, pp. 157-67.

FICTION

All Men Are Brothers [Shui Hu Chuan]. 2 vols., translated by Pearl S. Buck. New York: Grove Press, Inc., 1933, 1937.

Michener, James A. *Hawaii.* New York: Random House, Inc., 1959.

Okada, John. *No-No Boy.* Tokyo and Rutland, Vt.: Charles E. Tuttle, 1957.

Wu Ching-Tzu. *The Scholars.* Peking: Foreign Languages Press, 1957.